The Garden
Almanac
2026

Quarto

First published in 2025 by Frances Lincoln, an imprint of The Quarto Group.
One Triptych Place, London, SE1 9SH, United Kingdom
T (0)20 7700 9000
www.Quarto.com

EEA Representation, WTS Tax d.o.o., Žanova ulica 3, 4000 Kranj, Slovenia

RHS Books Publisher: Helen Griffin
RHS Head of Editorial: Tom Howard
RHS Books Editor: Simon Maughan
Authors: Zia Allaway and Guy Barter
Designer: Sarah Pyke
Publisher: Philip Cooper
Commissioning Editor: Alice Graham
Editor: Katerina Menhennet
Editorial Assistant: Izzy Toner
Senior Designer: Isabel Eeles
Senior Production Manager: Alex Merrett

The RHS would like to acknowledge:
Helen Bostock for consulting on the Garden benefactor pages.
Dr Nicholas Cryer for compiling the Temperature and rainfall charts.
James Curtis, RHS Head Chef, for the Recipe pages.
Dr Jassy Drakulic for advising on plant diseases.
Dr Hayley Jones for consulting on the Challenges pages.
James Lawrence for writing the Plants for difficult places pages.

MIX
Paper | Supporting responsible forestry
FSC® C004800

Printed in Dubai
OP/May/2025

The Royal Horticultural Society is the UK's leading gardening charity dedicated to advancing horticulture and promoting good gardening. Its charitable work includes providing expert advice and information in print, online and at its five major gardens and annual shows, training gardeners of every age, creating hands-on opportunities for children to grow plants and sharing research into plants, wildlife, wellbeing and environmental issues affecting gardeners. For more information visit www.rhs.org.uk or call 020 3176 5800.

RHS

Royal Horticultural Society

The Garden Almanac

2026

The month-by-month guide to
your best ever gardening year

Zia Allaway and Guy Barter

F FRANCES
LINCOLN

Introduction

Welcome to the 2026 edition of *RHS The Garden Almanac*, a celebration of the growing year and all it has to offer. Written by the Royal Horticultural Society's experts and horticulturists, this colourful guide offers month-by-month advice on what to sow, plant, harvest and make throughout the year. Packed with tips to help you garden sustainably while saving money, it also includes delicious seasonal recipes created by one of the RHS's top chefs.

The book also explores the often-hidden world of garden benefactors, the creatures and organisms that maintain a healthy ecosystem by keeping the soil healthy and unwanted insects at bay. Where problems do arise, our experts offer advice on how to identify and manage them.

You will find the average monthly temperatures and rainfall figures for your area, too, as well as sunrise and sunset times, to help you plan your garden's irrigation needs and monitor the light levels affecting plant growth. Moonrise and set times are also listed – some believe that sowing to coincide with moon phases improves crop yields, although it is not proven scientifically.

Other highlights include inspirational weekend projects that transform plants and recycled materials into beautiful natural gifts or features for the garden.

Keeping this invaluable gardening companion by your side throughout the coming year will help you to make the most of every season and ensure that all your plants and crops deliver on their promise.

Moon phases

A Moon cycle, or lunation, is the time it takes for the Moon to travel through all of its lunar phases, and lasts about 29½ days. Half of the Moon's surface is always illuminated by the Sun, but the surface area we can see changes as the Moon orbits the Earth. The eight phases in a lunar month are divided into four primary and four intermediate phases, as follows:

1 **NEW MOON** Primary phase: when the Moon is between the Sun and the Earth and cannot be seen because the whole surface is in shadow.

2 **WAXING CRESCENT MOON** Intermediate phase: the right edge can be seen in the UK and in the Northern Hemisphere.

3 **FIRST QUARTER MOON (HALF MOON)** Primary phase: the right half of the Moon is illuminated in the UK and Northern Hemisphere.

4 **WAXING GIBBOUS MOON** Intermediate phase: the right three-quarters is illuminated in the UK and Northern Hemisphere.

5 **FULL MOON** Primary phase: the Moon and the Sun are on opposite sides of the Earth and the whole Moon is illuminated.

6 **WANING GIBBOUS MOON** Intermediate phase: the left three-quarters is lit in the UK and Northern Hemisphere.

7 **THIRD QUARTER MOON (HALF MOON)** Primary phase: the left half is lit in the UK and Northern Hemisphere.

8 **WANING CRESCENT MOON** Intermediate phase: the left edge is lit in the UK and Northern Hemisphere.

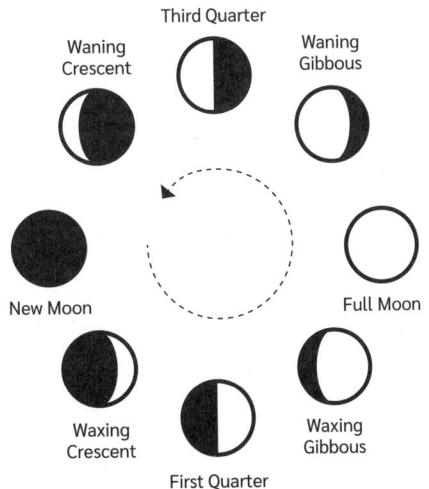

Third Quarter

Waning Crescent

Waning Gibbous

New Moon

Full Moon

Waxing Crescent

Waxing Gibbous

First Quarter

January

The garden slumbers under stormy skies. Perennials have gone to ground, their precious roots safely tucked up under the frozen soil, while gaunt trees and shrubs, stripped of their leafy cloaks, sway restlessly in the wind. Braving the cold, mahonia, witch hazel and sweet box flowers infuse the air with their heady scents, reminding us that nature's treasures abound, even in the depths of winter.

KEY EVENTS

New Year's Day, 1 January
Twelfth Night, 5–6 January
St Hilary's Day, 11 January (*said to be the coldest day of the year*)
Burns Night, 25 January
Big Garden Birdwatch, 23–25 January

What to do in January

New Year celebrations are followed by a period of rest in the garden, as growth slows or grinds to a halt during the cold, dark days of winter. However, you can venture outside on mild days to plant inexpensive bare-root plants, and use the long evenings to order seeds and plants, with their promise of flowers and crops in the warmer days to come.

In the garden

PLANT BARE-ROOT TREES AND SHRUBS, which are available from late autumn until the first weeks of March. Generally less expensive than plants grown in pots, they are dug up from a nursery field while dormant and will arrive with no soil around their roots, hence the name. Plant them as soon as they arrive, if the ground is neither frozen nor waterlogged, or set them temporarily in pots of used compost until conditions improve. Plant your trees and shrubs at the same level they were growing at in the field, indicated by the darker soil mark on the stems. **1**

GIVE BIRDS FRESH WATER every day, offering it in a shallow bowl so that small species can drink and bathe safely. Set the bowl in a sunny spot that's not easy to access by cats and other predators, where the birds have good all-round views. Replace the water and clean the bowl regularly with hot, soapy water, rinsing it afterwards, to prevent the spread of disease.

PLANT A WILDLIFE HEDGE, using bare-root plants. Choose a selection of native deciduous plants such as field

PRUNING TIP
Wisteria
For maximum flower power, wisterias are best pruned twice a year. In July or August, after flowering, cut back the whippy green shoots that grew earlier in the year so that five or six leaves remain on each stem. This controls the size of the plant, encourages better air circulation around the stems and allows more sunlight to reach the young growth where flowers will form the following year. In January, simply cut back the shoots you pruned in summer to two or three buds (see above).

maple (*Acer campestre*), hawthorn (*Crataegus monogyna*), and wild roses (*Rosa canina* and *Rosa rubiginosa*, for example), together with evergreens for winter cover and berries for birds, including yew (*Taxus baccata*) and holly (*Ilex aquifolium*).

RENOVATE CLIMBING AND RAMBLING ROSES while they are dormant. Remove all dead, diseased, dying and weak shoots, then cut some of the oldest stems down to the ground, retaining a maximum of six young, vigorous stems. Then shorten the side shoots of these remaining stems by one third to one half, and tie them into their supports. In spring, add a 5cm (2in) layer of well-rotted garden compost or manure (leaving a space around the stems).

CUT OFF HELLEBORE LEAVES showing signs of disease before or as the flowering stems appear. This prevents the spread of the fungal disease, hellebore leaf spot. ❷

In the fruit & veg patch

CHIT EARLY SEASON POTATOES Chitting simply means popping your seed potatoes on a tray or an old egg box in moderate light with the eyes (sunken areas or buds) facing upwards. Shoots will soon form and the potatoes can then be planted outside in March.

SOW MICROGREENS on a windowsill indoors or in a heated greenhouse for winter greens. Line a seed tray or clean food container with kitchen roll or felt and dampen it before sprinkling the

seeds on top. Water or mist carefully so the paper or felt remains damp but is not swimming in water. Shoots should develop in a few days or weeks, depending on the variety. When ready, snip them off at the base with scissors.

CLEAN OUT PLANT POTS in the quiet winter months, ready for the rush in spring when there is so much to do. Use hot, soapy water and a small scrubbing brush to remove old soil that may be harbouring diseases or unwanted insects.

ORDER SEEDS for sowing in the next few months. You sow some crops in February, so it's good to get ahead and order your favourites early. If you don't have much space for seeds or only

want a few tomato or courgette plants, for example, you can also order plug plants now, which will arrive a few weeks before they need to be planted outside.

Indoors

WATER HOUSEPLANTS SPARINGLY throughout the winter months when growth is slower.

CLEAN FOLIAGE of large-leaved houseplants with a soft, damp cloth to remove dust and allow them to photosynthesize effectively.

PLANT FORCED NARCISSUS AND HYACINTH bulbs in a sheltered spot in the garden or in a pot on a balcony after they have finished flowering indoors, and leave the foliage intact to die down naturally. This feeds the bulbs, promoting a good flower display next year. **3**

ENCOURAGE BUSHY GROWTH on Christmas cacti (*Schlumbergera*) after flowering by snipping off the tips of the stems, which will encourage more side shoots to form.

MONEY-SAVING IDEA
Buy bare-root perennials
Some perennials, including hardy geraniums, rudbeckias, echinacea (shown here) and hostas, are available in winter as bare-root plants. Just like shrubs and trees (see p.10), these tend to be much cheaper than those grown and sold in pots, and while the dormant plants may look less than promising when they arrive, they will soon perk up in spring and flower like their more expensive counterparts.

Plants of the month

1. Camellia (*Camellia japonica* pictured)
2. Winter daphne (*Daphne odora* 'Aureomarginata' pictured)
3. Heather (*Erica × darleyensis* pictured)
4. Witch hazel (*Hamamelis × intermedia* 'Jelena' pictured)
5. Lenten rose (*Helleborus × hybridus* Harvington hybrids pictured) .
6. Dwarf iris (*Iris reticulata* pictured)
7. Winter jasmine (*Jasminum nudiflorum*)
8. Mahonia (*Mahonia × media* 'Charity's Sister' pictured)
9. Sweet box (*Sarcococca hookeriana* var. *digyna* 'Purple Stem' pictured)
10. Viburnum (*Viburnum tinus*)
11. Pansy (*Viola* BEL VISO Series pictured)

Project: Make a macramé screen

Easy to make, this set of simple macramé pot-holders will accommodate a range of houseplants, while hanging them from hooks above a window will provide your collection with sufficient daylight during the winter months. You can make the holders to fit any small pot, up to about 15–20cm (6–8in) wide, using just a few lengths of thin rope or cord and this traditional method of tying knots. Easy to lift down for watering, they are also ideally suited to bathrooms, where warmth and humidity will suit air plants (*Tillandsia*) and exotic-looking cactus *Rhipsalis baccifera* or plants that like to cascade, such as *Philodendron scandens* or *Hoya linearis*.

YOU WILL NEED

Electric drill, Rawlplugs and screws
Hooks
16m (52ft) of strong, thin cord or rope (for each holder)
Scissors

1 Using the drill, Rawlplugs and screws, fix the hooks to the wall above the window or the ceiling. Hang four 4m (13ft) cords over a hook so they fall to eight equal lengths and tie together at the top to form a loop.

2 Separate the eight ends of the cord into pairs and, using an overhand knot, tie each pair 30cm (12in) below the top knot, making sure they are all in line.

3 For your second row of knots, separate out the cords from each pair and tie each with its neighbour instead. These knots should sit about 10–20cm (4–8in) below the first row. Take your time to ensure the knots are all at the same level.

4 Tie all the hanging cords together 15–20cm (6–8in) below the second row of knots. Pull tight and trim the ends so they are all the same length.

5 Raise the bottom knot to allow the cords above to open up, then slip your plant pot into the centre so it is held securely. As you get more confident, you can adjust the levels at which you tie the knots to hold larger or smaller pots.

Looking up

Sunrise and sunset

With just a few hours of sunlight each day, plant growth is very slow or stops altogether during the winter months, but evergreens soldier on in the low light.

DAY	LONDON		EDINBURGH	
	Sunrise	Sunset	Sunrise	Sunset
Thu, 1 Jan	8:03:56 am	4:04:12 pm	8:40:58 am	3:51:44 pm
Fri, 2 Jan	8:03:48 am	4:05:16 pm	8:40:41 am	3:52:58 pm
Sat, 3 Jan	8:03:36 am	4:06:23 pm	8:40:19 am	3:54:15 pm
Sun, 4 Jan	8:03:22 am	4:07:32 pm	8:39:54 am	3:55:35 pm
Mon, 5 Jan	8:03:04 am	4:08:44 pm	8:39:24 am	3:56:58 pm
Tue, 6 Jan	8:02:43 am	4:09:58 pm	8:38:51 am	3:58:24 pm
Wed, 7 Jan	8:02:19 am	4:11:14 pm	8:38:14 am	3:59:53 pm
Thu, 8 Jan	8:01:51 am	4:12:32 pm	8:37:32 am	4:01:25 pm
Fri, 9 Jan	8:01:20 am	4:13:53 pm	8:36:48 am	4:03:00 pm
Sat, 10 Jan	8:00:46 am	4:15:16 pm	8:35:59 am	4:04:38 pm
Sun, 11 Jan	8:00:09 am	4:16:41 pm	8:35:07 am	4:06:18 pm
Mon, 12 Jan	7:59:29 am	4:18:07 pm	8:34:11 am	4:08:00 pm
Tue, 13 Jan	7:58:46 am	4:19:36 pm	8:33:11 am	4:09:45 pm
Wed, 14 Jan	7:58:00 am	4:21:06 pm	8:32:09 am	4:11:31 pm
Thu, 15 Jan	7:57:11 am	4:22:37 pm	8:31:02 am	4:13:20 pm
Fri, 16 Jan	7:56:19 am	4:24:11 pm	8:29:53 am	4:15:11 pm
Sat, 17 Jan	7:55:24 am	4:25:45 pm	8:28:40 am	4:17:04 pm
Sun, 18 Jan	7:54:26 am	4:27:22 pm	8:27:24 am	4:18:58 pm
Mon, 19 Jan	7:53:26 am	4:28:59 pm	8:26:05 am	4:20:54 pm
Tue, 20 Jan	7:52:23 am	4:30:38 pm	8:24:43 am	4:22:52 pm
Wed, 21 Jan	7:51:17 am	4:32:18 pm	8:23:18 am	4:24:51 pm
Thu, 22 Jan	7:50:09 am	4:33:58 pm	8:21:50 am	4:26:51 pm
Fri, 23 Jan	7:48:58 am	4:35:40 pm	8:20:20 am	4:28:53 pm
Sat, 24 Jan	7:47:45 am	4:37:23 pm	8:18:47 am	4:30:56 pm
Sun, 25 Jan	7:46:29 am	4:39:07 pm	8:17:11 am	4:32:59 pm
Mon, 26 Jan	7:45:11 am	4:40:51 pm	8:15:32 am	4:35:04 pm
Tue, 27 Jan	7:43:50 am	4:42:36 pm	8:13:51 am	4:37:10 pm
Wed, 28 Jan	7:42:28 am	4:44:22 pm	8:12:08 am	4:39:16 pm
Thu, 29 Jan	7:41:03 am	4:46:09 pm	8:10:22 am	4:41:24 pm
Fri, 30 Jan	7:39:36 am	4:47:55 pm	8:08:34 am	4:43:31 pm
Sat, 31 Jan	7:38:06 am	4:49:43 pm	8:06:43 am	4:45:40 pm

Moonrise and moonset

Moon phases

○ **FULL MOON** 3 January   ● **NEW MOON** 18 January
◐ **THIRD QUARTER** 10 January   ◑ **FIRST QUARTER** 26 January

DAY	LONDON			EDINBURGH		
	Moonrise	Moonset	Moonrise	Moonrise	Moonset	Moonrise
1 Jan		6:28	13:25		07:20	12:59
2 Jan		07:45	14:27		08:40	13:58
3 Jan		08:42	15:47		09:32	15:24
4 Jan		09:20	17:17		10:02	17:03
5 Jan		09:45	18:47		10:18	18:41
6 Jan		10:03	20:12		10:29	20:14
7 Jan		10:17	21:32		10:36	21:40
8 Jan		10:28	22:48		10:42	23:02
9 Jan		10:39			10:47	
10 Jan	00:02	10:50		00:22	10:53	
11 Jan	01:14	11:02		01:41	10:59	
12 Jan	02:27	11:17		03:00	11:08	
13 Jan	03:41	11:36		04:21	11:20	
14 Jan	04:53	12:02		05:40	11:39	
15 Jan	06:00	12:39		06:53	12:11	
16 Jan	06:57	13:29		07:53	12:59	
17Jan	07:43	14:33		08:34	14:07	
18 Jan	08:16	15:46		09:01	15:28	
19 Jan	08:40	17:04		09:17	16:54	
20 Jan	08:58	18:24		09:28	18:21	
21 Jan	09:12	19:43		09:36	19:47	
22 Jan	09:25	21:02		09:42	21:12	
23 Jan	09:36	22:21		09:48	22:38	
24 Jan	09:48	23:43		09:54		
25 Jan	10:01				00:07	10:01
26 Jan		01:09	10:18		01:40	10:11
27 Jan		02:37	10:42		03:17	10:26
28 Jan		04:06	11:16		04:55	10:52
29 Jan		05:27	12:07		06:21	11:38
30 Jan		06:31	13:18		07:24	12:51
31 Jan		07:15	14:43		08:01	14:24

Average temperature & rainfall

This table shows the average minimum and maximum temperatures, indicated by the blue and red dots, together with the average rainfall and number of rainy days for this month. The horizontal rules show how the figures have varied over the past decade.

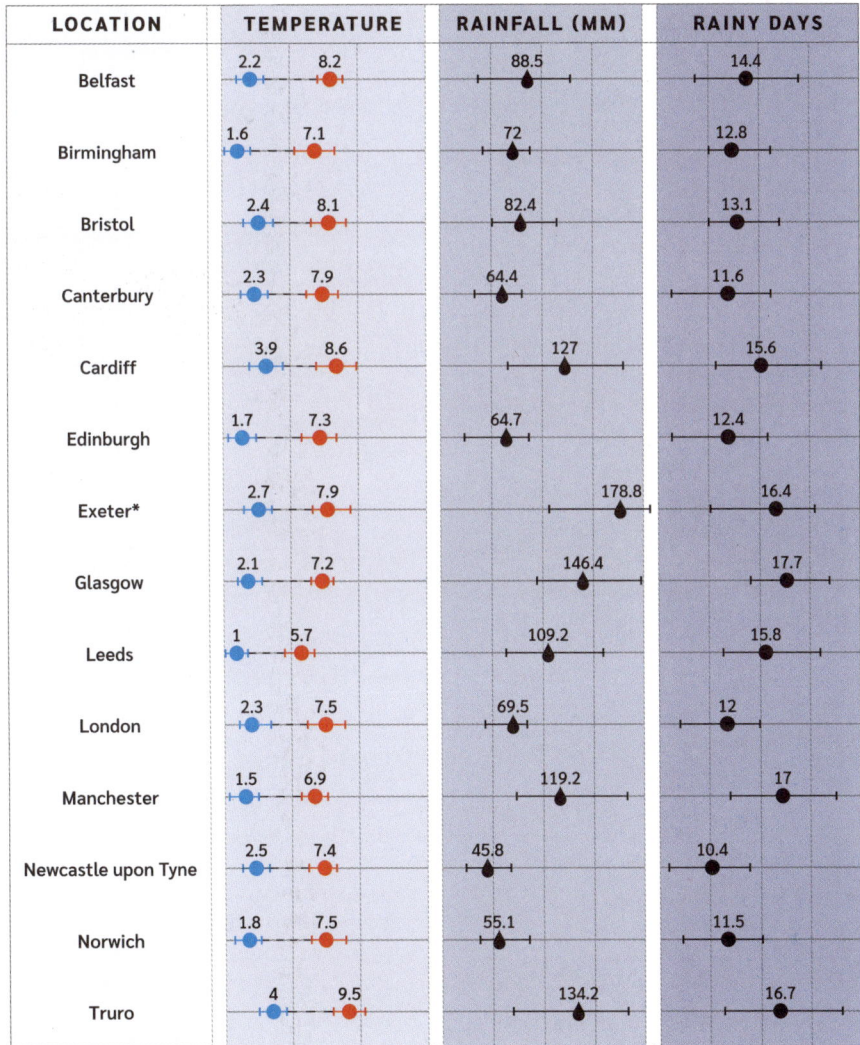

LOCATION	TEMPERATURE	RAINFALL (MM)	RAINY DAYS
Belfast	2.2 8.2	88.5	14.4
Birmingham	1.6 7.1	72	12.8
Bristol	2.4 8.1	82.4	13.1
Canterbury	2.3 7.9	64.4	11.6
Cardiff	3.9 8.6	127	15.6
Edinburgh	1.7 7.3	64.7	12.4
Exeter*	2.7 7.9	178.8	16.4
Glasgow	2.1 7.2	146.4	17.7
Leeds	1 5.7	109.2	15.8
London	2.3 7.5	69.5	12
Manchester	1.5 6.9	119.2	17
Newcastle upon Tyne	2.5 7.4	45.8	10.4
Norwich	1.8 7.5	55.1	11.5
Truro	4 9.5	134.2	16.7

* figures for Bovey Tracey

Temperature scale: 0   5   10
Rainfall scale: 50   100   150   200
Rainy days scale: 10   15   20

Sustainable gardening

Houseplants that last

Thriving, happy houseplants that live for many years not only give us great joy, they are also the more sustainable, since a failing houseplant that's quickly discarded has a relatively higher carbon footprint compared to one that's long-lived, especially if it and its pot end up in landfill. However, January can be a tricky time for these cosseted plants and they can begin to show signs of stress, having endured three months of central heating, low winter light levels and, possibly, overwatering.

Worse still, moribund houseplants leave owners feeling miserable, according to a 2022 research study by the RHS and Reading University, which looked at the mental health of over 500 UK adult houseplant owners. On the other hand, attractive, healthy plants had a highly positive effect, and while swift recycling and replacement of jaded plants restores people's spirits, plants that survive for a long period are preferable.

WATERING WITH CARE

So, how can we turn the table, and keep plants thriving and our spirits up during these cold, dark days? Watering is the trickiest part: plants look peaky, and it's easy to assume they need a drink, but in winter most need just enough moisture to keep the compost slightly damp.

Moth orchids are easy to grow, thriving in centrally heated homes and surviving periods of neglect.

Overwatering and soggy soils lead to fungal plant diseases that can be fatal, so make sure your houseplant is in a pot with drainage holes in the bottom. You can then set that pot in a decorative waterproof container, removing it to water your plant over the sink, then leaving it to drain before replacing it. If the plant is too big to move, irrigate lightly and check that water is not pooling in the waterproof container.

The simplest way to measure moisture is by assessing the weight of the inner pot: very light indicates excessively dry, while very heavy means the compost is sodden, and both extremes are best avoided. Another way to test the compost moisture level is with your finger – if the top feels damp, no more water is needed. If sogginess results despite your best efforts, a plant can sometimes be saved by tipping it out of the pot and drying the roots with some kitchen towel before repotting. Another good tip is to position your plants where you can see them easily, so that you remember to check them regularly.

If you don't have much time to nurture your plants, choose easy-care moth orchids (*Phalaenopsis*), which are happy in bright, warm rooms, or opt for shade-tolerant plants such as the ZZ plant (*Zamioculcas zamiifolia*) and spider plant (*Chlorophytum comosum*), which both tolerate periods of neglect. The rabbit's foot fern (*Davallia solida* var.

Only water when the top of the compost feels dry.

fejeensis), with its surface rhizomes, can also tolerate some drought, unlike most ferns – douse the rhizomes with water, too, as they also absorb moisture.

LET IN THE LIGHT

Light is important, too, and plants set near a north-facing window will often struggle in winter. As a rule, give plants as much light as possible now, until levels increase in April, moving flagging specimens closer to a sunnier window or setting them under grow lights. Good choices for gloomy areas that can't be avoided include the cast-iron plant (*Aspidistra*), golden pothos (*Epipremnum aureum*) and Boston fern (*Nephrolepis exaltata* 'Bostoniensis').

HEAT STRESS

Central heating and radiators stress houseplants, so move heat-stressed plants to a cooler or unheated room to recover, if possible. Plants that cope with heat, but need plenty of light include *Aloe vera*, Swiss cheese plant (*Monstera*) and flaming Katy (*Kalanchoe blossfeldiana*).

Having said all this, remember that popular houseplants are essentially weeds in their tropical homes, thriving beneath oppressive luxuriant vegetation or battling drought and dry air in the case of cacti and succulents. These are born survivors and most require just a little know-how to get them through tougher winter conditions.

Edible garden

While the temperatures are freezing outside, you can lift your spirits by sowing hardy crops indoors on a windowsill or in a conservatory if you don't have a heated greenhouse. Winter vegetables such as carrots and sprouts are also ready to be picked now.

Vegetables

SOW INDOORS Broad beans; lettuce; microgreens ❶; peas; radishes; spinach; summer cabbages.

PLANT OUTDOORS Asparagus crowns; garlic sets; Jerusalem artichokes; shallots.

HARVEST Brussels sprouts; carrots; cauliflowers (in mild regions); celeriac; chard; Jerusalem artichokes; kale; leeks; lettuce and radishes grown under a cloche or in a cool greenhouse, as well as hardy winter radishes grown outside; parsnips; sprouting broccoli; swedes; turnips; winter cabbages and savoys.

Fruit

PLANT OUTDOORS Bare-root hardy fruit trees such as apples, apricots, cherries, nectarines, peaches, pears, plums, quinces.

HARVEST Citrus fruits such as lemons and oranges grown under cover can be harvested now when ripe, as indicated by the colour of the skin.

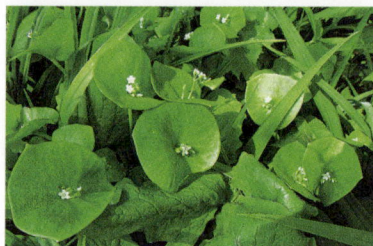

HERB OF THE MONTH: WINTER PURSLANE (*Claytonia perfoliata*)
Also known as miner's lettuce, this low-growing hardy herb can be harvested throughout the winter from a summer or early autumn sowing. Grow it in a sheltered spot where the round leaves and flowering shoots add a mild flavour, similar to lettuce, to salads and other dishes. If you allow some of the plants to flower, they will self-seed, or you can harvest the seed, to save buying more the following year. You can also sow winter purslane in spring to produce a crop in summer.

Challenges this month

The low temperatures in winter kill many unwanted creatures or they may lie low, hiding in crevices and other sheltered areas until spring arrives. However, houseplants can still be affected by fungus gnats and the wet weather outside encourages moss and algae.

ALGAE thrive in wet winter weather, producing a green film or powdery deposit on paths, decks and patios, and making them slippery and potentially hazardous. Likewise, moss and liverworts, which form flat, plate-like growths, can exacerbate the problem. These organisms collectively boost biodiversity, providing food and habitats for beetles, spiders and woodlice, as well as microscopic invertebrates, so only remove them where they may cause injury. As they all thrive in shade, removing overhanging branches will allow more sunlight to dry the surfaces. Also use a stiff broom or wire brush to remove established growths, and dig out moss from paving cracks with a pointed weeding tool or knife. Avoid chemical products, which can harm wildlife and the environment.

FUNGUS GNATS, also known as sciarid flies, are tiny greyish-brown flies often found in damp compost or flying around houseplants. Their larvae, which are whitish with black heads and about 6mm (¼in) in length, can sometimes damage seedlings and cuttings. While these flies can be a nuisance, the larvae do not harm established plants, and outside in the garden, they and the adults form an important part of a healthy ecosystem. Indoors, use potting media formulated for houseplants and in winter allow the surface to dry out between waterings. Always plant in a pot with drainage holes, and leave it to drain after watering (see p.18). Where larvae are eating seedlings and cuttings, try a biological control for fungus gnats, available from online suppliers.

SNAILS AND SLUGS (pictured) are active all year, but cause less damage to plants in winter. Snails stay mostly dormant in sheltered areas, while slugs spend winter underground. You may be able to provide an extra winter food source for birds while reducing the mollusc population by raking over the soil and removing patches of fallen leaves on beds and borders to expose slugs' and snails' eggs to their natural predators.

Garden benefactors

Song and mistle thrushes

Brightening up the winter garden with their spotted breasts and tuneful, whistling calls, thrushes are gardeners' friends in other ways, too, eating slugs, snails, caterpillars, and aphids that can threaten our plants.

These medium-sized birds include the song thrush (pictured) and mistle thrush, which is named after its penchant for mistletoe berries. The numbers of both species are on the decline, due largely to habitat loss and the use of insecticides, but the smaller song thrush is more abundant, while the mistle thrush is on the red list and at risk of extinction. Gardeners can help to reverse the downward trend in numbers by avoiding slug pellets, which kill the molluscs these beautiful birds rely on for food, and providing plants that will sustain them.

The song thrush favours snails and can be seen smashing them on rocks to access the flesh inside, so provide a few large stones for them to use. Mistle thrushes prefer slugs and insects, while both species eat berries, including those of holly (*Ilex*), hawthorn (*Crataegus*), rowan (*Sorbus*), ivy (*Hedera helix*), and mistletoe (*Viscum album*), as well as the fallen fruit from apple and pear trees.

Also provide plenty of nesting sites, such as hedges, shrubs and trees, and leave fallen foliage on the ground, as it harbours the insects and molluscs that support them and their chicks.

The birds start nesting from early to late spring. Song thrushes build a cup-shaped nest and lay between four to six glossy blue eggs, which hatch two weeks later. The chicks fledge a fortnight after hatching but still rely on their parents to feed them for some time after that. Mistle thrushes' nests are not as neat, and they lay three to six eggs, which also hatch after two weeks, while the chicks fledge two to three weeks later.

Design masterclass

Jo Thompson

One of the UK's most admired garden designers and plantswomen, Jo Thompson is a well-known face at the RHS Chelsea Flower Show, where she has created ten top award-winning show gardens, the most recent being 'The Glasshouse Garden' for the 2025 event. She also designed the Cool and new Winter Gardens at RHS Rosemoor in Devon, and collaborated with landscape architects Gustafson Porter + Bowman on the conservation of Highgate Cemetery, the resting place of George Eliot, Karl Marx, and George Michael, among many other famous figures.

Jo began her career as a teacher after studying modern languages at university, but soon found her true calling when she signed up for a design course at the English Gardening School. She established her practice in 1999 and has since enjoyed huge success, designing private gardens and public spaces here in the UK and abroad.

HOW TO DESIGN A SMALL GARDEN

Having designed many award-winning small gardens, Jo offers her tips on making the most of a restricted space.

▶ 'You may have a small floor area, but think of the volume in three dimensions and all the space above the ground that you can fill with climbers, trees and shrubs.'

▶ 'Clothe the boundaries with plants – roses, clematis, honeysuckle – that offer flower and leaf colour, while increasing privacy. Choose their supports carefully, too, keeping them simple and avoiding gimmicky features such as trellis with diamond-shaped apertures that attract the eye, accentuating the boundaries. Simple square trellis or horizontal wires have the opposite effect, blurring the boundaries and making the garden appear larger.'

▶ 'Take inspiration from surrounding buildings or countryside to create a design that suits its setting – a Moroccan-inspired courtyard, for example, will look out of place in a UK city, while a design that picks up on the colours of the surrounding masonry and echoes the street trees will be more fitting.'

Plants for difficult places

Soils prone to waterlogging

Despite the challenging conditions, there are plenty of plants that thrive in soils which experience periodic waterlogging.

Soils that are rich in clay are often prone to waterlogging because they drain poorly. In winter, they can be heavy and sticky and puddles may form on the surface after heavy rain, while in summer they often bake hard to form a crust with wide cracks in it. These extreme conditions make the soil difficult to cultivate, so avoid digging them at these times.

An annual application of well-rotted garden compost or other organic matter, applied as a mulch over the surface in autumn, will gradually make things easier (see also pp.36–7). As well as adding some nutrients, organic matter helps to open up a soil, improving its structure and increasing drainage, while also helping to prevent cracking. In this way, increasing the levels of organic matter in your soil over several years can ameliorate the extremes of winter wet and hard, dry, summer soils.

Saturated soils have insufficient oxygen to maintain healthy roots and only aquatic pond plants will survive if these conditions persist. However, other shrubs and perennials are adapted to cope with wet soils, so if your ground is always damp, but not permanently waterlogged, search for bog plants at rhs.org.uk for a selection that will thrive in your garden.

For clay soils that experience temporary waterlogging, but are reasonably dry for the rest of the time, consider the colourful stems of *Cornus* for winter interest and the showy summer flowers of *Hydrangea arborescens* 'Annabelle', which look stunning when set against the dark foliage of the ninebark *Physocarpus opulifolius* 'Diabolo'. Use perennials such as loosestrife and astrantias to help extend the interest at lower levels. Using the ethos of 'right plant, right place' to create a sustainable planting

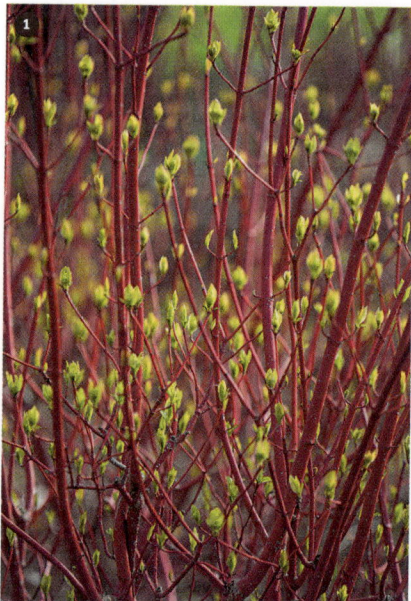

combination helps minimize waste and creates robust, long-lived schemes that benefit soil health and biodiversity.

PLANTING CHOICES FOR WET SOILS

① Siberian dogwood
(*Cornus alba* 'Sibirica')
This hardy, medium-sized deciduous shrub produces thickets of slender red stems that turn bright crimson in winter. Clusters of small, cream flowers appear in spring and summer among the green foliage, followed by blue-white berries. **H&S:** 1.5 × 1.5m (5 × 5ft)

Ninebark 'Diabolo'
(*Physocarpus opulifolius* 'Diabolo')
A deciduous hardy shrub, grown for its deep purple, lobed leaves and domed clusters of pink-tinged white flowers in summer. **H&S:** 1.5 × 1.5m (5 × 5ft)

Hydrangea 'Annabelle'
(*Hydrangea arborescens* 'Annabelle')
This large hydrangea is loved for its huge globes of creamy-white flowers, which appear in late summer and fade to pale lime in autumn, when the dark green foliage also turns yellow.
H&S: up to 2 × 2m (6ft 6in × 6ft 6in)

② Meadow rue (*Thalictrum delavayi*)
The slender dark purple stems of this tall, hardy perennial produce sprays of dainty little lilac-mauve flowers in late summer over delicate ferny foliage.
H&S: 1.2 × 0.6m (4 × 2ft)

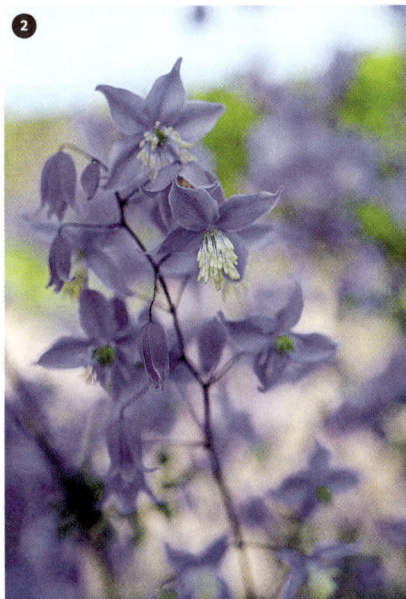

Purple loosestrife (*Lythrum salicaria*)
Stems of slim, willowy leaves are topped in summer with spikes of small purplish-pink flowers, which decorate this hardy perennial over a long period.
H&S: 90 × 75cm (3ft × 2ft 6in)

Great black masterwort
(*Astrantia major* 'Claret')
Dark red pincushion-shaped flowers appear on this hardy perennial in summer over deeply lobed, dark green leaves. **H&S:** 90 × 30cm (36 × 12in)

February

Love is in the air now, as frogs and toads take to the water to mate in February and birds begin their search for secure nesting sites. Sap is also rising, as buds on trees and shrubs begin to swell, stirring into life after their winter slumber. Beneath their branches, the nodding flowers of dainty snowdrops and early daffodils herald longer days and the promise of spring.

KEY EVENTS
Candlemas Day, 2 February
St Valentine's Day, 14 February
Maha Shivaratri, 15–16 February
Shrove Tuesday, 17 February
Lunar New Year, 17 February (*Year of the Horse*)
Start of Ramadan, 18 February

What to do in February

As the garden starts to wake from its winter slumber, we too must get back into action to keep pace with the quickening growth. While it's still a little cold for sowing seeds outside, you can make new beds and borders ready for the spring season, and continue planting bare-root plants (see p.10) for a show of colour later in the year.

SOW HARDY ANNUALS indoors in trays and pots this month for earlier flowers. Good choices include pot marigolds (*Calendula*), love-in-a-mist (*Nigella*), poppies (*Papaver*), wild carrot (*Daucus carota*) and baby blue eyes (*Nemophila menziesii*). The young seedlings can then be planted outside in late spring. ❶

TRIM BACK WINTER-FLOWERING HEATHERS after they have flowered. This will encourage new growth to develop and bushier plants that will produce more flowers in the winter. ❷

CUT BACK DECIDUOUS GRASSES, such as *Calamagrostis, Molinia caerulea* and *Stipa gigantea*, in late February or early March, taking the old, dry stems down to the ground, before the new growth appears. Delay pruning *Miscanthus sinensis* until next month and *Pennisetum orientale* until April, since they shoot a little later and the old stems protect the new growth from cold winter weather. After cutting, spread a thick mulch of organic matter around the clumps.

TAKE CUTTINGS of tender fuchsias and pelargoniums that have been overwintered indoors, when you see some new shoots developing. Remove a stem about 7–10cm

In the garden

PLANT SNOWDROPS IN THE GREEN
These little winter flowers can be grown from dry bulbs planted in autumn, but the best results usually derive from small clumps planted while in leaf after flowering. Look for them on sale this month, and plant them as soon as they arrive.

Use shredded bark chips for trees and large shrubs, and leave a gap around their woody stems.

In the fruit & veg patch

PREPARE VEGETABLE BEDS for planting in the coming months. Remove unwanted plants and debris, and apply a mulch of well-rotted garden compost or manure (see below, left). For areas on heavy clay soil, you may increase your harvests by planting in raised beds filled with imported topsoil mixed with plenty of organic matter.

(3–4in) long, cutting just beneath a leaf joint (node) on the new growth. Remove the lower leaves, leaving about three or four on the stem. Pop your cuttings in pots of gritty, peat-free cuttings compost, keep them moist, and new roots should develop within a few weeks. Repot them when they outgrow their original pot.

CUT BACK AUTUMN RASPBERRIES, removing the old stems that carried fruit the previous year. This will encourage new canes to grow in the spring. **3**

MULCH THE SOIL with a 5–8cm (2–3in) layer of well-rotted garden compost or farmyard manure. This will help to suppress weeds, retain soil moisture and improve the soil as it rots down further.

PRUNING TIP
Clematis
Clematis fall into three main groups and each is pruned in a different way. Group 1 comprises winter- and spring-flowering clematis, and need no regular pruning, except to keep large plants in check after flowering. Group 2 comprises large-flowered cultivars that bloom in May or June. Prune these lightly in February, taking each stem back to the first or second strong, healthy bud from the top. Removing the old blooms after flowering may also encourage a second flush in late summer. Group 3 clematis flower from midsummer to early autumn, and they are also pruned in February. Simply cut back all the stems to a healthy bud close to the ground. They will then flower on the new stems that form in the current year.

PROTECT BLOSSOM from frost on apricots, nectarines and peaches by covering the plants in hessian or horticultural fleece at night. Remove it in the morning to allow the sunlight in and bees to access the blooms. It takes some effort to do this, but you will be rewarded with heavier crops.

SOW SMALL-SEEDED TENDER VEG such as indoor tomatoes, aubergines and peppers indoors on a well-lit windowsill. Sow them thinly in trays or pots of peat-free seed compost, and keep the young seedlings moist as they grow. Also turn the pots and trays regularly so that they don't grow tall and spindly. When they have three or four leaves and can be handled, transfer the seedlings into individual containers and grow on. Keep these tender plants protected in a greenhouse or conservatory, where they will fruit later in the year.

SOW EARLY HARDY CROPS indoors in pots, following the instructions for tender veg above. Try pointed cabbages, sprouting broccoli (calabrese), cauliflowers, and salad leaves. When large enough, the young crops can be planted outside in April.

FEED FRUIT TREES with an organic-based potassium-rich fertilizer, including those made from seaweed, following the instructions on the pack.

Indoors

DIVIDE BEGONIA TUBERS when shoots start to appear in late February or early March. Cut into sections, each with at least one bud, then leave for a few hours for cuts to callous over before potting them up into individual containers. Plant with the top of the tuber level with the surface of the compost.

CHECK LIGHT LEVELS for houseplants that are looking lacklustre, or if their leaves are paler than usual. Cacti and succulents need a sunny position to thrive, while large-leaved plants can generally tolerate lower light levels and may scorch, given too much sun (see also pp.18–19 for more advice).

MONEY-SAVING IDEA
Buy small plants to grow on
Known as plugs, small seedling bedding plants and crops are on sale now from garden centres and online. They are generally cheaper than more mature plants, and you can bulk buy to fill your garden or allotment later in the season. You will need to repot them a few times, so save supermarket food containers and old containers to accommodate them and they will soon grow to the same size as the larger plants that cost two or three times as much.

Plants of the month

1. Bedding daisy
   (*Bellis perennis*)
2. Wintersweet
   (*Chimonanthus praecox*)
3. Winter-flowering
   clematis (*Clematis
   cirrhosa* var. *purpurascens*
   'Freckles' pictured)
4. Crocus (*Crocus*)
5. Daffodil (*Narcissus*
   'Peeping Tom' pictured)
6. Paperbush
   (*Edgeworthia chrysantha*)
7. Winter aconite
   (*Eranthis hyemalis*)
8. Snowdrop (*Galanthus*
   'Dionysus' pictured)
9. White-stemmed bramble
   (*Rubus cockburnianus*)
10. Forbes' squill
    (*Scilla forbesii*)
11. Hacquetia
    (*Sanicula epipactis*)

Project: Weave a willow cone

Quick and easy to make, this natural plant support is constructed from willow or hazel stems. You can also tailor the circumference and height of your cone to suit the plants it will need to support, such as annual sweet peas and perennial clematis, or climbing crops, including French or runner beans. Try using your own willow, but do not use fresh stems, which will root when plunged into the soil. Cut them in January and leave to dry – stripping the bark from the bases also reduces rooting. Or buy rods and flexible stems, known as withies, from specialist willow suppliers – you may need to soak the latter first. Also check out RHS workshops that teach the art of willow weaving at rhs.org.uk/findanevent.

YOU WILL NEED
Length of plywood
Electric drill
Secateurs
Willow rods and
    withies
Cable tie or wire

2 Bundle together the vertical rods at the top, checking that they are directly above the centre of the cone, and secure tightly with a long cable tie or wire.

3 To stiffen the whole structure, weave another band of withies about 30cm (12in) below the cable tie. Trim off any loose ends around the band with secateurs.

1 Make a circle of holes in the plywood with a drill to the diameter you require (we made 16 here with a 90cm (3ft) diameter), large enough to hold the upright willow rods. Make a slanting cut at the end of each rod to make them easier to push into the ground, and insert them in the holes. Weave a twig band 15cm (6in) above the base of the rods, as shown.

Looking up

Sunrise and sunset

The days are growing longer more quickly this month, with the increase in light levels lifting our spirits and prompting plants to stir into growth in the garden.

DAY	LONDON		EDINBURGH	
	Sunrise	Sunset	Sunrise	Sunset
Sun, 1 Feb	7:36:35 am	4:51:31 pm	8:04:51 am	4:47:49 pm
Mon, 2 Feb	7:35:02 am	4:53:19 pm	8:02:57 am	4:49:58 pm
Tue, 3 Feb	7:33:27 am	4:55:07 pm	8:01:00 am	4:52:08 pm
Wed, 4 Feb	7:31:50 am	4:56:56 pm	7:59:01 am	4:54:18 pm
Thu, 5 Feb	7:30:11 am	4:58:45 pm	7:57:01 am	4:56:29 pm
Fri, 6 Feb	7:28:30 am	5:00:34 pm	7:54:59 am	4:58:39 pm
Sat, 7 Feb	7:26:48 am	5:02:23 pm	7:52:55 am	5:00:50 pm
Sun, 8 Feb	7:25:04 am	5:04:13 pm	7:50:49 am	5:03:01 pm
Mon, 9 Feb	7:23:18 am	5:06:02 pm	7:48:42 am	5:05:12 pm
Tue, 10 Feb	7:21:31 am	5:07:51 pm	7:46:33 am	5:07:23 pm
Wed, 11 Feb	7:19:42 am	5:09:41 pm	7:44:22 am	5:09:34 pm
Thu, 12 Feb	7:17:52 am	5:11:30 pm	7:42:10 am	5:11:45 pm
Fri, 13 Feb	7:16:00 am	5:13:20 pm	7:39:57 am	5:13:56 pm
Sat, 14 Feb	7:14:07 am	5:15:09 pm	7:37:42 am	5:16:07 pm
Sun, 15 Feb	7:12:12 am	5:16:58 pm	7:35:26 am	5:18:18 pm
Mon, 16 Feb	7:10:16 am	5:18:47 pm	7:33:09 am	5:20:28 pm
Tue, 17 Feb	7:08:19 am	5:20:35 pm	7:30:50 am	5:22:39 pm
Wed, 18 Feb	7:06:21 am	5:22:24 pm	7:28:30 am	5:24:49 pm
Thu, 19 Feb	7:04:22 am	5:24:12 pm	7:26:09 am	5:26:59 pm
Fri, 20 Feb	7:02:21 am	5:26:01 pm	7:23:47 am	5:29:09 pm
Sat, 21 Feb	7:00:20 am	5:27:49 pm	7:21:24 am	5:31:18 pm
Sun, 22 Feb	6:58:17 am	5:29:36 pm	7:19:00 am	5:33:27 pm
Mon, 23 Feb	6:56:13 am	5:31:24 pm	7:16:35 am	5:35:36 pm
Tue, 24 Feb	6:54:09 am	5:33:11 pm	7:14:09 am	5:37:45 pm
Wed, 25 Feb	6:52:03 am	5:34:58 pm	7:11:42 am	5:39:54 pm
Thu, 26 Feb	6:49:57 am	5:36:45 pm	7:09:14 am	5:42:02 pm
Fri, 27 Feb	6:47:50 am	5:38:31 pm	6:31:15 am	5:44:10 pm
Sat, 28 Feb	6:45:42 am	5:40:17 pm	7:04:16 am	5:46:17 pm

Moonrise and moonset

Moon phases

○ **FULL MOON** 1 February   ● **NEW MOON** 17 February
◐ **THIRD QUARTER** 9 February   ◑ **FIRST QUARTER** 24 February

DAY	LONDON			EDINBURGH		
	Moonrise	Moonset	Moonrise	Moonrise	Moonset	Moonrise
1 Feb		07:45	16:13		08:23	16:03
2 Feb		08:06	17:42		08:35	17:40
3 Feb		08:22	19:05		08:44	19:10
4 Feb		08:34	20:24		08:50	20:36
5 Feb		08:45	21:41		08:56	21:58
6 Feb		08:56	22:55		09:01	23:19
7 Feb		09:08			09:07	
8 Feb	00:10	09:21		00:40	09:15	
9 Feb	01:24	09:39		02:01	09:25	
10 Feb	02:37	10:02		03:22	09:41	
11 Feb	03:47	10:34		04:39	10:07	
12 Feb	04:49	11:18		05:44	10:48	
13 Feb	05:39	12:17		06:33	11:49	
14 Feb	06:16	13:27		07:04	13:05	
15 Feb	06:44	14:44		07:24	14:31	
16 Feb	07:04	16:05		07:37	15:59	
17 Feb	07:20	17:26		07:45	17:27	
18 Feb	07:33	18:46		07:52	18:54	
19 Feb	07:44	20:07		07:58	20:22	
20 Feb	07:56	21:30		08:04	21:52	
21 Feb	08:09	22:56		08:11	23:24	
22 Feb	08:25			08:19		
23 Feb		00:24	08:46		01:01	08:33
24 Feb		01:53	09:16		02:39	08:54
25 Feb		03:15	10:00		04:09	09:32
26 Feb		04:23	11:02		05:18	10:33
27 Feb		05:13	12:21		06:02	11:58
28 Feb		05:47	13:48		06:28	13:34

Average temperature & rainfall

This table shows the average minimum and maximum temperatures, indicated by the blue and red dots, together with the average rainfall and number of rainy days for this month. The horizontal rules show how the figures have varied over the past decade.

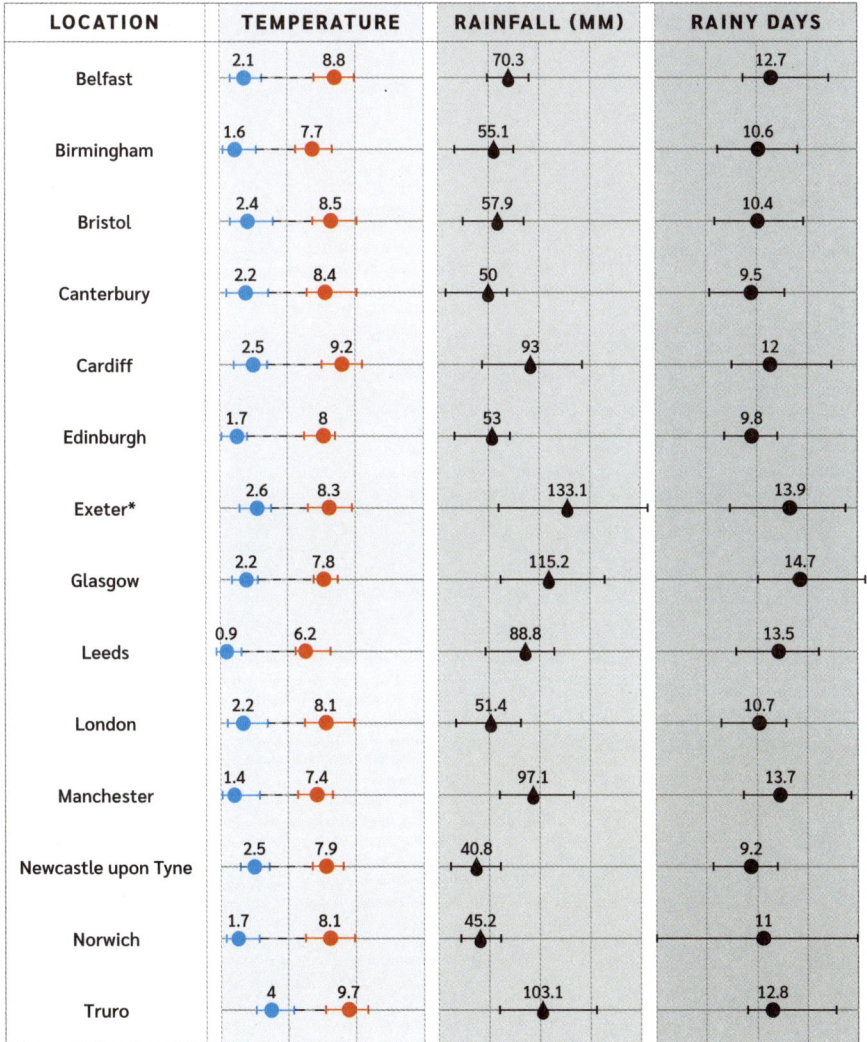

LOCATION	TEMPERATURE	RAINFALL (MM)	RAINY DAYS
Belfast	2.1 8.8	70.3	12.7
Birmingham	1.6 7.7	55.1	10.6
Bristol	2.4 8.5	57.9	10.4
Canterbury	2.2 8.4	50	9.5
Cardiff	2.5 9.2	93	12
Edinburgh	1.7 8	53	9.8
Exeter*	2.6 8.3	133.1	13.9
Glasgow	2.2 7.8	115.2	14.7
Leeds	0.9 6.2	88.8	13.5
London	2.2 8.1	51.4	10.7
Manchester	1.4 7.4	97.1	13.7
Newcastle upon Tyne	2.5 7.9	40.8	9.2
Norwich	1.7 8.1	45.2	11
Truro	4 9.7	103.1	12.8

* figures for Bovey Tracey   0   5   10   50   100   150   200   5   10   15

Sustainable gardening

Caring for soil sustainably

Many people give soil little thought but, in fact, this humble brown material comprises a complex ecosystem and it is key to the health of both plants and the planet. As well as providing plants with access to food, water and anchoring their roots, soil is an exceptionally rich wildlife habitat, home to a wide variety of creatures and microorganisms. It is also a carbon sink, helping to combat climate change – in the UK alone, soil stores ten billion tonnes of carbon and plays an essential role in mitigating the effects of climate change.

So, what is soil and how does it nurture plants and the environment? The average garden soil is composed of minerals, air, water and organic matter, the latter inhabited by fungi, bacteria, microbes, protozoa, worms and a host of other organisms. The minerals range

Sandy soil will fall apart when you try to roll it.

from coarse sand to fine clay particles, and these define the texture of soil and influence its individual properties. For example, a soil rich in clay minerals is generally moisture-retentive and fertile, while sandy soils are free-draining and hold fewer plant nutrients; silty soils are somewhere in between, with more nutrients than sand but slightly better drainage than clay. Loams have a good balance of clay, sand and silt particles and form the well-drained, water-retentive soil we all hanker after.

A good starting point for gardeners is to check the texture of your soil by digging up a sample from just below the surface and rolling it between your fingers. Clay soil feels sticky, has a shiny finish when rubbed, and can be rolled into a sausage shape. Sandy soil feels gritty and will fall apart when you try to roll it. Silt soils, which are rare in domestic gardens, have a slippery, soapy texture, and cannot be rolled into a sausage.

IMPROVING MATTERS
While there are plants adapted to thrive in all types of soil, you can broaden your choices by improving the way the particles are held together, known as its structure. Heavy clays that become waterlogged in winter, and dry to form a hard, cracked surface in summer, can be very challenging, but they can be improved by applying a layer at least

Improve your soil with an organic mulch.

water clings to them for longer, allowing plants time to absorb the moisture before it drains away. Using mulches in this way also eliminates the need to dig organic matter into the soil, which can release the greenhouse gas, carbon dioxide, into the atmosphere, while also destroying fungal networks and soil organisms essential for plant growth.

The 'no-dig' approach can reduce weeding, too, since any weed seeds that fall on the mulch remain on the surface, where many will be eaten by birds, ants and other garden creatures. Some unwanted plants will inevitably take root, but hoeing off the seedlings regularly is easy and less disruptive than digging out mature plants.

NATURE'S FERTILIZERS

Like us, plants need food to grow and thrive. The nutrients they require are nitrogen, potassium and phosphorus, with some magnesium and sulphur, and tiny traces of other elements. RHS research shows that the nutrients in garden soil are sufficient to sustain most plants, especially if it is mulched. However, hungry fruit, vegetables and some roses will benefit from fertilizers. Organic-based fertilizers, applied as directed by the manufacturer, will be effective, and a soil analysis every five years can be a good investment – see rhs.org.uk for details.

5cm (2in) deep of organic matter such as rotted compost or manure over the surface (known as mulching) in spring or autumn. The same treatment will also help a very free-draining sandy soil to retain more water and nutrients.

Soil organisms devour the organic matter you apply and their remains and secretions act as 'glue' that binds tiny clay minerals into lumps called peds, allowing roots, air and water to penetrate it. This glue also covers the surface of larger sand particles so that

Edible garden

Start sowing tender crops such as aubergines and chillies that require a long season of growth for the fruits to mature, and, in mild areas, also start off hardy crops under cloches or in a cold frame. In the fruit garden, cheaper bare-root plants are still available.

Vegetables

SOW INDOORS Aubergines; Brussels sprouts; chillies; cucumbers; kale; lettuce; onions; peppers; spinach; tomatoes.

SOW OUTDOORS UNDER CLOCHES OR IN A COLD FRAME Bolt-resistant beetroots; broad beans; carrots; lettuce; onions; peas; radishes; peas; spinach; spring onions; summer cabbages.

PLANT NOW Asparagus crowns; garlic sets; brown onion sets at end of month.

HARVEST NOW Brussels sprouts; cauliflowers (in mild areas); carrots; celeriac ❶; chard; kale; leeks; lettuce and radishes grown under a cloche or in a cool greenhouse; parsnips; sprouting broccoli; swedes; winter cabbages.

Fruit

PLANT NOW Bare-root hardy fruit trees such as apples, cherries, peaches, pears, plums, quinces; rhubarb (older, unproductive rhubarb plants can be lifted and divided now, too).

HARVEST Citrus fruits such as lemons and oranges, when their skins colour up.

❶

HERB OF THE MONTH: CHAMOMILE (*Chamaemelum nobile*)
Long used as a relaxant, the leaves of chamomile make a soothing cuppa that will help you fall asleep. This herb is a hardy perennial that will deliver a crop of leaves year after year. You can buy young plants now or sow seed in trays or pots under cover or wait until the soil warms up in April to sow them directly outside. Chamomile requires free-draining soil and a sunny site to thrive, and the little white and yellow daisies that appear in summer also attract pollinators.

Challenges this month

Winter may be coming to a close, but temperatures are generally still low, reducing the activity of herbivorous creatures and some plant diseases, but weeds that persist through winter can be kept in check before warmer conditions prompt their rapid growth.

CHICKWEED (*Stellaria media*) is a native annual plant with small green leaves and tiny white flowers, produced throughout the year, that form thousands of seeds, causing it to spread rapidly. Bees enjoy the nectar-rich blooms and birds such as chaffinches eat the seeds, so leave a small patch in winter to feed wildlife. However, in spring, it can quickly overwhelm gardens if not kept in check by pulling plants out or hoeing seedlings before they set seed. Mulching with an 8cm (3in) layer of bark chips and adding groundcover plants that outcompete chickweed will also help.

VOLES are small rodents, similar in appearance to mice but with shorter tails, which live in our gardens and eat a wide range of plants, including spring bulbs, corms, peas, beans and sweetcorn. In winter, when vegetation is frozen and less palatable, they often eat the bark of woody-stemmed species, which may kill young plants. Tell-tale signs of vole activity are bumps in the lawn and small heaps of soil on borders, where they have been tunnelling just beneath the surface. It is unlikely that you will have many voles in your garden, and the damage they cause is generally minimal, so it is best to leave them be,

as they support biodiversity and provide vital food for predators such as owls. If they are nibbling your prized plants, fit biodegradable tree spirals around young trees, or cover vulnerable plants with mesh netting, buried 25cm (10in) deep into the ground.

NON-NATIVE FLATWORMS (pictured) have found their way to our shores in the past 60 years and, unlike our four native species, many eat a diet almost entirely made up of earthworms, although current research shows that they do not seem to be affecting ecosystems, as was originally feared. The long, flat-bodied worms can range in length from 2–20cm (¾–8in) and may find their way into your garden in or under the pots of new plants and via plant swaps, but they can be tolerated if you spot them.

Garden benefactors

Spiders

For arachnophobes, or people who fear spiders, this group of invertebrates may be far from welcome when they venture into your home, but in the garden, they are our best friends.

There are over 600 species of spider in the UK, and these eight-legged carnivores consume a wide range of prey, including aphids, flies, gnats, wasps, mosquitoes, and even snails, thereby helping to control many unwanted insects that eat our flowers and crops.

Spiders also decorate our gardens with their intricate webs, which look like delicate lace doilies when embellished with frost or dew. However, not all arachnids use their silk webs to catch and bind their prey. Some are stalkers and hide among the flowers, taking their prey by surprise, while jumping spiders leap on their targets, and cannibalistic pirate spiders mimic the behaviour of an insect on another's web to lure the owner closer before staging an attack.

The silken threads spiders produce are also used as suspension lines to allow them to travel from place to place, and to wrap and protect their eggs.

To encourage a healthy population of spiders in your garden, do not use pesticides, which can kill them and their prey. You can also make protective habitats for them, such as log piles and areas of leaf litter, and grow dense shrubs and climbers. Hunting spiders also benefit from patches of bare soil so leave some beds unmulched.

Avoid breaking spiders' webs, too, since it takes a lot of energy to produce them, and leave unharmed the silk bundles of eggs you may find suspended on glasshouse window frames or elsewhere. Also handle any spiders you find in the house with care, popping a glass or cup over them and sliding a piece of card underneath, before rehoming them in a shed, garage or other garden building.

Design masterclass

Tom Stuart-Smith OBE

A multi-award-winning landscape architect, Tom Stuart-Smith's work combines naturalism with modernity, and includes high-profile public parks and landscapes, and private gardens, both here in the UK and worldwide.

Tom has been awarded nine gold medals for his RHS Chelsea Flower Show gardens, and three 'Best in Shows'. He was made a Vice President of the RHS in 2017 and produced the masterplan for RHS Garden Bridgewater, which opened in 2021 to much acclaim. Earlier work includes the design for the Bicentenary Glasshouse Garden at RHS Garden Wisley, Her Majesty the Queen's Jubilee Garden at Windsor Castle, and Trentham Gardens in Staffordshire.

Tom studied Zoology at Cambridge University before completing a postgraduate degree in Landscape Design. He then worked for the celebrated landscape architect and former President of the RHS, Elizabeth Banks, before establishing his own design studio in 1998.

HOW TO DESIGN A GARDEN IN SHADE
Taking inspiration from Tom's many plant-rich gardens, he offers his advice on planting shady areas.

▶ 'Making shady gardens look good in spring with a collection of bulbs is relatively easy, but it's more difficult to continue the show into late summer. Try *Kirengeshoma palmata* with its yellow bells, wild ginger *(Saruma henryi)*, which has heart-shaped leaves and small yellow flowers, and the baneberries *(Actaea)* for late-season interest.'

▶ 'Low-growing evergreens are very useful as a counterpoint to herbaceous fluff. Try *Daphne pontica* or *D. laureola*, *Skimmia anquetilia*, and some of the shrubby ivies such as *Hedera colchica* 'Fall Favourite'.'

▶ 'Include one or two plants that hold the composition together and have a quiet presence throughout the year. The Japanese forest grass, *Hakonechloa macra*, and epimediums, with their overwintering leaves, are the perfect foils for more showy plants.'

Plants for difficult places

Windy, exposed sites

Gardens in exposed or coastal areas tend to experience the most damaging winds and gales, although wind tunnels created by buildings can also cause problems in urban areas inland, too. Wind can be a problem because it dries out plants by stripping moisture from the leaves and the soil surface, but, as with all adverse environmental conditions, there are plants that have adapted to survive these effects.

Mulching the surface of your beds, preferably with homemade compost, can help maintain soil moisture in windy areas, allowing a broader range of plants to survive, while also suppressing unwanted seedlings. Spread a thick 5cm (2in) layer in autumn or spring after rain has wet the soil (see also pp.36–7).

Many garden-worthy plants have some natural resistance to wind. Adaptations include robust, glossy or waxy, thick leaves, as seen on *Escallonia* and *Elaeagnus*. Others, such as *Salvia, Phlomis* and *Stachys,* have hairy leaves, which provide insulation, protecting them from moisture loss. *Miscanthus* and other ornamental grasses have narrow leaves with less surface area from which to lose moisture, and they also provide interest by rustling in the breeze. The flowers of asters, which also have small leaves, help to prolong the interest for people, while also supporting bees and other pollinators.

By choosing plants that are adapted to windy locations, you can keep your borders looking good and growing well, and once established, they will reduce the need for watering.

PLANT CHOICES FOR WINDY AREAS

❶ *Escallonia* 'Apple Blossom'
This medium-sized hardy evergreen shrub has small, dark green, glossy leaves and clusters of pale pink flowers in summer. **H&S:** 2.5 × 2.5m (8 × 8ft)

Oleaster (*Elaeagnus* × *submacrophylla*)
A useful evergreen hedging plant, this hardy shrub produces shiny green leaves with silvery undersides and small but highly scented creamy-white flowers that appear in autumn.
H&S: 4 × 4m (13 × 13ft).

❷ Aster 'King George'
(*Aster amellus* 'King George')
Sprays of long-lasting, yellow-centred, violet-blue daisies top the slim stems of this hardy perennial throughout late summer and autumn.
H&S: 45 × 45cm (18 × 18in)

❸ Eulalia 'Cindy'
(*Miscanthus sinensis* 'Cindy')
A hardy ornamental grass, it produces a compact fountain of narrow, arching green leaves that turn light brown in winter. Pinky-red feathery flower plumes appear in late summer and mature to silvery seedheads.
H&S: 1.5 × 1.5m (5 × 5ft)

Balkan clary 'Amethyst'
(*Salvia nemorosa* 'Amethyst')
In summer and autumn, spikes of small, lilac-purple, hooded flowers appear over small, green, aromatic foliage. **H&S:** 90 × 60cm (3 × 2ft)

Lamb's ear (*Stachys byzantina*)
A spreading evergreen perennial with white woolly stems and soft grey leaves. Spikes of small pink flowers appear in summer. **H&S:** 45 × 45cm (18 × 18in)

March

Celebrations are in full swing as we leave winter's dark days behind us. Trees decked with flowers like blushing brides lift the spirits, while below them the garden is awash with spring bulbs, their jewel colours ushering in spring. As light levels increase, it's time to sow flowers and crops, their seeds a promise of good things to come.

KEY EVENTS

St David's Day, 1 March
First day of meteorological spring, 1 March
Masi Magam, 2–3 March
Mother's Day (UK), 15 March
St Patrick's Day, 17 March
End of Ramadan, 19 March
Eid al-Fitr, 19–20 March
Vernal equinox, 20 March
British Summer Time begins, 29 March

What to do in March

The first days of spring herald a surge in growth, as the light and warmer temperatures spur on germination and prompt buds to burst. Sowing and planting outside can start in earnest now, and lawns will benefit from raking to remove unwanted moss. Continue to protect vulnerable plants, too, as frosty nights are still a certainty.

In the garden

PLANT SUMMER BULBS AND TUBERS such as lilies and dahlias in pots. Use a 3:1 mix of peat-free multipurpose or peat-free John Innes No. 2 compost and horticultural grit. Plant dahlias with the old flower stem facing upwards and the sausage-like tubers spread out on a layer of compost, and fill in around them to just cover the stem. Keep dahlias under cover until the frosts have passed. **1**

Plant lily bulbs, pointed side facing up, at a depth of three times the height of the bulb, and place them outside in a sheltered spot. Water your lilies regularly during dry spells.

SOW HARDY ANNUALS OUTSIDE in mild periods in March – sowing under biodegradable fleece or a cloche will help to protect them during inclement conditions. For gardens in cold regions or with heavy clay soil, sow indoors in modules, placing them outside once they have germinated and grown so the roots are binding the potting compost.

PLANT OUT SWEET PEAS that were sown in autumn and overwintered under cover. Delay this until April in

PRUNING TIP
Shrub roses
Roses are pruned in March to promote more flowering stems in summer. First, cut out dead, diseased and weak stems. For hybrid teas (roses with one flower per stem), prune the remaining stems back to 4–6in (10–15cm) from the ground. Floribunda roses (multiple flowers per stem) should be cut to about 6in (15cm) from the ground. Make sloping cuts just above a bud so that rain will drain away and not cause rot.

cold regions. A simple support made from canes or bean poles and twine will show the plants off beautifully. **2**

SOW TENDER FLOWER SEED indoors, but check you have space to grow on the seedlings until they can be planted outside in late May.

DIVIDE PERENNIALS that have formed congested clumps. Dig up the whole clump and then prise it apart into sections using your hands, a sharp knife or back-to-back forks for large plants. Discard any dead, diseased or weak sections and replant small clumps of healthy stems and roots in their new positions or in pots.

CUT BACK SHRUBS that flower in late summer on stems produced during the current year. These include *Buddleja*

davidii, Ceratostigma, Hydrangea paniculata, Lavatera, and *Leycesteria.* All can be pruned back hard to a short framework of stems, which will then produce new flowering growth.

In the fruit & veg patch

PLANT ONION AND SHALLOT SETS but delay planting red varieties until mid-April. Sets are simply young bulbs, and they should be planted 15cm (6in) apart and in rows 30cm (12in) apart, with the tips just showing above the soil surface. Firm the soil and cover with birdproof netting.

REMOVE UNWANTED PLANTS such as bindweed, dandelions and docks that compete with your crops. Dig them out or smother them with cardboard and mulch (see p.135).

SMOTHER GREEN MANURES such as winter clover and trefoil, which were sown in late summer or autumn, with a mulch or hoe them off and leave the stems and leaves on the surface to rot down. Alternatively, incorporate them by digging them into the top layers of soil.

FEED BLUEBERRY PLANTS growing in containers with a fertilizer designed for acid soil-loving plants.

MULCH RHUBARB PLANTS with a 5–8cm (2–3in) layer of well-rotted garden compost or manure from an organic source, to help conserve soil moisture during the warmer months and suppress the growth of unwanted plants.

PLANT OUT FIRST EARLY POTATOES that you chitted indoors in January (see p.11). Choose an open, sunny site that's not prone to frost, and dig in some rotted garden compost or manure. Then add a 8cm (3in) layer of garden or peat-free compost. Plant the tubers in rows 60cm (2ft) apart, allowing 30cm (1ft) between them, and deep enough so there is 5cm (2in) of soil over the tips of the sprouts.

Indoors

START FEEDING and watering your houseplants every few weeks, now that they are growing again. Use a feed that's rich in potassium for flowering plants, a general seaweed-based fertilizer for leafy types and a special feed designed for cacti and succulents, and orchids.

MONEY-SAVING IDEA
Raising herbs from seed
Growing hardy herbs such as chervil, parsley, coriander and dill from seed is easy and cheaper than buying mature plants in pots or stems from the supermarket. In March, sow the seed in pots or trays of peat-free seed compost and leave outside in a sheltered spot – on a dining table, for example – or set in a cold frame to germinate. When seedlings appear, pot on small clumps into their own containers of peat-free multipurpose compost to grow on, and harvest the leaves as needed. Sow batches from now until summer for a continuous supply of leaves.

DIVIDE CONGESTED HOUSEPLANTS such as Boston ferns (*Nephrolepis*) and *Anthurium* to make new plants for free. Water well, then remove the plant from its pot and prise apart small sections with your hands or a sharp knife, discarding any stems or roots that look dead or diseased. Repot clumps of healthy leaves and roots in clean containers with drainage holes in the base and fresh compost.

TRY GROWING CALADIUM PLANTS from tubers. Plant with the growing tip about 5cm (2in) below the soil level and the knobbly side facing up. Place the pots in a warm area indoors in bright, indirect light and water regularly.

Plants of the month

1. White forsythia
   (*Abeliophyllum distichum*)
2. Winter windflower
   (*Anemone blanda*)
3. Japanese quince
   (*Chaenomeles × superba*
   pictured)
4. Armand clematis
   (*Clematis armandii*)
5. Hyacinth (*Hyacinthus
   orientalis* 'King of the
   Blues' pictured)
6. Chinese witch hazel
   (*Loropetalum chinense* var.
   rubrum 'Blush' pictured)
7. Magnolia (*Magnolia*
   'Caerhays Surprise'
   pictured)
8. Grape hyacinth (*Muscari
   latifolium* pictured)
9. Lily-of-the-valley bush
   (*Pieris japonica*)
10. Pear tree, blossom
    (*Pyrus communis*)
11. Species tulip (*Tulipa*
    'Little Beauty' pictured)

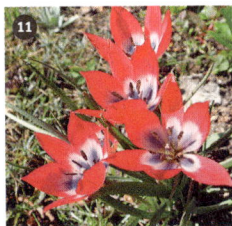

Project: Make a stepladder display

This easy project makes use of an old stepladder to display a range of seasonal plants, such as spring bulbs and herbs. A great idea for a small garden where ground space is at a premium, try placing your ladder where you can enjoy it from inside your house, as well as outside. You can also exchange the pots so that you always have some flowers in bloom, storing bulbs such as daffodils or muscari in a quiet corner when they are dormant. Another option is to use a free-standing ladder in a bed or border that needs a focal point.

YOU WILL NEED
Ladder
Exterior wood paint (optional)
Terracotta pots
Selection of plants and flowers
Large stone or brick (optional)

1 You can use a ladder of any size and leave it unpainted for a rustic look, as we have done here, or add a lick of exterior wood paint for a more polished finish. Lean it against a sturdy fence, boundary wall or your house. You may also wish to secure the legs at the base with a large stone or brick.

2 Repot your plants in terracotta pots of different shapes and sizes, if you want to create a unified display, making sure that they will fit securely on the rungs of the ladder.

3 Adjust the display, placing the larger pots on the bottom rungs, until you are happy with the final look. Water regularly during dry spells.

Looking up

Sunrise and sunset

Longer days allow more time for gardening and taking a moment to enjoy all that spring has to offer. British Summer Time also begins at the end of the month.

DAY	LONDON		EDINBURGH	
	Sunrise	Sunset	Sunrise	Sunset
Sun, 1 Mar	6:43:33 am	5:42:03 pm	7:01:46 am	5:48:24 pm
Mon, 2 Mar	6:41:23 am	5:43:49 pm	6:59:15 am	5:50:31 pm
Tue, 3 Mar	6:39:13 am	5:45:34 pm	6:56:43 am	5:52:38 pm
Wed, 4 Mar	6:37:02 am	5:47:19 pm	6:54:11 am	5:54:44 pm
Thu, 5 Mar	6:34:51 am	5:49:04 pm	6:51:38 am	5:56:50 pm
Fri, 6 Mar	6:32:38 am	5:50:49 pm	6:49:05 am	5:58:56 pm
Sat, 7 Mar	6:30:26 am	5:52:33 pm	6:46:31 am	6:01:02 pm
Sun, 8 Mar	6:28:13 am	5:54:17 pm	6:43:56 am	6:03:07 pm
Mon, 9 Mar	6:25:59 am	5:56:01 pm	6:41:22 am	6:05:12 pm
Tue, 10 Mar	6:23:45 am	5:57:45 pm	6:38:46 am	6:07:17 pm
Wed, 11 Mar	6:21:30 am	5:59:28 pm	6:36:11 am	6:09:21 pm
Thu, 12 Mar	6:19:15 am	6:01:11 pm	6:33:34 am	6:11:25 pm
Fri, 13 Mar	6:17:00 am	6:02:54 pm	6:30:58 am	6:13:29 pm
Sat, 14 Mar	6:14:44 am	6:04:37 pm	6:28:21 am	6:15:33 pm
Sun, 15 Mar	6:12:28 am	6:06:19 pm	6:25:44 am	6:17:37 pm
Mon, 16 Mar	6:10:12 am	6:08:01 pm	6:23:07 am	6:19:40 pm
Tue, 17 Mar	6:07:56 am	6:09:44 pm	6:20:29 am	6:21:43 pm
Wed, 18 Mar	6:05:39 am	6:11:26 pm	6:17:51 am	6:23:47 pm
Thu, 19 Mar	6:03:22 am	6:13:07 pm	6:15:14 am	6:25:49 pm
Fri, 20 Mar	6:01:05 am	6:14:49 pm	6:12:35 am	6:27:52 pm
Sat, 21 Mar	5:58:48 am	6:16:31 pm	6:09:57 am	6:29:55 pm
Sun, 22 Mar	5:56:31 am	6:18:12 pm	6:07:19 am	6:31:57 pm
Mon, 23 Mar	5:54:14 am	6:19:53 pm	6:04:41 am	6:34:00 pm
Tue, 24 Mar	5:51:56 am	6:21:34 pm	6:02:02 am	6:36:02 pm
Wed, 25 Mar	5:49:39 am	6:23:15 pm	5:59:24 am	6:38:04 pm
Thu, 26 Mar	5:47:22 am	6:24:56 pm	5:56:45 am	6:40:06 pm
Fri, 27 Mar	5:45:05 am	6:26:37 pm	5:54:07 am	6:42:09 pm
Sat, 28 Mar	5:42:48 am	6:28:18 pm	5:51:29 am	6:44:11 pm
Sun, 29 Mar*	6:40:31 am	7:29:59 pm	6:48:51 am	7:46:13 pm
Mon, 30 Mar	6:38:14 am	7:31:40 pm	6:46:13 am	7:48:15 pm
Tue, 31 Mar	6:35:58 am	7:33:20 pm	6:43:35 am	7:50:17 pm

*Note: clocks go forward by 1 hour.

Moonrise and moonset

Moon phases

○ **FULL MOON** 3 March   ● **NEW MOON** 19 March
◐ **THIRD QUARTER** 11 March   ◑ **FIRST QUARTER** 25 March

DAY	LONDON			EDINBURGH		
	Moonrise	Moonset	Moonrise	Moonrise	Moonset	Moonrise
1 Mar		06:10	15:15		06:43	15:09
2 Mar		06:27	16:39		06:53	16:41
3 Mar		06:40	18:00		07:00	18:08
4 Mar		06:52	19:17		07:05	19:32
5 Mar		07:03	20:33		07:11	20:54
6 Mar		07:14	21:49		07:16	22:16
7 Mar		07:27	23:04		07:23	23:38
8 Mar		07:43			07:32	
9 Mar	00:19	08:03		01:01	07:46	
10 Mar	01:31	08:31		02:20	08:07	
11 Mar	02:37	09:10		03:31	08:41	
12 Mar	03:31	10:02		04:27	09:33	
13 Mar	04:14	11:07		05:05	10:43	
14 Mar	04:45	12:21		05:28	12:04	
15 Mar	05:08	13:40		05:44	13:31	
16 Mar	05:25	15:01		05:54	14:59	
17 Mar	05:39	16:22		06:01	16:27	
18 Mar	05:51	17:44		06:08	17:56	
19 Mar	06:03	19:08		06:14	19:27	
20 Mar	06:16	20:35		06:20	21:01	
21 Mar	06:31	22:05		06:29	22:39	
22 Mar	06:51	23:36		06:40		
23 Mar	07:18				00:19	06:59
24 Mar		01:03	07:58		01:55	07:31
25 Mar		02:17	08:55		03:12	08:25
26 Mar		03:12	10:09		04:04	09:44
27 Mar		03:50	11:32		04:33	11:16
28 Mar		04:16	12:58		04:51	12:50
29 Mar*		05:34	15:22		06:02	15:21
30 Mar		05:48	16:42		06:09	16:48
31 Mar		06:00	17:59		06:15	18:11

*Note: clocks go forward by 1 hour.

Average temperature & rainfall

This table shows the average minimum and maximum temperatures, indicated by the blue and red dots, together with the average rainfall and number of rainy days for this month. The horizontal rules show how the figures have varied over the past decade.

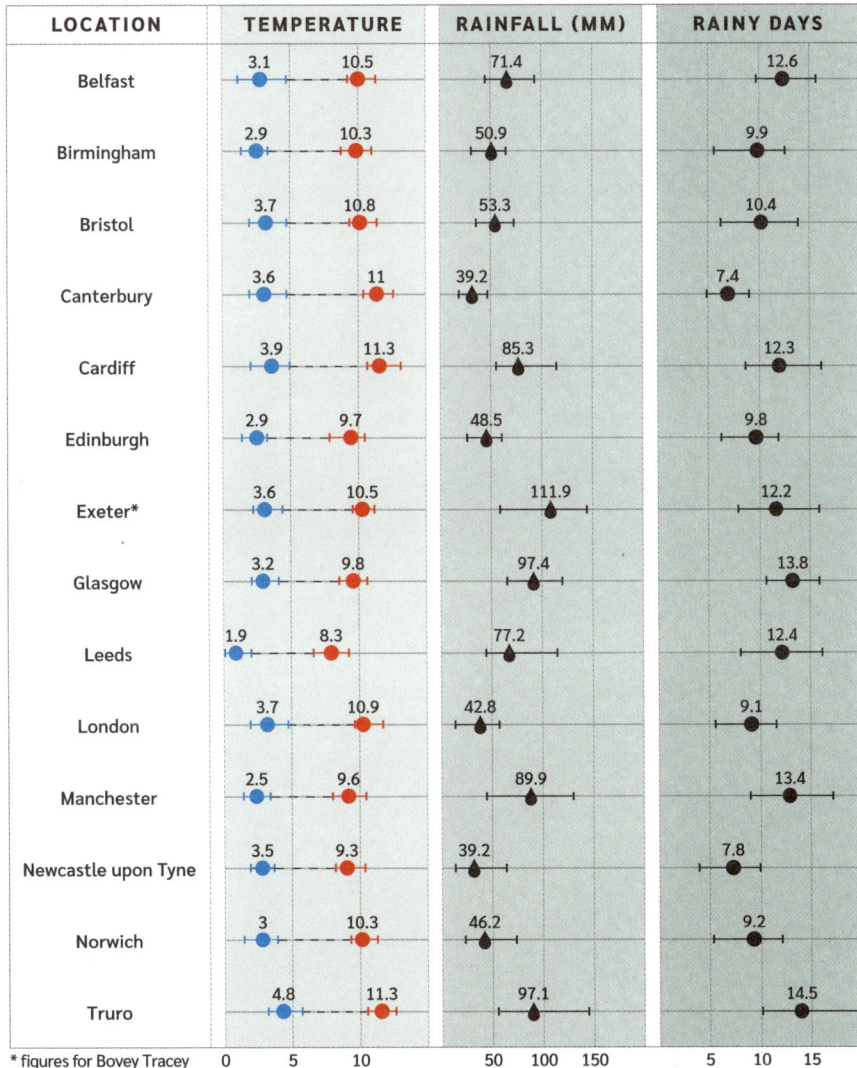

LOCATION	TEMPERATURE		RAINFALL (MM)	RAINY DAYS
Belfast	3.1	10.5	71.4	12.6
Birmingham	2.9	10.3	50.9	9.9
Bristol	3.7	10.8	53.3	10.4
Canterbury	3.6	11	39.2	7.4
Cardiff	3.9	11.3	85.3	12.3
Edinburgh	2.9	9.7	48.5	9.8
Exeter*	3.6	10.5	111.9	12.2
Glasgow	3.2	9.8	97.4	13.8
Leeds	1.9	8.3	77.2	12.4
London	3.7	10.9	42.8	9.1
Manchester	2.5	9.6	89.9	13.4
Newcastle upon Tyne	3.5	9.3	39.2	7.8
Norwich	3	10.3	46.2	9.2
Truro	4.8	11.3	97.1	14.5

* figures for Bovey Tracey

Temperature scale: 0 5 10
Rainfall scale: 50 100 150
Rainy days scale: 5 10 15

Sustainable gardening

Pollution-busting propagation

Filling our outdoor spaces with plants that absorb carbon dioxide and lock it up in the soil helps to combat climate change. Growing lots of different plants also promotes biodiversity. However, not all gardening activities make a positive contribution to the environment. Buying potted plants is a case in point, and comes at a cost to the planet, as well as your bank balance. The energy, plastic, water and chemicals used to grow a plant in a pot has an impact, and while this can be partly offset by the plants themselves, an eco-friendlier option is to sow seed or propagate them. This may sound daunting to new gardeners, but growing plants in this way is actually very easy.

SEEDS OF SUCCESS

Producing a packet of seed is much more sustainable than growing a plant in a plastic pot, and many flowers and crops such as cosmos, love-in-a-mist (*Nigella*), radishes and courgettes will germinate in no time. Sow the seed, following the instructions on the pack, in used, clean food trays with drainage holes punched into the base, card rolls, egg boxes, or biodegradable pots, filled with peat-free seed compost.

Even better, collect seeds from your existing plants or even supermarket veg such as chillies, tomatoes and peppers.

Verbena bonariensis is a prolific self-seeder.

Seed harvested from F1 hybrid plants often results in offspring that lacks the parents' quality, but it can be worth experimenting to see what you get. Other plants will do the job for you and self-seed. *Verbena bonariensis*, for example, produces a host of baby plants from its scattered seed that you can then dig up and plant elsewhere.

VALUABLE OFFSHOOTS

Many garden plants spread via their roots and shoots, and you can simply dig up and remove the new growth that arises from them. Asters, now variously called *Aster, Callistephus, Eurybia, Kalimeris* and *Symphyotrichum*, are good examples, producing offshoots that can be cut from the edges of clumps. Force your spade between the emerging stems to remove a section, and replant clumps with healthy roots and shoots.

Similarly, plants that produce suckers, where a new plant pops up close to the parent, can be used. Bay (*Laurus nobilis*), *Clerodendrum* and *Sarcococca* make new plants in this way for you to use.

Gooseberries and climbing hydrangeas (*Hydrangea anomala* subsp. *petiolaris*) produce drooping branches that root from the tips, where they touch the soil, making strong plants that can be lifted and planted elsewhere. Low shoots can often be bent down and pegged into the soil to root, too, in a process known as layering (see rhs.org.uk for details of how to do this).

THE PERFECT CUT

Most garden plants can be propagated from cuttings. These are stems or roots taken from the parent and plunged into water, soil or compost, from which new roots and stems will form. Try popping a few non-flowering stems in jars of water on a windowsill and wait for roots to form. Or fill small pots or trays with cuttings compost. Use a dibber or blunt pencil to make a hole in the compost, insert your cuttings, firm them in, and then leave them in a warm, light place, out of direct sunlight. A heated propagator will speed things up.

Deciduous plants, currants (*Ribes*) for example, are rooted from soft growth taken in spring and early summer (see p.106–7), while deciduous shrubs such as roses and buddleja can be grown from hardwood cuttings, taken in winter (see p.204). Evergreen plants, including *Choisya* and lavender, do best from semi-ripe cuttings taken in late summer and early autumn (see p.184).

Some plants are protected by legal restrictions, including Plant Breeders' Rights, and these can only be propagated in the UK for your own use – even giving some to friends is prohibited – but others are free to take and to give, at no cost to you and very little to the environment.

Sow in biodegradable pots filled with seed compost.

Edible garden

March is a busy month in the productive garden, with many crops to sow both indoors and outside in prepared beds in sheltered spots. However, many areas are still too cold for direct sowing outside, unless you can protect seedlings with a cloche or cold frame. The last winter crops are also ready to harvest, and rhubarb is ripe for picking, too.

Vegetables

SOW INDOORS Outdoor aubergines; cabbages; cauliflowers; celeriac; celery; chillies; courgettes; indoor cucumbers; kohlrabi; leeks; lettuce; peppers; outdoor tomatoes, turnips.

SOW OUTDOORS, UNDER CLOCHES OR IN COLD FRAMES Bolt-resistant beetroots; broad beans; broccoli; carrots; chard; leeks; lettuce; onions; parsnips; peas, including mange-tout and sugar snaps; radishes; rocket; salad crops; spinach; spring onions; turnips.

PLANT OUT Broad beans; early potatoes; hardy plants sown indoors in February or bought in, including asparagus crowns ❶; garlic sets, onion sets and shallots; lettuce; peas; radishes; spinach ❷; spring onions.

HARVEST NOW Brussels sprouts; cauliflowers; chard; kale; leeks; lettuce; overwintered spinach; spring cabbages; purple and white sprouting broccoli.

TOP TIP
Warm the soil
Encourage early crops by warming up the soil in March, where a few extra degrees can make all the difference. Cover the ground with biodegradable or re-used fleece, which prevents heat gained during the day from escaping at night. Peg it down with stones or bricks, and leave in place for a few weeks before sowing beneath it. Alternatively, make a cloche with a wire hoops covered with fleece, which can also be used to protect seedlings from cold temperatures and inclement weather.

Fruit

PLANT NOW Bare-root and potted hardy fruit trees such as apples, cherries, medlars, mulberries, pears, plums, quinces; apricot and peach trees in a sheltered spot; blackberry and raspberry canes (tie to supports) **3**; strawberries from runners.

HARVEST Rhubarb. **4**

HERB OF THE MONTH: CHERVIL (*Anthriscus cerefolium*)
This relative of parsley, with its milder taste and hint of aniseed, produces feathery leaves that help to flavour many savoury dishes, including eggs, fish and chicken, or add it to soups and salads. Maturing in as little as nine weeks, sow the seed outdoors *in situ* in batches throughout the spring and summer for a continuous supply up to the first frosts. You can extend the harvest into winter, too, if you grow it under a cloche.

Recipe

SUMMER BERRIES WITH GREEK YOGURT, HONEY AND SUNFLOWER GRANOLA

You can make this delicious recipe and enjoy the taste of summer all year round if you freeze some of your soft fruits. Nutritious and naturally sweet, it makes a great breakfast or dessert.

1   Preheat the oven to 150°C/130°C fan/gas 3.

2   Mix all ingredients for the granola, except for the dried cranberries, in a large mixing bowl.

3   Spread the granola mix evenly on a baking tray and bake for 15 minutes. Mix in the dried cranberries and bake for a further 10 minutes. (The cooled granola can be stored in an airtight container for up to a month.)

4   Once cool, layer the granola, clear honey, Greek yogurt and berries in a glass bowl and serve. This dish can be served individually or in large decorative glass bowls.

INGREDIENTS
For the granola
225g oatmeal
115g sunflower seeds
35g ground flaxseed
75g dried cranberries
75g slivered almonds
75g shredded coconut
3 tbsp peanut butter
½ tsp fine sea salt
170g clear honey
½ tsp vanilla

Berry mixture
100g strawberries
100g raspberries
100g blueberries
100g blackberries
50g redcurrants

50g clear honey
500g Greek yogurt

FREEZING BERRIES
It's easy to freeze summer berries so that you can enjoy them throughout the winter and spring. Simply lay out your freshly picked berries on a tray lined with parchment paper, making sure they are not touching. Place in the freezer for at least three hours, but no longer than twelve, then remove and place the berries in freezer bags. Blackberries, strawberries, raspberries, blueberries and cranberries can all be frozen in this way.

Challenges this month

The arrival of spring heralds fresh new growth in the garden, but this also means that unwanted plants are flourishing now, too. The abundant soil moisture can lead to root rots in waterlogged areas, while other diseases are also on the rise in March.

FOXES are a common sight in urban gardens, and for many people, their antics and those of their cubs in spring, are fun to watch. However, they can cause heartache if they dig up your plants, excavate large holes in your borders, or rip a lawn in search of chafer grubs. Foxes are generalists, which means they eat a wide variety of foods, including birds, small mammals, earthworms, fruit and nuts. While it's best to simply enjoy them in your garden, since no fence or wall is likely to keep them out, you can help to prevent them causing too much damage by avoiding fertilizers made from animal products such as bonemeal and chicken manure, which may cause them to dig up plants in search of food. Fill in any holes as quickly as possible, too, as this will stop them from making dens.

SHEPHERD'S PURSE (*Capsella bursa-pastoris*) is an annual UK native that produces a rosette of straight and wavy-edged green leaves and branching stems, about 50cm (20in) in height, covered with tiny white flowers, followed by distinctive heart-shaped seedheads. While the blooms offer food for pollinators, including butterflies, and seeds for birds, it can spread quickly through the garden, smothering

low-growing ornamentals and crops. However, it is easy to pull out or hoe off during dry weather, but perhaps leave some plants around larger trees and shrubs that will not be overwhelmed through winter to feed hungry wildlife.

CLEMATIS SLIME FLUX (pictured) is a bacterial infection that can affect most clematis species, especially in spring and early summer, when the bacteria enter through a wound caused by frost, wind or other disturbance. Symptoms include yellowing and wilting of the foliage and a frothy or slimy, foul-smelling substance oozing from the stems. The disease can be fatal, but plants can sometimes be saved by pruning out the affected parts. If a clematis dies from it, you can dig out the plant and roots, together with some of the soil, and replant with a new one.

Garden benefactors

Ground beetles

The British Isles are home to over 4,000 species of beetle, including over 370 types of ground beetle, many of which reside in our gardens. As well as adding to the biodiversity of our plots, this group of largely ground-dwelling insects are allies, munching on creatures that feast on our plants and crops, including aphids, caterpillars, slugs, snails, leatherjackets and cutworms. Some beetles act as pollinators as they travel from flower to flower in search of food, while the burrows they make in the ground help to improve the soil structure and availability of nutrients for garden plants.

Ground beetles measure from just 2mm (1/16in) in length to 2.5cm (1in) and have long antennae and legs, and black, brown or colourful metallic shell-like exoskeletons that help to protect them from predators.

Largely flightless, ground beetles are most active from March to October, and rest under logs, stones and pots, and in leaf litter during the day, emerging at night to chase down their prey, which they devour with their strong jaws.

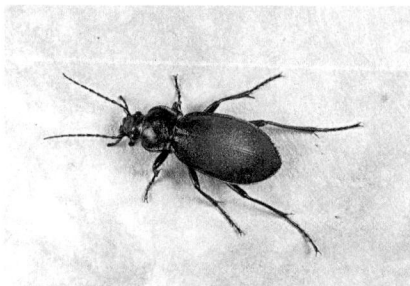

The life cycles of ground beetles vary depending on the species, with some breeding in the summer or autumn and overwintering as larvae, and others breeding in the spring and overwintering as adults. They can live from one to several years. Their caterpillar-like larvae have pincers at the tail end and are also carnivorous, helping to keep the insect populations in gardens in check.

Many species of ground beetle are protected under conservation laws here in the UK, due to the benefits they offer and the fact that their numbers are in decline as a result of habitat loss, pollution and climate change.

To encourage this army of predators into your garden, provide suitable habitats such as stones, wood piles, areas of leaf litter, and compost heaps, and never use insecticides, which threaten them and their prey.

Design masterclass

Charlotte Harris & Hugo Bugg

The combined talents of Charlotte Harris and Hugo Bugg have earned their multi-award-winning practice Harris Bugg Studio a reputation for design excellence and they have delivered a host of prestigious projects both here in the UK and abroad.

The pair have won four gold medals at the RHS Chelsea Flower Show, with a 'Best in Show' award for their 2023 Horatio's Garden. Other projects include the innovative walled Kitchen Garden at RHS Garden Bridgewater and a masterplan for the Royal Botanic Garden in Jordan, as well as numerous smaller urban and country gardens for private clients.

Charlotte worked in fund-raising before changing careers to study garden design at Merrist Wood College in Surrey, and then joined Tom Stuart-Smith's practice

where she honed her craft. Hugo studied garden design at Falmouth University and won the title RHS Young Designer of the Year in 2010. The duo pooled their skills to form Harris Bugg Studio in 2017, and have been lauded as the most 'pioneering design talents of their generation'.

DESIGNING A PRODUCTIVE GARDEN
The designers won many accolades for their productive garden at RHS Garden Bridgewater and offer advice to those creating their own veg patch.

▶ 'Think beyond annual crops, which often need more watering and time than perennial veg and herbs that have deeper roots and are generally pretty self-sufficient. Our favourites include perennial kale, globe artichokes and lemon verbena.'

▶ 'Your soil is the foundation for plant growth and health. Taking a no-dig approach (see p.37) builds organic layers on top of the soil, which improves its structure, encourages beneficial organisms, and enhances water retention and fertility, thereby delivering better yields, without any backbreaking digging.'

▶ 'Experiment, and put aside worries of making mistakes. A garden is forgiving, offering the chance to try again. It's a place to learn, adapt and grow, encouraging us to discover what works and what doesn't.'

Plants for difficult places

Plants for acid soil

Alkaline, neutral or mildly acidic soils suit most plants, but only ericaceous plants thrive in acidic soils. Acidity and alkalinity are defined as pH – over pH7 is alkaline and below pH5.5 is very acidic – and you can measure your soil's pH with a simple garden-centre test kit. Looking at plants thriving nearby can also give you a clue, since healthy camellias, rhododendrons and *Pieris* are good indicators of acid soils, and they are more generally found in south-western England, Wales and Scotland.

Many acid-loving plants have spring flowers but, with some careful selection, it is possible to extend the interest across different seasons. *Enkianthus*, for example, has clusters of small cream or reddish bell-shaped flowers in late spring but good autumn leaf colour, too.

Rhododendrons provide glossy evergreen foliage and showy late spring flowers, while their near cousins azaleas often have scented blooms and some appear a little later in early summer. *Pieris* also flowers in spring but provides additional colour with its newer growth, which is often flushed red.

For groundcover, you can select a heath (*Erica*), heather (*Calluna*) and *Glandora*, which will offer colour at your feet, while the roots also knit together the soil, preventing it from eroding. Groundcover plants help to reduce moisture loss by evaporation from the soil surface, too, and suppress weed growth.

PLANTS FOR ACIDIC CONDITIONS

1 Redvein enkianthus (*Enkianthus campanulatus*)
A large, deciduous, hardy shrub with small green leaves that turn bright red, orange and yellow in autumn. Clusters of small cream or reddish, bell-shaped flowers appear from late spring to midsummer.
H&S: 2.5 × 2.5m (8 × 8ft)

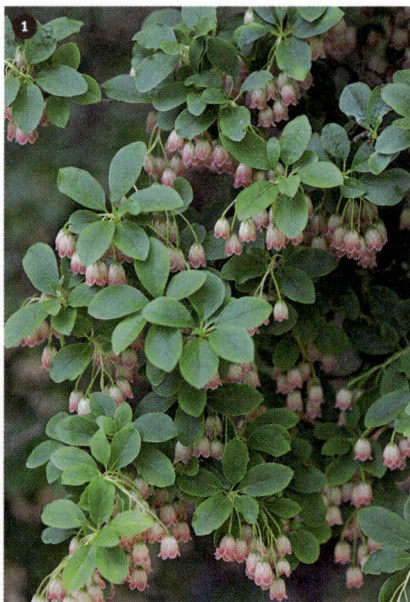

2 *Rhododendron luteum*
This beautiful deciduous azalea features green leaves that turn orange, purple and red in autumn, and very fragrant yellow flowers in late spring and early summer.
H&S: up to 1.2 × 1.2m (4 × 4ft)

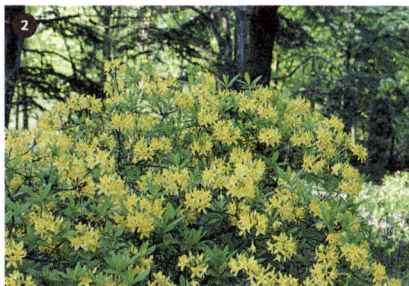

3 *Pieris japonica* 'Valley Valentine'
A decorative medium-sized hardy evergreen shrub with dark green, glossy foliage and arching stems of long-lasting dusky red, bell-shaped flowers in spring.
H&S: 1.5 × 1.5m (5 × 5ft)

Prickly heath 'Bell's Seedling'
(*Gaultheria mucronata* 'Bell's Seedling')
Forming a mound of dark green prickly leaves, this compact shrub produces clusters of small white flowers in late spring and early summer, followed by dark red berries. **H&S:** 1.2 × 1.2m (4 × 4ft)

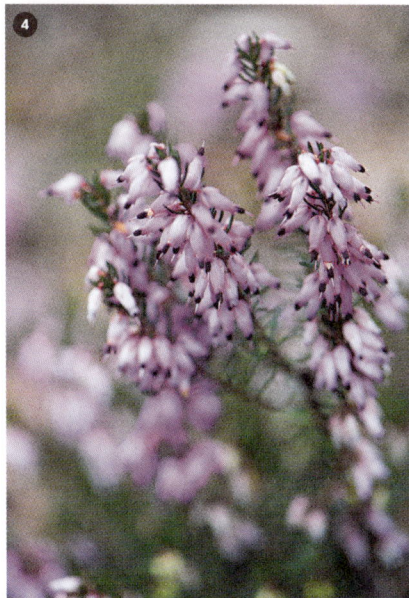

Heather 'Kerstin'
(*Calluna vulgaris* 'Kerstin')
Downy grey foliage with yellow and red tips provide interest in spring before this hardy evergreen shrub produces spikes of mauve flowers in late summer and autumn. **H&S:** 20 × 30cm (8 × 12in)

4 Heath 'March Seedling' (*Erica carnea* f. *carnea* 'March Seedling')
This small, hardy, evergreen shrub features dark green evergreen foliage and spikes of rose-pink to purple flowers in spring. **H&S:** 25 × 40cm (10 × 16in)

April

As the Earth turns and days lengthen, the increasing light prompts a flurry of activity in the garden. Carpets of foliage and flowers cover the soil, as the sun's warm rays bolster growth. For gardeners, this is the busiest time of year – planting, sowing and tending our plots – while enjoying the spring flowers and preparing the ground for those yet to come.

KEY EVENTS

Passover, 1–9 April
Good Friday, 3 April
Easter Day, 5 April
St George's Day, 23 April

What to do in April

One of the best months for sowing and planting, the longer days fuel rapid growth above ground, while warmer, damp soils encourage the roots below. Sow fast-maturing crops such as lettuce and radishes fortnightly for harvests throughout summer, and annual flowers in batches until mid-May for a long season of blooms.

In the garden

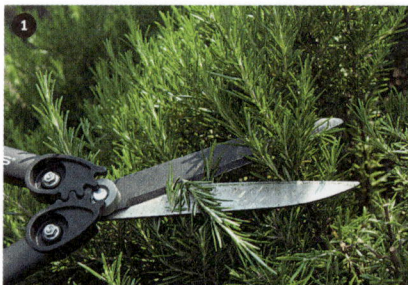

CUT BACK EVERGREEN SHRUBS Prune Mediterranean shrubs such as lavender and rosemary in April, cutting them back to healthy buds – do not prune into old, lifeless wood, which may not reshoot. Also lightly prune evergreens that flower late in the year, including *Fatsia*, *Hebe* and *Escallonia*, if they need a trim, but leave those that are currently in bloom or about to flower, such as *Ceanothus*, *Choisya*, *Daphne*, *Mahonia* and rhododendrons until May, after they have bloomed. **1**

DEADHEAD DAFFODILS and other spring bulbs after the flowers have faded. This diverts their energy from making seed into bulking up the bulbs for a good display next year.

SOW WILD FLOWERS in pots and plant the seedlings when they have established a few sets of leaves in a sunny bed or border where they will help to feed butterflies, moths and other pollinators. This is an easy way to incorporate them into the garden if you don't have space for a meadow.

MONEY-SAVING IDEA
Recycle old potting compost
Bags of compost can be expensive and when sowing and planting in spring, costs mount up. Good quality seed compost is worth the investment, but consider reusing old potting compost for more mature plants in containers. For the best results, mix spent potting compost with fresh material, or try sieving garden soil and mixing it with homemade compost or leaf mould. Adding some organic general-purpose fertilizer will boost the nutrient levels, too.

PRICK OUT TENDER PLANTS sown indoors last month. 'Pricking out' simply means transferring each seedling into its own module or pot to grow on. Once seedlings have a few leaves, hold one by a leaf, and use a blunt pencil or dibber (shown above) to loosen the roots. Replant in peat-free multipurpose compost, and grow on indoors until all risk of frost has past, before planting outside. ➋

DIVIDE WATER LILIES that have outgrown their allocated space. After removing the plant, use a sharp knife to cut the root ball into sections, each with at least one shoot and some roots. Replant the divided clumps into pond baskets filled with aquatic compost.

WATER PATIO PLANTS during dry spells and feed shrubs and perennials

growing in pots with an all-purpose organic fertilizer, following application rates recommended on the packaging.

In the fruit & veg patch

SOW PEAS in a sunny, sheltered spot. Shorter varieties are ideal for small spaces: sow them in a flat-bottomed trench 5cm (2in) deep and 15cm (6in) wide, and space them 7.5cm (3in) apart in a single row, or in two rows 30cm (1ft) apart. Plunge twiggy stems – the prunings from garden shrubs will work well – next to the seeds to support the growing stems.

PLANT OUT SECOND EARLY and maincrop potatoes from mid-April, following the advice on p.48. Plant second earlies 30cm (12in) apart, in rows 60cm (24in) apart, and maincrops

SOW CARROTS AND CABBAGES in prepared beds. Cover your crops with fleece or insect-proof mesh to protect them from carrot fly, the larvae of which tunnels into the roots, and cabbage white butterfly, whose larvae eat the leaves of brassicas such as cabbages, broccoli and Brussels sprouts.

SOW AUTUMN SQUASHES indoors. Set the seeds in pots of peat-free seed compost. The resulting seedlings should be planted outside 90cm (3ft) apart, or 1.5m (5ft) for trailing varieties, after the last frosts in May.

MULCH RASPBERRY CANES with organic matter such as garden compost, or add a high nitrogen organic fertilizer such as dried poultry manure pellets.

Indoors

START FEEDING CITRUS PLANTS now, using a specialist fertilizer designed for these fruit plants. After the frosts, set your plants outside in pots with drainage holes in the bottom. **4**

WATER HOUSEPLANTS MORE FREQUENTLY during warm spells, but take care not to overwater them. If their pots have drainage holes, place them in a sink, water them well, then leave them to drain. Further watering advice can be found on pp.18–19.

37cm (15in) apart, in rows 75cm (30in) apart. Meanwhile mound up soil around the emerging stems of first earlies, a process known as 'earthing up', which protects the stems from cold weather and encourages more tubers to form. Do the same when the potatoes you have just planted start to grow.

PROTECT YOUNG CROPS with cloches or cover plants with a double layer of biodegradable fleece when frost is forecast. The new growth of potatoes and strawberries is particularly vulnerable, as are tender crops growing in unheated greenhouses. **3**

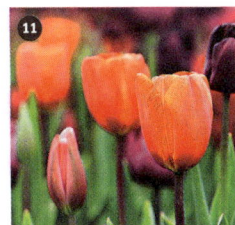

Plants of the month

1 Bergenia (*Bergenia cordifolia* 'Rosa Zeiten' pictured)
2 Siberian bugloss (*Brunnera macrophylla* 'Silver Heart' pictured)
3 Crab apple, blossom (*Malus × zumi* 'Golden Hornet' pictured)
4 Dog's tooth violet (*Erythronium* 'Pagoda' pictured)
5 Pearlbush (*Exochorda × macrantha* 'Niagara' pictured)
6 Persian lily (*Fritillaria persica*)
7 Ornamental cherry, blossom (*Prunus* 'Accolade' pictured)
8 Lungwort (*Pulmonaria* 'Barfield Regalia' pictured)
9 Rhododendron (*Rhododendron* 'Saint Tudy' pictured)
10 Flowering currant (*Ribes sanguineum* 'Atrorubens' pictured)
11 Tulip (*Tulipa*)

Project: Grow pizza in a pot

This fun project is a great way for children to learn about where their food comes from. Combining the tomatoes and herbs will allow you to make a fresh pizza topping when the fruits ripen later in the year. You can start now with small plug plants, if you didn't sow tomato seed earlier in the year (see p.30), and buy young herb plants from the garden centre. Remember that the tomato and basil plants are tender, so keep them indoors until after the frosts in May.

YOU WILL NEED
Outdoor tomato plant
Basil seed or plug
    plants
Oregano plug plants
Rosemary plug plants
Nasturtium seed
    (optional)

1 Fill a large pot, at least 30 x 40cm (12 x 15in) in height and diameter, with multipurpose peat-free compost, to about 7.5cm (3in) below the rim. Leaving this gap allows plenty of space for watering.

2 Plant a young tomato plant at the back of the container. Add a tall cane and tie the stems to it, if growing a cordon variety. Fill in around the front with a selection of herbs, making sure that the taller rosemary will not overshadow the shorter plants. Add a few nasturtium seeds for extra colour – these will germinate and grow during the summer.

3 Fill in around the plants with more compost to cover the root balls, and firm gently with your hands. Water well. Keep the container in a warm, bright spot indoors until about two weeks before the last frost, then set it outside during the day and bring it in at night, or cover with two layers of fleece or an old sheet overnight if frost is forecast.

4 After the risk of frost has passed, stand the pot outside day and night in a sheltered, sunny spot. Keep well-watered and apply a potassium-rich fertilizer when the flowers appear on the tomato plant.

Looking up

Sunrise and sunset

Spring is well under way, with longer days to spend in the garden and relax outside in the evening. The sun's warmth will dry the soil rapidly, so keep on top of watering.

DAY	LONDON		EDINBURGH	
	Sunrise	Sunset	Sunrise	Sunset
Wed, 1 Apr	6:33:41 am	7:35:01 pm	6:40:57 am	7:52:19 pm
Thu, 2 Apr	6:31:25 am	7:36:41 pm	6:38:20 am	7:54:21 pm
Fri, 3 Apr	6:29:10 am	7:38:22 pm	6:35:43 am	7:56:23 pm
Sat, 4 Apr	6:26:54 am	7:40:03 pm	6:33:06 am	7:58:25 pm
Sun, 5 Apr	6:24:39 am	7:41:43 pm	6:30:29 am	8:00:27 pm
Mon, 6 Apr	6:22:24 am	7:43:24 pm	6:27:53 am	8:02:29 pm
Tue, 7 Apr	6:20:10 am	7:45:04 pm	6:25:17 am	8:04:31 pm
Wed, 8 Apr	6:17:56 am	7:46:45 pm	6:22:42 am	8:06:33 pm
Thu, 9 Apr	6:15:43 am	7:48:25 pm	6:20:07 am	8:08:35 pm
Fri, 10 Apr	6:13:30 am	7:50:06 pm	6:17:32 am	8:10:38 pm
Sat, 11 Apr	6:11:18 am	7:51:47 pm	6:14:58 am	8:12:40 pm
Sun, 12 Apr	6:09:06 am	7:53:27 pm	6:12:25 am	8:14:42 pm
Mon, 13 Apr	6:06:55 am	7:55:08 pm	6:09:52 am	8:16:45 pm
Tue, 14 Apr	6:04:44 am	7:56:48 pm	6:07:19 am	8:18:47 pm
Wed, 15 Apr	6:02:35 am	7:58:29 pm	6:04:47 am	8:20:50 pm
Thu, 16 Apr	6:00:26 am	8:00:10 pm	6:02:16 am	8:22:52 pm
Fri, 17 Apr	5:58:17 am	8:01:50 pm	5:59:46 am	8:24:55 pm
Sat, 18 Apr	5:56:10 am	8:03:31 pm	5:57:16 am	8:26:58 pm
Sun, 19 Apr	5:54:03 am	8:05:11 pm	5:54:48 am	8:29:00 pm
Mon, 20 Apr	5:51:57 am	8:06:52 pm	5:52:20 am	8:31:03 pm
Tue, 21 Apr	5:49:52 am	8:08:32 pm	5:49:53 am	8:33:06 pm
Wed, 22 Apr	5:47:49 am	8:10:12 pm	5:47:26 am	8:35:08 pm
Thu, 23 Apr	5:45:46 am	8:11:53 pm	5:45:01 am	8:37:11 pm
Fri, 24 Apr	5:43:44 am	8:13:33 pm	5:42:37 am	8:39:14 pm
Sat, 25 Apr	5:41:43 am	8:15:13 pm	5:40:13 am	8:41:16 pm
Sun, 26 Apr	5:39:43 am	8:16:53 pm	5:37:51 am	8:43:18 pm
Mon, 27 Apr	5:37:44 am	8:18:33 pm	5:35:30 am	8:45:21 pm
Tue, 28 Apr	5:35:47 am	8:20:12 pm	5:33:10 am	8:47:23 pm
Wed, 29 Apr	5:33:51 am	8:21:52 pm	5:30:51 am	8:49:25 pm
Thu, 30 Apr	5:31:56 am	8:23:31 pm	5:28:34 am	8:51:26 pm

Moonrise and moonset

Moon phases

○ **FULL MOON** 2 April
◑ **THIRD QUARTER** 10 April

● **NEW MOON** 17 April
◐ **FIRST QUARTER** 24 April

DAY	LONDON			EDINBURGH		
	Moonrise	Moonset	Moonrise	Moonrise	Moonset	Moonrise
1 Apr		06:11	19:14		06:21	19:33
2 Apr		06:22	20:30		06:26	20:54
3 Apr		06:34	21:45		06:33	22:16
4 Apr		06:48	23:00		06:41	23:39
5 Apr		07:07			06:53	
6 Apr	00:14	07:32		01:00	07:10	
7 Apr	01:23	08:06		02:15	07:39	
8 Apr	02:22	08:53		03:17	08:23	
9 Apr	03:09	09:52		04:02	09:26	
10 Apr	03:44	11:02		04:30	10:42	
11 Apr	04:10	12:18		04:49	12:05	
12 Apr	04:29	13:36		05:01	13:31	
13 Apr	04:44	14:55		05:09	14:57	
14 Apr	04:57	16:16		05:16	16:24	
15 Apr	05:09	17:38		05:22	17:54	
16 Apr	05:22	19:04		05:29	19:27	
17 Apr	05:36	20:35		05:37	21:05	
18 Apr	05:54	22:08		05:47	22:47	
19 Apr	06:18	23:41		06:03		
20 Apr	06:54				00:29	06:31
21 Apr		01:03	07:47		01:57	07:18
22 Apr		02:07	08:57		03:00	08:31
23 Apr		02:51	10:20		03:36	10:01
24 Apr		03:20	11:46		03:57	11:36
25 Apr		03:41	13:10		04:10	13:08
26 Apr		03:56	14:30		04:19	14:35
27 Apr		04:08	15:47		04:25	15:58
28 Apr		04:19	17:02		04:31	17:18
29 Apr		04:30	18:16		04:37	18:38
30 Apr		04:42	19:30		04:43	19:59

Average temperature & rainfall

This table shows the average minimum and maximum temperatures, indicated by the blue and red dots, together with the average rainfall and number of rainy days for this month. The horizontal rules show how the figures have varied over the past decade.

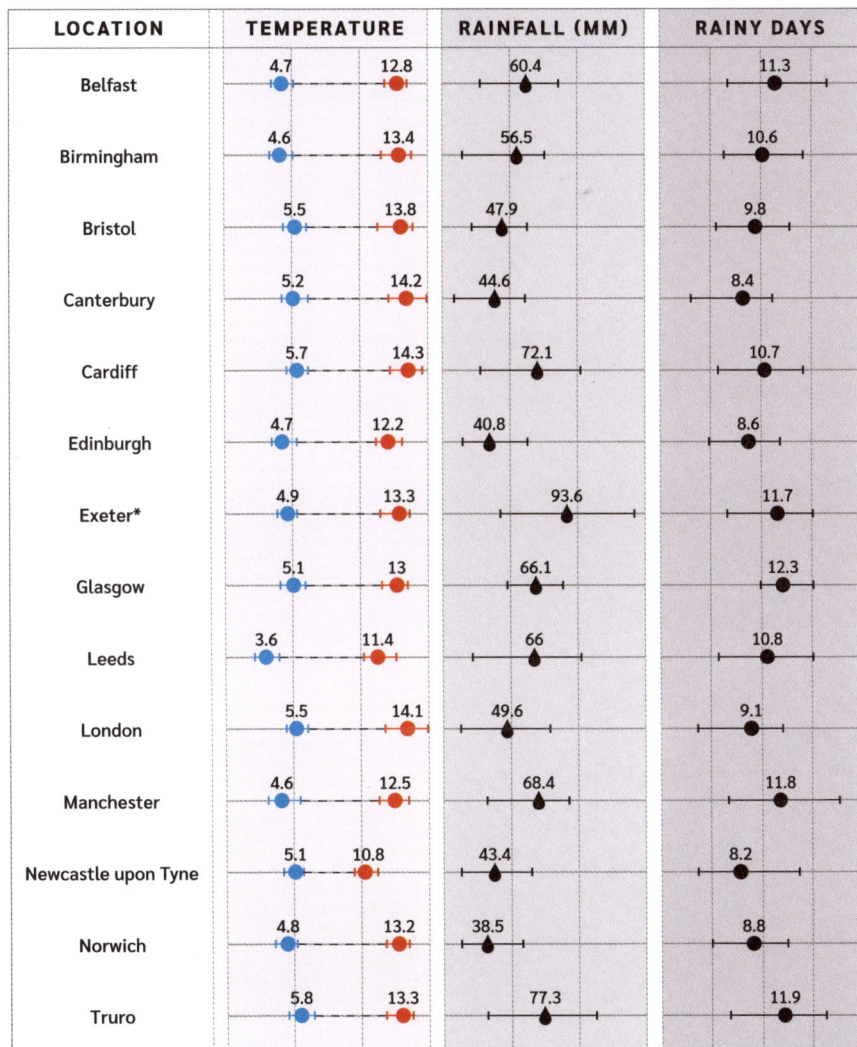

LOCATION	TEMPERATURE		RAINFALL (MM)	RAINY DAYS
Belfast	4.7	12.8	60.4	11.3
Birmingham	4.6	13.4	56.5	10.6
Bristol	5.5	13.8	47.9	9.8
Canterbury	5.2	14.2	44.6	8.4
Cardiff	5.7	14.3	72.1	10.7
Edinburgh	4.7	12.2	40.8	8.6
Exeter*	4.9	13.3	93.6	11.7
Glasgow	5.1	13	66.1	12.3
Leeds	3.6	11.4	66	10.8
London	5.5	14.1	49.6	9.1
Manchester	4.6	12.5	68.4	11.8
Newcastle upon Tyne	5.1	10.8	43.4	8.2
Norwich	4.8	13.2	38.5	8.8
Truro	5.8	13.3	77.3	11.9

* figures for Bovey Tracey

Temperature scale: 0 5 10
Rainfall scale: 50 100
Rainy days scale: 5 10 15

Sustainable gardening

Planting for pollinators

Bees, butterflies, moths and other pollinating insects are vital to almost every ecosystem on the planet. They ensure that flowering plants and crops reproduce effectively, thereby supporting all the creatures further up the food chain that depend on this vegetation for food and shelter – it is estimated that one third of the world's food production depends on bees alone. These insects also form part of that food chain and are an important source of food for birds, amphibians, mammals and reptiles.

However, populations of pollinating insects are in decline, due to habitat loss, intensive farming practices and changes in weather patterns, leaving them, and us, very vulnerable. One way to reverse this worrying trend is to stock up on plants in our gardens that provide food for these creatures.

BUSY BEES
Bees and other insects shift pollen from the male to the female parts of a flower, allowing fertilization to take place and seeds and fruits to form. Plants reward their insect helpers with nectar, a sugary liquid specifically produced to lure pollinators, who also help themselves to some, but not all of the protein-rich pollen. Even partially self-fertile plants

such as broad beans produce more crops when pollinated by insects. Bees, including bumble and solitary bees, as well as honey bees, are the most important pollinating insects, while many flies, such as houseflies and hoverflies, are effective too and second only to bees. Beetles, butterflies, moths and wasps also play a part.

CHOOSING PLANTS FOR POLLINATORS
Native flowers, including cowslips (*Primula veris*), devil's bit scabious (*Succisa pratensis*), hawthorn (*Crataegus*) and ivy (*Hedera*), are especially valuable to pollinating insects, not only offering nectar and pollen, but also supporting insect larvae such as caterpillars that browse their roots and foliage.

Less useful are blowsy double blooms, with extra petals that resemble flowers within flowers, which lack accessible

Single-flowered dahlias are loved by bees.

pollen and nectar. Use these sparingly, even though they may be more showy and slower to fade than the beneficial single flowers. However, do not dismiss all exotic plants, many of which are also valuable. For example, single-flowered dahlias and fuchsias supply stores of nectar and pollen in late summer when most natives have finished blooming.

Early flowers are important, too, offering sustenance to insects building up their energy reserves in readiness for summer. The blossom of apple, pear, and cherry trees, willow catkins, flowering currants, grape hyacinths, hellebores, and snowdrops all offer early food sources.

For an easy reference of plants that support pollinators, download the free *RHS Plants for Pollinators* project lists from rhs.org.uk. Seed and plant suppliers also use the bee symbol to label plants on these lists.

HELPFUL 'WEEDS'

So-called weeds can help pollinators, although removing them before they set seed set is wise. Red deadnettle (*Lamium purpureum*), perennial sowthistle (*Sonchus arvensis*) and wood avens (*Geum urbanum*) are good examples of rampant, but pollen- and nectar-rich plants to retain while they are in flower. Delay mowing parts of lawns to allow daisies,

Plant a variety of flowers for a long season of nectar.

dandelions, buttercups and other insect-friendly meadow plants to thrive. Only mow when flowering is over, in late summer. You can also leave some cabbages, radishes, carrots, parsnips and leeks to flower.

Finally, provide fresh water in a shallow dish that insects can access and leave a few areas of bare earth for wild bees to make nests for their eggs. Containers packed with hollow stems or drilled logs also make valuable wild bee habitats.

Edible garden

Mid-spring is a busy month for sowing and planting, but it is also dubbed the 'hunger gap', since few crops are ready to harvest at this time of year, when winter vegetables are over and the new season's crops have yet to mature. However, it is the season for succulent asparagus spears, and early sown cabbages will be maturing, too.

Vegetables

SOW INDOORS IN A SHADED GREENHOUSE Outdoor aubergines; basil; broccoli (calabrese); Brussels sprouts; cabbages for summer and autumn harvests and storing, including red cabbages; cardoons; cauliflowers; celeriac; celery; globe artichokes; hardy herbs including chervil, coriander, dill, parsley, savoury (winter and summer) and thyme; kohlrabi; leeks; outdoor peppers; tomatoes.

In the second half of the month: Cardoons; courgettes; cucamelons; cucumbers; edible flowers; French and runner beans; globe artichokes; gherkins; marrows, pumpkins, summer and winter squash; sweetcorn.

SOW OUTDOORS Artichokes; beetroots; broad beans; broccoli (calabrese); carrots; chard; leeks, lettuce; onions; parsnips; peas ❶, including sugarsnaps and mangetout; radishes; rocket; salad crops; spinach; spring onions; turnips.

PLANT OUT Hardy plants sown indoors in February and March, including asparagus, beetroot, cabbages, carrots,

HERB OF THE MONTH: PEPPERMINT (*Mentha × piperita*)
Adding a fresh, minty taste to salads, savoury and sweet dishes, and cocktails, peppermint is one of the easiest herbs to grow. This hardy perennial produces purple-flushed green leaves from spring to autumn, before the foliage dies down in the winter, returning again in spring. It tolerates some shade, too, but it's invasive and best restricted to a pot of its own. Congested plants can be divided in autumn or spring.

cauliflowers, celeriac, celery, chard, kohlrabi; globe and Chinese artichokes; lettuce and salad leaves; onion sets; parsnips; peas; maincrop potatoes; radishes; rocket; shallots.

HARVEST NOW Asparagus; chard; kale; lettuce; radishes; shrubby herbs such as rosemary and sage ❷; spinach; spring cabbages; purple and white sprouting broccoli; spring onions.

Fruit

SOW INDOORS Melons; watermelons.

PLANT NOW Potted fruit trees and bushes; blackberry and raspberry canes (at the beginning of the month); strawberry plants.

HARVEST Rhubarb.

TOP TIP
Eco-friendly herb patch
Growing herbs by the back door offers easy access to their leaves for use in the kitchen. A quick and inexpensive idea is to collect together empty food cans, old washing up bowls, buckets and crates, and make drainage holes in the base of each with an electric drill. Sow seed of annuals in the food cans, and plant shrubby and large herbs such as sage, rosemary and sweet cicely in the other vessels in peat-free loam-based compost mixed with a few handfuls of horticultural grit for extra drainage. The cans can also be attached to trellis with some raffia to create a living wall. The recycled containers will soon be disguised beneath the herbs' leafy stems. Just remember to water the plants regularly during dry spells.

🍲 Recipe

SERVES 4

MOROCCAN RUMP OF LAMB WITH POACHED RHUBARB

Using spring lamb, now in season, and sticks of fresh rhubarb, which are ready to harvest now, this recipe makes a change from a traditional Sunday roast, or serve it at a dinner party.

1   Rub the lamb all over with a teaspoon of olive oil and pinch of salt and pepper. Also add some sprigs of fresh thyme.

2   Starting fat side down, sear the lamb in a non-stick frying pan on a medium-high heat for ten minutes, turning regularly until gnarly all over but blushing in the middle, or use your instincts to cook to your liking.

3   Remove to a plate to rest. Then, with the frying pan on a low heat, make a liquor by stirring in a splash of water and a little red wine vinegar to pick up the sticky bits, leaving it to simmer gently until needed.

4   For the poached rhubarb, mix the caster sugar with 250ml of water in a saucepan and bring to the boil. Meanwhile, cut the rhubarb into 5–10cm (2–4in) batons and finally slice the shallot.

5   Add the batons and shallot to the boiling sugar syrup, then immediately remove the pan from the heat. Leave the rhubarb batons in the syrup as it cools, then remove them with a slotted spoon.

6   Set the lamb on flatbreads, with a drizzle of liquor, the rhubarb syrup and rhubarb batons. Add the yoghurt and garnish with cucumber, spinach leaves and coriander.

INGREDIENTS

For the pan-seared lamb rump
2 x 200-240g lamb rumps
1 tsp olive oil
Salt and black pepper to taste
2 sprigs of thyme
Splash of red wine vinegar
150g caster sugar
400g rhubarb
1 shallot

For the garnish
4 flatbreads
100g Greek yoghurt
1 cucumber (peeled ribbons)
50g baby spinach
Fresh coriander

Challenges this month

The garden comes alive as temperatures and light levels increase, prompting a surge in creatures that may damage your ornamentals and crops. Diseases are also on the rise this month, while late frosts can adversely affect fruits and other plants.

SPRING FROSTS can damage the blossom and young fruit on trees and bushes, leading to few or no fruits. On large trees, there is little you can do to avoid this, but covering smaller soft fruit bushes, espaliered trees and strawberries for two weeks after flowering begins, if severe frosts are forecast, will help. Use a double layer of fleece – or cloches if practical – and remove during the day to allow pollinators to access the flowers. Trained fruit grown on walls and fences can be covered with two or three layers of horticultural fleece, hessian or shade netting. Use canes to keep the material from touching the flowers and roll it up during the day. Remove the covers as soon as the danger of frost is over.

ANNUAL MEADOW GRASS (*Poa annua*) is a coarse annual grass that self-seeds into borders and lawns. While it can make a lawn look uneven, it has many benefits for wildlife, feeding butterfly caterpillars, while birds such as finches feed on the seeds. Leave some to grow and set seed in informal lawns, curbing its spread by raking in more lawn seed now. For more formal lawns, mow regularly to keep meadow grass in check and use a collection box for clippings, which may contain the seed.

APPLE SCAB (pictured) and the similar pear scab are fungal diseases that cause dark, scabby marks on the fruit and leaves of these crops. Scab is spread by airborne spores that overwinter on fallen leaves which reinfect the tree, causing olive-green spots or blotches, darkening over time, on the foliage. It also causes stems to crack and blister, and when the fungus enters the plant, it can cause apple canker, a more serious disease (see rhs.org.uk for more details). Diseased fruits may be distorted but scab does not usually affect the flavour, although cracked apples don't store well. To control the disease, remove blistered or cracked twigs and dispose of fallen leaves and infected fruits to reduce incidences the following year. Replace susceptible trees with scab-resistant varieties, but avoid fungicides (including organic types) that reduce biodiversity.

Garden benefactors

Earthworms

Responsible for maintaining a healthy soil packed with nutrients, earthworms are key to plant growth and welfare.

There are about 30 species of earthworm in Britain, and while they vary in size and colour, all help to create good soil structure and improve fertility. They perform this trick by eating soil and organic matter such as decaying plants, roots and leaves, which are then broken down into smaller particles as the worms digest them, before being returned to the soil in their droppings, known as casts. The casts are then worked on by bacteria and fungi, which break them down further into a nutrient package that plants can absorb, with five times more nitrogen, seven times more phosphorus, and a thousand times more beneficial bacteria than the original soil.

Worms' activity also benefits the soil structure, their burrows helping to break up large particles, while creating tunnels that air and water can pass through, thereby increasing the oxygen supply to plants' roots and improving drainage. They also mix up the soil layers and incorporate organic matter such as fallen leaves, which they drag down into their burrows. In addition, these little creatures provide food for a wide variety of garden wildlife, including toads, frogs, blackbirds, robins, beetles, and hedgehogs.

Earthworms breed in the warmer months of the year and deposit their eggs in the soil in lemon-shaped egg sacks. These hatch into small worms that increase in size over time. Brandling or tiger worms live in compost heaps or areas of rotting organic matter, while a variety of other species live at varying depths in the soil.

You will not need to add worms to your garden, since they are present in all soils, but are found in fewer numbers in very acidic or waterlogged conditions. However, you can encourage them by mulching, leaving leaf litter on your borders and beneath trees, and growing cover crops or green manures on bare ground. Also, minimize digging and avoid the use of all pesticides.

Design masterclass

Tom Massey

With five RHS Chelsea Flower Show gardens under his belt, Tom Massey is one of the most celebrated designers in the UK, known for his bold, thought-provoking, ecologically sensitive gardens. In 2023, he wrote his first book, *RHS Resilient Garden,* which explores ways of future-proofing our plots and helping to mitigate the effects of climate change. He then wrote a second book, *RHS Waterwise Garden,* in 2025, showing how we can sustainably manage water in our gardens and landscapes.

Tom is also widely recognized for his appearances on the BBC2 television series *Your Garden Made Perfect,* on which he pitched his ideas against other garden designers to homeowners.

Tom developed a love and appreciation for the natural world while exploring the Roseland Peninsula in Cornwall, where he spent holidays as a child. After completing an Animation degree, he pursued a number of jobs before switching careers to garden design. He graduated with a distinction from the London College of Garden Design and opened his practice in 2015.

HOW TO DESIGN A WATERWISE GARDEN

Inspired by his recent book, Tom explains how to conserve water while reducing flooding.

▶ 'Redirect the downpipes on your house and outbuildings into water butts, a rainwater harvesting tank or rain garden. This reduces the risk of stormwater runoff causing flooding on your property or overwhelming mains sewers. It also provides a free water source to irrigate your plants.'

▶ 'Use permeable surfaces such as gravel, porous pavers or decking that allow water to soak into the ground to reduce runoff. If you have large areas of existing paving, consider replacing some pavers with planting pockets.'

▶ 'Opt for more plants and less paving. Planting areas allow water to infiltrate into the soil, helping to recharge groundwater supplies and supporting ecosystems, while reducing stormwater runoff.'

Plants for difficult places

Fruit and veg for shade

Most crops demand full sun to generate a good harvest, but there are few stalwarts that you can grow successfully in shady gardens, such as urban plots surrounded by buildings.

The reason why many vegetables and fruits are less productive in shade is that most crops have a high demand for sunlight, which helps to feed and develop them. For some garden owners, it may be possible to increase light levels, and your choices, by pruning back trees or large shrubs to allow more sun into your space. Or, if your garden is shaded by walls or fences, painting the surfaces white may help to reflect more light into it.

If these options are not open to you, thankfully some plants tolerate lower light levels and still produce a good harvest. Members of the *Ribes* genus, including currants and gooseberries, tend to do well in some shade, probably because the wild plants from which they were bred grew on the edges of forests and woodlands.

Peas referred to as early croppers, which often only need twelve weeks between planting and harvest, tend to be slightly more tolerant of some shade than maincrop varieties. Sowing these peas in batches every two weeks can also extend their cropping season.

Leafy crops such as kale and lettuce grow well in partial shade and the more consistent temperatures here can also reduce bolting. This is when plants run to seed quickly because they are stressed, often due to very hot or cold temperatures, which are more common on more open, sunny sites.

No two gardens will ever be the same so try experimenting with other crops, too, including carrots, chard, rocket and raspberries, all of which have some shade tolerance.

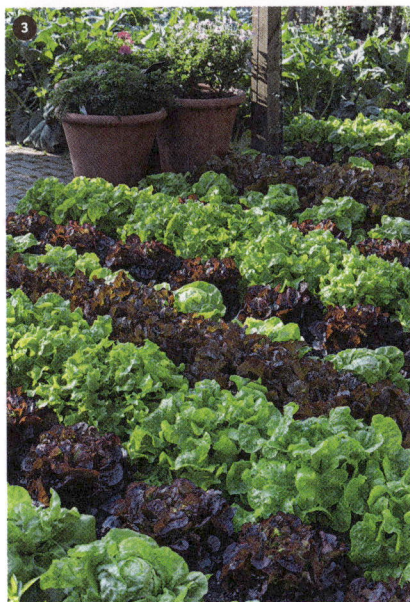

CHOOSING CROPS FOR SHADE

❶ Redcurrant 'Rovada'
One of the best redcurrants, this cultivar produces exceptionally heavy crops, with long strings of large fruit in late summer. **H&S:** 1.2 × 1.2m (4 × 4ft)

❷ Gooseberry 'Hinnonmäki Röd'
Unusual deep red gooseberries are produced on disease-resistant bushes and ready to harvest in mid-July. **H&S:** 2.5 × 1.5m (8 × 5ft)

Blackcurrant 'Ben Tirran'
The sweet currants on this high-yielding variety usually ripen at the end of July or early August, thereby extending the cropping season. **H&S:** 1.2 × 1.2m (4 × 4ft)

Kale 'Reflex'
The dark green, highly nutritious edible leaves of this kale variety are extremely winter hardy and can be picked over a long period from October to February. **H&S:** 90 × 60cm (3 × 2ft)

Kohlrabi
Choose between the green and purple varieties of this cabbage-like, compact crop. The swollen stems can be eaten raw in salads or cooked like turnips. **H&S:** 45 × 40cm (18 × 16in)

❸ Lettuce 'Salad bowl'
The frilly-edged, lime-green leaves of this variety and its sister 'Red Salad Bowl' can be used as a cut-and-come-again lettuce or left to develop a full head. **H&S:** 30 × 30cm (12 × 2in)

May

The garden is buzzing with activity as spring moves into summer. Birds are feeding their young with caterpillars plucked from luscious leaves, while bees flit from flower to flower in search of nectar. Planting with these visitors in mind benefits us, too, offering free plant protection and bountiful crops, while their calming presence delivers precious moments of peace.

KEY EVENTS

May Day Bank Holiday, 4 May
Ascension Day, 14 May
RHS Chelsea Flower Show, 19–23 May
Shavuot, 21–23 May
Whit Sunday, 24 May
Spring Bank Holiday, 25 May
Eid al-Adha, 27 May

What to do in May

As the threat of frost passes towards the end of the month, tender flowers and crops can be planted outside in their final positions. Lawns will need mowing regularly now if you want a level sward, or leave them to grow for a few months, allowing the wild flowers embedded in them to bloom and feed pollinators such as bees and butterflies.

In the garden

CONTINUE TO SOW HALF-HARDY ANNUALS in pots indoors or in a protected spot outside, where they are less likely to be eaten by slugs and snails. Once they form robust plants, they are not as appetising to these molluscs and can be planted in beds and patio containers to flower until the frosts return in autumn.

SHADE GREENHOUSES and conservatories, which can become very hot during late spring and summer, causing plants to scorch and wilt. Use shade netting inside the greenhouse or paint the panes with special paint, available from the garden centre or online – this can then be washed off in autumn. Blinds are another, but more expensive, option. **1**

HARDEN OFF SEEDLINGS for two weeks in mid-May to acclimatize them, placing them outside during the day and bringing them indoors at night. Cover plants outside with a double layer of fleece in week one, and a single layer in week two. Alternatively, keep under well-ventilated cloches or cold frames, before planting outside after the frosts.

SOW HARDY ANNUALS in gaps in your borders. This is a great way to fill a new bed with colour while you wait for the permanent plants to fill out. Ensure the seedlings will have space and light to establish well.

PLANT UP PATIO POTS with summer flowers grown earlier indoors and hardened off (see left). Also consider planting long-flowering hardy perennials such as *Coreopsis* and hardy geraniums in containers. These offer good value since they overwinter and flower year after year.

GIVE POTTED SPRING BULBS A BOOST with a dose of seaweed-based fertilizer and leave the foliage to wither naturally.

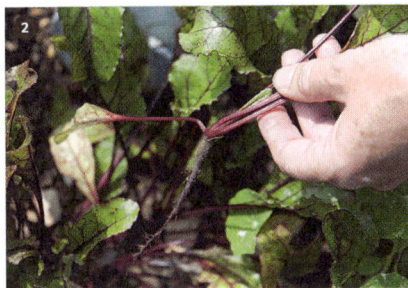

PRUNING TIP
Spring-flowering shrubs
Prune shrubs such as *Kerria*, *Choisya* (pictured here), *Spiraea*, *Ribes*, and Japanese quince (*Chaenomeles*) in May, after they have finished flowering. Remove one in three of the oldest stems and shorten those that remain to a healthy bud. The shrubs then have time to grow new flowering stems for next spring's display.

In the fruit & veg patch

SOW SPROUTING BROCCOLI AND OVERWINTERED CAULIFLOWERS at the end of month indoors in cell trays for a harvest next spring. After about six weeks, transplant the seedlings to a sunny or very lightly shaded fertile spot outside. Plant them through a mulch of well-rotted garden compost, allowing 60cm (2ft) between rows and 45cm (18in) between plants. Use card collars to protect them against cabbage root fly and cover with butterfly netting (see p.157).

THIN OUT CROPS that you sowed outside in March and April, using the thinnings of leafy vegetables such as broccoli, carrots and beetroots, to add to your salads. **2**

PINCH OUT THE GROWING TIPS of broad beans when small pods have started to form. The plants will then focus on developing more pods instead of taller stems, and it helps to reduce blackfly, which loves the tender tips.

DIRECT SOW TENDER BEANS in a prepared bed in a sunny spot. For climbing French and runner beans, make a wigwam support with four or five canes, about 2.5m (8ft) tall, and sow two seeds at the base of each cane – remove the weakest one after they have germinated. Try sowing dwarf beans in large pots of peat-free compost, spacing the seed 15–20cm (6–8in) apart. These compact plants need no supports, and are ideal for a productive patio. Alternatively sow dwarf French beans in rows 45cm (18in) apart, thinning the seedlings to 15cm (6in) between plants.

Indoors

PLACE HARDIER HOUSEPLANTS outside at the end of the month in a partly shaded sheltered area, checking that yours will cope with the night temperatures in your area. The fresh, humid air outside helps to boost growth, but ensure the plants are housed in pots with drainage holes at the bottom.

REPOT PLANTS that are flagging due to congested roots. Tease out the roots gently with your fingers, and plant in a pot one size larger than the original, with fresh peat-free compost. **3**

MOVE PLANTS AWAY FROM DIRECT SUN to avoid scorching. Even sun-lovers such as cacti and succulents can scorch in a hot, bright conservatory or greenhouse during the long days from May to August.

MONEY-SAVING IDEA
Propagate houseplants
You can make new plants for free from leaf cuttings. Remove a few leaves from *Sansevieria* and *Streptocarpus* and cut into horizontal strips. Then insert them on their cut ends, up to a third deep, in houseplant potting compost, and roots will grow from the severed edges. For begonias, lay the leaves face down and make several cuts at right angles across each vein. Place the leaf face up on a bed of houseplant compost, and use wire or paperclips to keep the cut surface in contact with the soil. Pot up the new plants that form into individual containers.

Plants of the month

1 Ornamental onion (*Allium hollandicum* 'Purple Sensation' pictured)

2 Columbine (*Aquilegia chrysantha* 'Yellow Queen' pictured)

3 Trailing bellflower (*Campanula poscharskyana* 'E.H. Frost' pictured)

4 California lilac (*Ceanothus thyrsiflorus* 'Mystery Blue' pictured)

5 Clematis (*Clematis* 'Daniel Deronda' pictured)

6 Chinese dogwood (*Cornus kousa* var. *chinensis*)

7 Martin's spurge (*Euphorbia* × *martini*)

8 English bluebell (*Hyacinthoides non-scripta*)

9 Honesty (*Lunaria annua*)

10 Peony (*Paeonia lactiflora* 'Sword Dance' pictured)

11 Chinese wisteria (*Wisteria sinensis* 'Prolific' pictured)

Project: Make a container pond

If you don't have space for a full-size pond, this miniature planted pool is a great alternative. Bringing colour and interest to a garden or patio, it will also attract a range of wildlife, including birds, aquatic insects, and frogs, if you set shorter pots around it to allow them to hop in. Choose a large pot to fit a few plants, and if opting for terracotta, keep it in a sheltered area close to the house, where frost won't damage it.

YOU WILL NEED
Large pot (this one is 40 x 40 x 40cm/ 15 x 15 x 15in)
Selection of pond plants such as: *Sagittaria latifolia*; *Iris laevigata* 'Variegata'; a miniature bulrush (*Typha minima*); *Veronica beccabunga;* and the miniature water lily *Nymphaea* 'Pygmaea Helvola'
Cork or pond liner
Silicone-based sealer
Yacht varnish
Pond baskets
Aquatic compost

1 First seal your pot if it has a drainage hole in the bottom. Either insert a cork into a round hole or place a piece of pond liner over it and fix it in place with a silicone-based sealer to make the container watertight.

2 Also seal the insides by applying two or three coats of yacht vanish. This will protect terracotta, which is porous and prone to frost damage.

3 Plant your aquatics in individual pond baskets, available from water garden suppliers, and aquatic compost – peat-free multipurpose is too rich in nutrients for these plants. Place all the plants on top of bricks or upturned pots so that the tops of their baskets will be just below the water surface, apart from the water lily, which can sit on the base.

4 Before filling the pot with water, move it to a sunny, sheltered location. Keep the water level topped up during the warmer months. You can lift and divide the plants every year or two to keep them in check.

Looking up

Sunrise and sunset

The long days bring more warmth, but beware of late frosts which can strike earlier in the month. Also keep unwanted plants, which will be growing rapidly, in check.

DAY	LONDON		EDINBURGH	
	Sunrise	Sunset	Sunrise	Sunset
Fri, 1 May	5:30:02 am	8:25:10 pm	5:26:18 am	8:53:28 pm
Sat, 2 May	5:28:10 am	8:26:48 pm	5:24:03 am	8:55:29 pm
Sun, 3 May	5:26:19 am	8:28:27 pm	5:21:50 am	8:57:30 pm
Mon, 4 May	5:24:30 am	8:30:05 pm	5:19:38 am	8:59:31 pm
Tue, 5 May	5:22:42 am	8:31:42 pm	5:17:27 am	9:01:31 pm
Wed, 6 May	5:20:56 am	8:33:19 pm	5:15:18 am	9:03:30 pm
Thu, 7 May	5:19:11 am	8:34:56 pm	5:13:11 am	9:05:29 pm
Fri, 8 May	5:17:28 am	8:36:32 pm	5:11:06 am	9:07:28 pm
Sat, 9 May	5:15:47 am	8:38:08 pm	5:09:02 am	9:09:26 pm
Sun, 10 May	5:14:07 am	8:39:43 pm	5:07:00 am	9:11:23 pm
Mon, 11 May	5:12:29 am	8:41:17 pm	5:05:00 am	9:13:20 pm
Tue, 12 May	5:10:53 am	8:42:50 pm	5:03:02 am	9:15:16 pm
Wed, 13 May	5:09:19 am	8:44:23 pm	5:01:06 am	9:17:11 pm
Thu, 14 May	5:07:47 am	8:45:55 pm	4:59:12 am	9:19:05 pm
Fri, 15 May	5:06:17 am	8:47:27 pm	4:57:20 am	9:20:58 pm
Sat, 16 May	5:04:49 am	8:48:57 pm	4:55:30 am	9:22:50 pm
Sun, 17 May	5:03:23 am	8:50:26 pm	4:53:42 am	9:24:41 pm
Mon, 18 May	5:01:59 am	8:51:55 pm	4:51:57 am	9:26:30 pm
Tue, 19 May	5:00:37 am	8:53:22 pm	4:50:14 am	9:28:18 pm
Wed, 20 May	4:59:18 am	8:54:48 pm	4:48:34 am	9:30:05 pm
Thu, 21 May	4:58:01 am	8:56:13 pm	4:46:56 am	9:31:51 pm
Fri, 22 May	4:56:46 am	8:57:36 pm	4:45:21 am	9:33:35 pm
Sat, 23 May	4:55:33 am	8:58:58 pm	4:43:49 am	9:35:17 pm
Sun, 24 May	4:54:24 am	9:00:19 pm	4:42:19 am	9:36:57 pm
Mon, 25 May	4:53:16 am	9:01:38 pm	4:40:53 am	9:38:36 pm
Tue, 26 May	4:52:11 am	9:02:56 pm	4:39:29 am	9:40:13 pm
Wed, 27 May	4:51:09 am	9:04:12 pm	4:38:08 am	9:41:47 pm
Thu, 28 May	4:50:09 am	9:05:26 pm	4:36:50 am	9:43:20 pm
Fri, 29 May	4:49:12 am	9:06:39 pm	4:35:35 am	9:44:50 pm
Sat, 30 May	4:48:18 am	9:07:50 pm	4:34:24 am	9:46:18 pm
Sun, 31 May	4:47:27 am	9:08:59 pm	4:33:16 am	9:47:43 pm

Moonrise and moonset

Moon phases

○ **FULL MOON** 1 May　　● **NEW MOON** 16 May　　○ **FULL MOON** 31 May
◑ **THIRD QUARTER** 9 May　　◐ **FIRST QUARTER** 23 May

DAY	LONDON			EDINBURGH		
	Moonrise	Moonset	Moonrise	Moonrise	Moonset	Moonrise
1 May		04:55	20:45		04:50	21:21
2 May		05:12	21:59		05:01	22:42
3 May		05:35	23:10		05:17	
4 May		06:06		00:00	05:41	
5 May	00:12	06:48		01:07	06:20	
6 May	01:04	07:43		01:57	07:15	
7 May	01:43	08:49		02:31	08:27	
8 May	02:11	10:01		02:52	09:46	
9 May	02:32	11:17		03:06	11:09	
10 May	02:48	12:34		03:16	12:33	
11 May	03:02	13:51		03:24	13:57	
12 May	03:14	15:11		03:30	15:23	
13 May	03:26	16:33		03:36	16:52	
14 May	03:39	18:00		03:43	18:26	
15 May	03:55	19:32		03:53	20:06	
16 May	04:17	21:07		04:06	21:50	
17 May	04:47	22:37		04:28	23:29	
18 May	05:33	23:52		05:06		
19 May	06:38				00:45	06:10
20 May		00:45	08:00		01:34	07:38
21 May		01:21	09:29		02:01	09:16
22 May		01:45	10:56		02:17	10:51
23 May		02:02	12:19		02:27	12:21
24 May		02:16	13:37		02:35	13:46
25 May		02:27	14:52		02:41	15:07
26 May		02:38	16:06		02:46	16:27
27 May		02:50	17:20		02:52	17:46
28 May		03:03	18:34		02:59	19:07
29 May		03:19	19:48		03:09	20:28
30 May		03:39	20:59		03:23	21:47
31 May		04:08	22:04		03:45	22:57

Average temperature & rainfall

This table shows the average minimum and maximum temperatures, indicated by the blue and red dots, together with the average rainfall and number of rainy days for this month. The horizontal rules show how the figures have varied over the past decade.

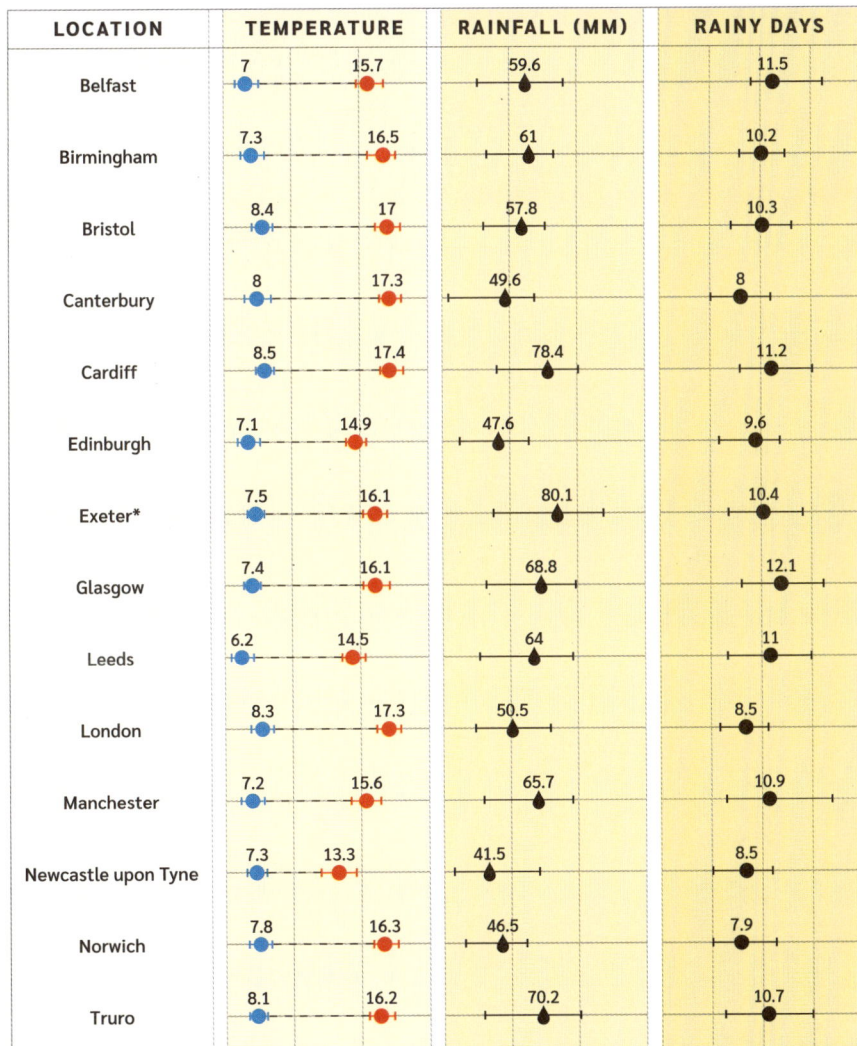

LOCATION	TEMPERATURE		RAINFALL (MM)	RAINY DAYS
Belfast	7	15.7	59.6	11.5
Birmingham	7.3	16.5	61	10.2
Bristol	8.4	17	57.8	10.3
Canterbury	8	17.3	49.6	8
Cardiff	8.5	17.4	78.4	11.2
Edinburgh	7.1	14.9	47.6	9.6
Exeter*	7.5	16.1	80.1	10.4
Glasgow	7.4	16.1	68.8	12.1
Leeds	6.2	14.5	64	11
London	8.3	17.3	50.5	8.5
Manchester	7.2	15.6	65.7	10.9
Newcastle upon Tyne	7.3	13.3	41.5	8.5
Norwich	7.8	16.3	46.5	7.9
Truro	8.1	16.2	70.2	10.7

* figures for Bovey Tracey

Temperature scale: 5 10 15
Rainfall scale: 50 100
Rainy days scale: 5 10 15

Sustainable gardening

Growing your own food

Growing your own food can be highly sustainable and even 'circular', with homemade garden compost providing all the nutrients crops need, and any garden and kitchen waste then returned to the compost bin for the next crop. It's easy, too, and anyone can grow herbs or salad crops, even if they have just a window box or small courtyard garden.

Although supermarket carrots, parsnips, cabbages and other winter crops are probably cheaper to buy than to grow, other produce, such as salads and soft fruit, for example, can save you money. Many of these crops are flown in from abroad, adding to their carbon footprint, so those raised in your backyard will be more eco-friendly.

Onions laid out to dry after harvesting.

Just remember that most crops are harvested from midsummer to mid-autumn and that supplies diminish in winter, petering out almost entirely from mid-April to mid-May, when you may have to supplement your home-grown produce with fruit and vegetables from the shops.

TOP CHOICES

Lettuces are cheap and easy to grow, with packs often containing a thousand seeds. Sowing some every few weeks directly in the ground in a sunny spot enriched by homemade compost can give a good supply of salad leaves from June until October. The same goes for other undemanding but relatively costly produce, such as radishes, rocket and salad onions. More unusual vegetables such as endive, chicory, lamb's lettuce and radicchio are equally valuable and make nutritious autumn salads.

In small gardens with limited space, try adding edibles to the flower borders – as well as utilizing the beds efficiently, mixing plants together in this way often reduces the incidence of attacks by unwanted insects and diseases.

Rewarding winter crops include leeks, purple sprouting broccoli and kale, which have to be picked by hand commercially, making them relatively expensive to buy. Sown in late spring or summer, they occupy the ground for many months so are best for larger plots, although in spring salads can be grown between them or 'intercropped'.

Imported produce such as mangetout peas and French beans are also easy to grow in the summer. To save space, train taller climbing cultivars up fences or over teepees made from canes. The seed of these crops is relatively costly, but both plants are self-fertile and will come 'true to type' from home-saved seeds.

Tomatoes, sweet peppers and chillies are popular crops and here some investment will be beneficial – a polythene tunnel or a second-hand greenhouse, sometimes available for free from recycling websites, will aid these heat-loving crops. Ideally raise your own plants from seed on a sunny windowsill initially, or buy young tomato plants, which can be cost effective if you only want one or two.

EASY FRUITS

While supermarkets offer in-season strawberries and raspberries at relatively good prices, both are easy to grow. Other fruits are more costly to buy because they don't store well but they, too, are easy crops and you can pick them as needed. Examples include blackberries, gooseberries, figs (in the south), and all types of currants, which are reasonably heavy cropping and very undemanding, if you're strapped for time. You could also try more unusual berries, seldom seen in supermarkets, such as honeyberries (similar to blueberries but easier to grow), and hybrids such as loganberries, tayberries and jostaberries, the latter taste like a cross between a gooseberry and blackcurrant.

To ensure the birds do not devour your crops, these berries will need to be covered, but if you put away the nets carefully after the harvest, they will last for many years.

If you have never grown these crops before, you may be surprised at their fresher taste, as the journey from garden to plate is only a few minutes, rather than days, improving their flavour.

Blackberry 'Karaka Black' crops over a long time.

Edible garden

The spring harvests get under way this month, with fresh cabbages, cauliflowers and turnips ready to pick from a sowing the previous summer. Many vegetables, including tender types, can also be sown directly outside after the frosts in late May.

Vegetables

SOW INDOORS Butternut squash; calabrese; cauliflowers; courgettes; cucamelons; cucumbers; marrows; pumpkins; peppers; sprouting broccoli; summer and winter squash; sweetcorn.

SOW OUTDOORS Beetroots; broad beans; broccoli; calabrese; carrots; cauliflowers; chicory for forcing; Florence fennel; French beans; globe artichokes; lettuce; parsnips; peas; radishes; rocket; runner beans; salad crops; spinach; spring onions; turnips; winter crops such as late winter cabbages and savoys, and sprouting broccoli.

PLANT OUT Hardy plants sown indoors in March, including Brussels sprouts, cabbages, cardoons, cauliflowers, celeriac, celery, globe artichokes; kohlrabi, lettuce; maincrop potatoes.

After the last frosts from mid-May or crops grown under cloches: Basil, courgettes; marrows, pumpkins, summer and winter squash; outdoor cucumbers; outdoor tomatoes; peppers; sweetcorn.

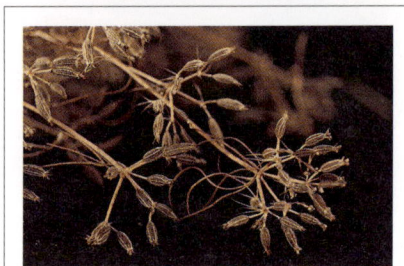

HERB OF THE MONTH: CARAWAY
(*Carum carvi*)
This hardy biennial is grown mainly for its aromatic seeds, which can be added to various dishes and baked goods. The young leaves are also delicious in salads. Sow the seed this month in free-draining soil in full sun, and transplant seedlings when small to prevent plants from flowering prematurely (bolting). The flowers and seeds will then appear next year, in their second summer.

TOP TIP
Try the Three Sisters planting combo
Used by Native American tribes, this grouping
is pretty and fun. Plant sweetcorn, climbing
beans and pumpkins or squash together in one
plot. Leave about double the recommended
space between each plant so they won't shade
one another. The beans can clamber up the
sweetcorn plants but will need trimming so
they don't smother them, while the pumpkins'
foliage shades out weeds. Plant through a
mulch of well-rotted organic matter.

HARVEST NOW Asparagus; chard;
lettuce and salad leaves; radishes **1**;
shrubby herbs; spinach; spring
cabbages; overwintered spring
cauliflowers; spring onions; turnips. **2**

Fruit

PLANT NOW Potted fruit trees and
bushes such as blueberries and
blackberries; long cane raspberries to
crop later this year; 60-day strawberry
plants for later summer strawberries.

HARVEST Rhubarb; first early
strawberries in late May. **3**

🍲 Recipe

PAN FRIED SALMON AND ASPARAGUS

This fresh, simple recipe combines fresh asparagus, which is in season in May, with lettuce and turnips that are ready to pick. If you froze your own peas last summer, you can add those, too.

1 Preheat the oven to 200°C/fan 180°C/gas 6.

2 Place a large frying pan over a medium to high heat. Once hot, add a splash of olive oil and slowly lower each fillet, skin side down, into the pan. Apply a little pressure to the fish so it doesn't curl and all of the skin is touching the pan.

3 Allow to cook for 2–3 minutes so the skin becomes crispy, then cook in the preheated oven for a further 4–5 minutes.

4 Meanwhile, heat the fish stock in a saucepan, adding the new potatoes and asparagus, then the turnip and peas a couple of minutes later.

5 Finish by adding the baby lettuce leaves and herbs. Add the butter to emulsify the fish stock and make a rich buttery sauce.

6 Remove the salmon fillets from the oven and leave them to rest for two or three minutes before serving with the vegetables and sauce.

7 Garnish with pea shoots, lemon wedges and chive flowers.

INGREDIENTS
4 salmon fillets, 180g each
1 turnip, thinly sliced
1 baby lettuce
8 asparagus, peeled
300g new potatoes, cooked and quartered
50g peas
100ml fish stock
100g butter
10g dill, chopped
10g chives, chopped
10g tarragon, chopped
Salt and pepper to season
Olive oil

For the garnish
Pea shoots
Wedge of lemon
Chive flowers

Challenges this month

Keeping on top of unwanted plants that may smother your ornamentals and crops is a priority, as they will be growing rapidly now. Also check ornamental plants and crops regularly for signs of disease that may require immediate action.

ASH DIEBACK is a devastating fungal disease that affects ash trees (*Fraxinus excelsior*) of all ages and eventually kills them. Now widespread in many areas of the UK, if you own a tree, you should be vigilant for signs of the disease, which include black blotches on the foliage and wilted leaves; cankers on stems and branches; and, in some cases, dark lesions at the base of the trunk. The whole tree then starts to die back. Visit the Forestry Commission website (forestresearch.gov.uk) for advice on what to do if a tree succumbs to the disease, and how you can help with research into its effects. An affected tree can topple and cause harm, so engage a qualified arboriculturist to make it safe.

CREEPING THISTLE (*Cirsium arvense*) is a tall native perennial plant, up to a metre (39in) in height, with spiny leaves and purple thistle-like flowers, followed by fluffy seedheads. Often regarded as a weed due to its ability to spread quickly, it is listed on the Weeds Act 1959, which aims to control plants that adversely affect agricultural land. However, in gardens, creeping thistle also has many benefits and supports a wide range of wildlife, so you may wish to cultivate a few plants in a quiet area, while keeping others under control. First, deadhead the flowers before they set seed and hoe off seedlings. Dig out young plants and their roots, and place in your council green waste, as home composting may not kill them. If larger plants are hard to remove, pull off the top growth and smother with a 10cm (4in) bark or woodchip mulch or several thicknesses of cardboard. Avoid weedkillers, which harm the environment.

PEA AND BEAN WEEVILS cause distinctive U-shaped notches along the leaf edges of pea and broad bean plants in spring (pictured), while the larvae feed on plants' root nodules. The damage from both the adults and their larvae is usually limited, but you can boost affected crops, if their growth is significantly checked by weevils, by covering the plants with fleece and watering them.

Garden benefactors

Hoverflies

These masters of disguise are often mistaken for wasps or bees, and like their doppelgangers, they play a vital role in the management of a healthy garden, while also helping to keep unwanted creatures at bay.

There are about 280 species of hoverfly in Britain, and they vary in size from a few millimetres to about 2cm (¾in) in length. The majority of adults feed on nectar and pollen and are important pollinators, while the larvae of six species eat aphids, as well as other plant sap-sucking insects such as leafhoppers, whiteflies and scale insects, protecting plants in the same way as ladybirds. The larvae of some species feed on decaying organic matter and help to recycle plant nutrients and increase soil fertility in the process.

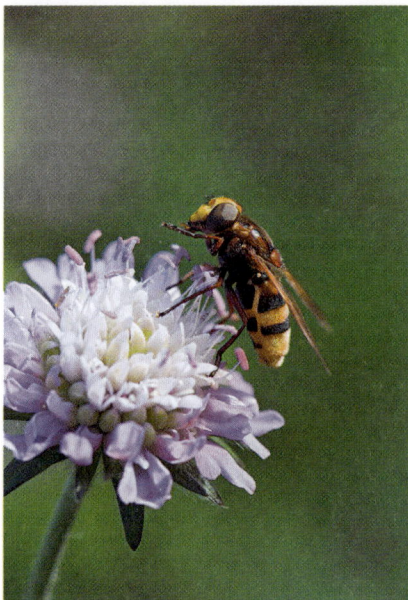

The adults' ability to hover in mid-air gives rise to their name, and they often sport yellow and black stripes, imitating stinging insects to ward off predators. However, unlike wasps and bees, hoverflies are harmless to humans. You can identify which is which by counting their wings when the insects are at rest: hoverflies have just two wings (one pair), while bees and wasps have four (two pairs).

Hoverflies are most active from spring to autumn, and produce several generations per year. The adult lays eggs near either a source of aphids or rotting wood or water, depending on the species, which then hatch into legless larvae. After pupating, they emerge as adults, most of which then live for a week or two.

To encourage hoverflies, plant a range of flowers that offer a succession of easily accessible pollen and nectar throughout the year and avoid using insecticides. Plants that hoverflies particularly like include *Echium vulgare*, coreopsis, Japanese anemones, buddleia, marigolds (*Calendula)*, hebes, poppies (*Papaver*), wild carrot (*Daucus carota),* marjoram and brambles. Add a log pile or area of stagnant water rich in decaying leaves or plants for the larvae.

Design masterclass

Cleve West

One of the most successful RHS Chelsea Flower Show designers of all time, Cleve West has won seven gold medals and is the only person to have been awarded 'Best in Show' two years in succession. He also designed the first garden for the charity Horatio's Garden, which creates outdoor spaces at spinal injury centres for the patients and staff.

A committed vegan, Cleve's respect and concern for the environment and all its life forms inform his approach to design. His gardens support wildlife by increasing habitats and biodiversity, while also demonstrating his keen sense of artistry and planting skill.

Cleve grew up in Somerset and the magic of Exmoor has been a life-long influence on his work. After studying Art and PE, he began his career maintaining gardens, but was soon drawn to design. He studied at Kew and with the late John Brookes before setting up his studio in 1990. He now splits his time between designing and his allotment, where he gardens organically and without animal products.

HOW TO DESIGN A WILDLIFE GARDEN

Wildlife habitats take centre stage in all of Cleve's designs and here he suggests the best ways to make a home for all manner of creatures in your garden.

▶ 'Ponds, even small ones, are magnets for wildlife, and easy to install. Create a gentle slope on one side, and shelves or piles of debris around the edge to make your pond easier for creatures to access.'

▶ 'If you want an instant wildlife spectacle, find an oak post, drill lots of holes of various sizes in it, and "plant" it vertically in a hole, where it will get some sun. Then stand back and watch solitary bees jostle for a new home in which to breed.'

▶ 'A native hedge has so much to offer wildlife by way of habitat, food and cover. Try a combination of native shrubs and trees, such as field maple (*Acer campestre*), hawthorn (*Crataegus monogyna*) and a wild rose. Avoid blackthorn, unless you have lots of space, as it can produce unwanted suckers in a small space.'

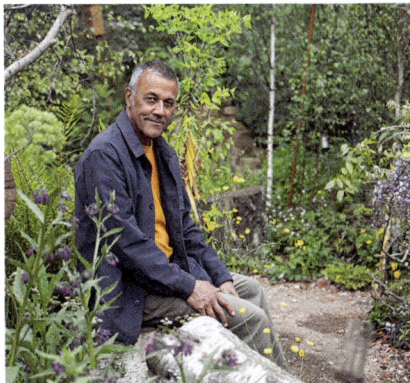

Plants for difficult places

Slug- and snail-proof plants

Most gardeners will have experienced the disappointment of seeing a much-loved plant damaged or even killed by slugs or snails. Not all molluscs are the culprits, and many species of slug feed on decomposing organic matter, such as dead leaves, dung, and even dead slugs and snails. These beneficial creatures perform a valuable function in the composting process and provide an important food source for other garden wildlife such as birds, frogs, toads, hedgehogs, slow-worms and ground beetles. However, some slugs and snails are partial to ornamental plants and crops, causing much heartache.

Protecting vulnerable plants, such as seedlings and the young shoots of herbaceous plants, is the best strategy. Growing seedlings on a table or ledge offers some protection, and letting them grow bigger and sturdier before planting out can allow them to tolerate a bit of nibbling. Torchlight searches for these nocturnal creatures can be effective, especially in damp weather. Place suspects in a pot and rehome them in another area, such as the compost heap, where they can help to turn plant waste into a useful soil conditioner.

The other, easier option is to choose plants that are less palatable to slugs and snails, such as shrubs, trees and

some perennials with natural adaptations that act as deterrents. Shrubs with glossy leaves such as California lilacs (*Ceanothus*) and some hydrangeas are more resistant to slugs and snails. Plants with high levels of essential oils such as lavender, rosemary and other herbs are rarely affected, too, while those with hairy or furry leaves such as lamb's ears (*Stachys*) are not often on their menu.

By choosing more resilient plants and managing those that are vulnerable, you should limit the damage and may even start to appreciate molluscs' value in the wider natural environment.

CHOOSING MOLLUSC-PROOF PLANTS

❶ Montbretia 'Paul's Best Yellow' (*Crocosmia* 'Paul's Best Yellow') Sword-shaped leaves provide a foil for the arching stems of golden-yellow tubular flowers that appear on this perennial from late summer to early autumn. **H&S:** 90 × 90cm (3 × 3ft)

2 Cranesbill 'Orion' (*Geranium* 'Orion')
Cranesbills or hardy geraniums are slug- and snail-resistant perennials, and this one is particularly beautiful with its lobed leaves and large blue summer flowers with purple veins and a white centre. **H&S:** 50 × 90cm (20 × 36in).

California lilac 'Burkwoodii' (*Ceanothus* 'Burkwoodii')
Loved for their round clusters of small blue flowers, most California lilacs bloom in spring, but this one produces flowers in late summer and autumn between glossy, dark, evergreen leaves. **H&S:** 1.5 × 2m (5ft × 6ft 6in)

English lavender 'Hidcote' (*Lavandula angustifolia* 'Hidcote')
A compact, floriferous lavender, ideal for a low hedge, with narrow grey-green evergreen foliage that's joined by spikes of highly scented blue-purple flowers in summer. **H&S:** 45 × 45cm (18 × 18in)

3 *Hydrangea macrophylla* 'Lanarth White'
The flowers of this elegant lacecap hydrangea are pink, or blue if grown on acid soil, surrounded by white, petal-like ray-florets.
H&S: 1.5 × 1.5m (5 × 5ft)

Wallich spurge (*Euphorbia wallichii*)
The dark-green leaves, often with a purple-flushed edge, and bright yellow flowerheads that appear in summer make this easy-going perennial a popular choice for sunny sites.
H&S: 60 × 60cm (2 × 2ft)

June

Fuelled by long hours of bright sun, the garden is buoyant with bouquets of jewel-like flowers and leafy crops. Now that the frosts have passed, it's time to set out your stores of tender plants and produce, and to immerse yourself in the shimmering colours of early summer. Roses and peonies are the stars of the show, their big, blowsy blooms taking centre stage.

KEY EVENTS

Father's Day, 21 June
Islamic New Year, 16 June
Windrush Day, 22 June
Midsummer's Day, 24 June

What to do in June

The long, warm days of early summer prompt many plants to burst into bloom, creating a cacophony of colour in the garden. Deadheading helps to keep the show going, while removing the shoot tips of late-summer and autumn-flowering perennials encourages bushier growth and more blooms later in the year.

In the garden

WATER NEW AND YOUNG PLANTS regularly during dry spells. Make sure you irrigate plants in pots even after rain, since the leaves often shield the compost, which may remain dry. Install water butts to harvest the rain running off the roofs of your house and outbuildings. Leave them half empty to capture summer downpours.

SOW AUTUMN BEDDING PLANTS such as violas and bellis daisies in pots and seed trays indoors or outside, as well as biennials, including wallflowers (*Erysimum*) and sweet williams (*Dianthus barbatus*), for a garden full of flowers next spring.

CUT BACK HARDY GERANIUMS after the flowers have faded, removing the old flowering stems at the base. This encourages fresh, new leaves to form and sometimes a second flush of blooms.

REMOVE UNWANTED PLANTS such as bindweed (*Calystegia sepium*), docks (*Rumex obtusifolius*) (pictured), cleavers (*Galium aparine*) and chickweed (*Stellaria media*), that threaten to swamp your plants and crops. Hoe, dig them out, or smother them with mulch. Collect and destroy uprooted plants, and avoid using weedkillers, which can cause environmental harm. **1**

TAKE SOFTWOOD CUTTINGS to boost your stocks of hardy perennials and deciduous shrubs. Remove a non-flowering shoot about 10cm (4in) long, cutting just above a leaf joint or bud. Fill a pot or module tray with cuttings compost, then trim the stem just below

PRUNING TIP
Prunus trees
The best time to prune trees in the *Prunus* genus is between May and July to protect them against disease. Plants that fall into this category include ornamental cherries, damsons, plums and almonds, which are all susceptible to silver leaf disease, the spores of which are less prevalent during these months. Wounds also heal quickly now, minimizing the risk of infection. Prune out dead, diseased and crossing stems, and trim others lightly to form a balanced shape, if required.

a leaf or stem bud (node), remove the lower leaves, and pinch out the soft tip. Make a hole in the compost with blunt pencil or dibber and pop the cutting in, up to its first set of leaves, then firm gently. Repeat with a few cuttings around the edge of the pot. Label and place in a shaded propagator or cover the pot or tray with a clear, used plastic bag, held up with sticks. Keep the compost moist and when shoots appear, remove the plastic bag. Roots should develop within four or five weeks. **2**

DEADHEAD REPEAT-FLOWERING ROSES regularly. Remove single blooms from a head by cutting where its short stem meets the stems of the other flowers, or, if a whole cluster has gone over, make a cut just above a leafy stem below it. **3**

In the fruit & veg patch

VENTILATE GREENHOUSES by opening doors and windows during hot, sunny weather and add more shading, where possible. Be ready to introduce biological controls to counter red spider mite that favours hot conditions.

SOW SALAD CROPS in the evenings and during cool weather, since germination rates are inhibited when the soil temperatures reach 22°C (72°F) or more.

PLANT OUT TENDER CROPS such as outdoor tomatoes, chillies and cucumbers in northern gardens, now that all risk of frost should be over.

SOW AUTUMN AND WINTER CROPS such as calabrese, pak choi, Chinese cabbage, mustard greens, swedes, kohlrabi and carrots in prepared beds. Protect them all with insect-proof netting, ensuring it has no holes that the cabbage white butterfly or carrot fly can get through to lay their eggs. **4**

MONEY-SAVING IDEA
Make trailing houseplants for free
Collect stems about 10cm (4in) long and trim them below a leaf, then remove a few of the lower leaves and the soft tip. Place in a jar of water and wait for roots to form. Then fill a pot with cuttings compost and use a blunt pencil or dibber to make holes around the edge. Insert a cutting in each hole, up to the lower leaf. Place a used, clear plastic bag over the pot, propping it up with four sticks. Keep the compost moist and remove the bag once a week to allow air to circulate. Remove the bag when new shoots start to appear.

Indoors

DEADHEAD FLOWERING HOUSEPLANTS such as *Streptocarpus* and African violets (*Saintpaulia*) regularly to sustain the show over a few months.

TRIM TRAILING HOUSEPLANTS, including the silver-inch plant (*Tradescantia zebrina*), pothos (*Epipremnum aureum*) and string of beads (*Curio rowleyanus*) to keep them in check. Snip the stems just below a leaf and use them for cuttings (see above).

CONTINUE TO WATER AND FEED regularly to keep your indoor plants healthy and growing well.

Plants of the month

1. Yarrow (*Achillea millefolium* NEW VINTAGE VIOLET pictured)
2. Sweetshrub (*Calycanthus* 'Aphrodite' pictured)
3. Delphinium (*Delphinium* 'Holly Cookland Wilkins' pictured)
4. Deutzia (*Deutzia* × *hybrida* 'Strawberry Fields' pictured)
5. Foxglove (*Digitalis purpurea*)
6. Dusky cranesbill (*Geranium phaeum* 'Chocolate Chip' pictured)
7. Catmint (*Nepeta* 'Chettle Blue' pictured)
8. White gaura (*Oenothera lindheimeri* PAPILLON pictured)
9. White laceflower (*Orlaya grandiflora*)
10. Jacob's ladder (*Polemonium foliosissimum* 'Scottish Garden' pictured)
11. Vervain (*Verbena officinalis* var. *grandiflora* 'Bampton' pictured)

Project: Plant an edible den

Rather than filling the garden with plastic play equipment, why not plant a living den with your children, who can then experience the thrill of watching the plants grow to make a leafy tent? The beans are the added bonus, which your young ones can harvest in summer for their dinner. If you did not sow beans in pots indoors earlier in the year, young plants are available to buy in trays from the garden centre.

YOU WILL NEED
5 large pots
Peat-free multipurpose compost
5 long canes or pruned stems
Garden twine
5 runner or French bean plants

1 Fill each of the pots with the compost and set them out in a circle. Add a tall cane or pruned stem to each pot. Draw the canes together at the top and tie them with strong garden twine.

2 Plant one bean in each of the pots – you may have to tie in the stems initially to their cane supports but they will soon twine around them of their own accord. Water them in.

3 Wrap more twine around the uprights to create a network of strings for the beans to climb along and make an enclosure. Leave a space for the children to enter the den when it is covered with plants.

4 Water the plants regularly, and harvest the beans later in the summer when they are young and tender. Also leave a few pods and sow the bean seeds next year.

Looking up

Sunrise and sunset

The sun is at its most intense now, quickly drying out the soil around vulnerable young and new plants, and those in pots, so ensure you water them regularly.

DAY	LONDON		EDINBURGH	
	Sunrise	Sunset	Sunrise	Sunset
Mon, 1 Jun	4:46:38 am	9:10:05 pm	4:32:11 am	9:49:06 pm
Tue, 2 Jun	4:45:52 am	9:11:10 pm	4:31:10 am	9:50:27 pm
Wed, 3 Jun	4:45:09 am	9:12:13 pm	4:30:12 am	9:51:44 pm
Thu, 4 Jun	4:44:29 am	9:13:13 pm	4:29:17 am	9:52:59 pm
Fri, 5 Jun	4:43:52 am	9:14:11 pm	4:28:27 am	9:54:11 pm
Sat, 6 Jun	4:43:18 am	9:15:07 pm	4:27:39 am	9:55:20 pm
Sun, 7 Jun	4:42:47 am	9:16:00 pm	4:26:56 am	9:56:26 pm
Mon, 8 Jun	4:42:19 am	9:16:51 pm	4:26:16 am	9:57:28 pm
Tue, 9 Jun	4:41:54 am	9:17:40 pm	4:25:40 am	9:58:27 pm
Wed, 10 Jun	4:41:32 am	9:18:26 pm	4:25:08 am	9:59:23 pm
Thu, 11 Jun	4:41:13 am	9:19:09 pm	4:24:40 am	10:00:16 pm
Fri, 12 Jun	4:40:57 am	9:19:49 pm	4:24:16 am	10:01:05 pm
Sat, 13 Jun	4:40:45 am	9:20:27 pm	4:23:56 am	10:01:50 pm
Sun, 14 Jun	4:40:35 am	9:21:02 pm	4:23:40 am	10:02:31 pm
Mon, 15 Jun	4:40:29 am	9:21:34 pm	4:23:27 am	10:03:09 pm
Tue, 16 Jun	4:40:25 am	9:22:03 pm	4:23:19 am	10:03:43 pm
Wed, 17 Jun	4:40:25 am	9:22:29 pm	4:23:15 am	10:04:14 pm
Thu, 18 Jun	4:40:28 am	9:22:53 pm	4:23:15 am	10:04:40 pm
Fri, 19 Jun	4:40:34 am	9:23:13 pm	4:23:18 am	10:05:02 pm
Sat, 20 Jun	4:40:43 am	9:23:30 pm	4:23:26 am	10:05:21 pm
Sun, 21 Jun	4:40:55 am	9:23:44 pm	4:23:38 am	10:05:35 pm
Mon, 22 Jun	4:41:10 am	9:23:55 pm	4:23:54 am	10:05:45 pm
Tue, 23 Jun	4:41:28 am	9:24:03 pm	4:24:13 am	10:05:52 pm
Wed, 24 Jun	4:41:49 am	9:24:08 pm	4:24:37 am	10:05:54 pm
Thu, 25 Jun	4:42:13 am	9:24:09 pm	4:25:04 am	10:05:52 pm
Fri, 26 Jun	4:42:40 am	9:24:08 pm	4:25:35 am	10:05:46 pm
Sat, 27 Jun	4:43:09 am	9:24:03 pm	4:26:10 am	10:05:36 pm
Sun, 28 Jun	4:43:42 am	9:23:55 pm	4:26:49 am	10:05:23 pm
Mon, 29 Jun	4:44:17 am	9:23:44 pm	4:27:31 am	10:05:05 pm
Tue, 30 Jun	4:44:55 am	9:23:30 pm	4:28:17 am	10:04:43 pm

Moonrise and moonset

Moon phases

◑ **THIRD QUARTER** 8 June
● **NEW MOON** 15 June
◐ **FIRST QUARTER** 21 June
○ **FULL MOON** 30 June

DAY	LONDON			EDINBURGH		
	Moonrise	Moonset	Moonrise	Moonrise	Moonset	Moonrise
1 Jun		04:46	22:59		04:19	23:53
2 Jun		05:37	23:42		05:09	
3 Jun		06:40		00:32	06:16	
4 Jun	00:13	07:50		00:57	07:33	
5 Jun	00:36	09:05		01:13	08:55	
6 Jun	00:54	10:20		01:23	10:17	
7 Jun	01:08	11:35		01:31	11:39	
8 Jun	01:20	12:52		01:38	13:01	
9 Jun	01:32	14:10		01:44	14:26	
10 Jun	01:44	15:32		01:51	15:54	
11 Jun	01:58	16:59		01:58	17:29	
12 Jun	02:16	18:30		02:09	19:09	
13 Jun	02:41	20:03		02:26	20:51	
14 Jun	03:19	21:27		02:55	22:20	
15 Jun	04:14	22:32		03:46	23:23	
16 Jun	05:31	23:16		05:06		
17 Jun	07:00	23:46			00:00	06:43
18 Jun	08:32				00:21	08:24
19 Jun		00:06	10:00		00:34	10:00
20 Jun		00:21	11:22		00:42	11:29
21 Jun		00:34	12:40		00:49	12:53
22 Jun		00:45	13:55		00:55	14:14
23 Jun		00:57	15:09		01:01	15:34
24 Jun		01:09	16:23		01:08	16:55
25 Jun		01:24	17:37		01:17	18:16
26 Jun		01:44	18:50		01:29	19:35
27 Jun		02:09	19:57		01:48	20:49
28 Jun		02:45	20:55		02:18	21:50
29 Jun		03:32	21:42		03:04	22:33
30 Jun		04:32	22:16		04:06	23:01

Average temperature & rainfall

This table shows the average minimum and maximum temperatures, indicated by the blue and red dots, together with the average rainfall and number of rainy days for this month. The horizontal rules show how the figures have varied over the past decade.

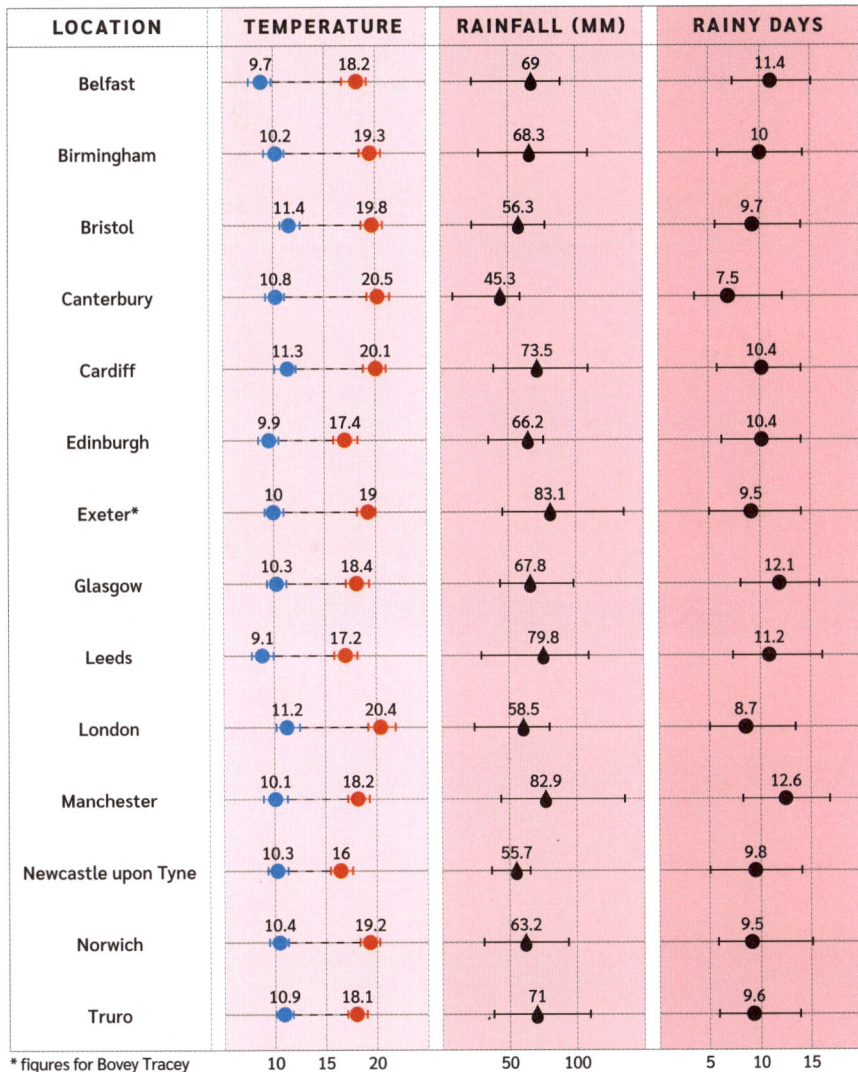

LOCATION	TEMPERATURE		RAINFALL (MM)	RAINY DAYS
Belfast	9.7	18.2	69	11.4
Birmingham	10.2	19.3	68.3	10
Bristol	11.4	19.8	56.3	9.7
Canterbury	10.8	20.5	45.3	7.5
Cardiff	11.3	20.1	73.5	10.4
Edinburgh	9.9	17.4	66.2	10.4
Exeter*	10	19	83.1	9.5
Glasgow	10.3	18.4	67.8	12.1
Leeds	9.1	17.2	79.8	11.2
London	11.2	20.4	58.5	8.7
Manchester	10.1	18.2	82.9	12.6
Newcastle upon Tyne	10.3	16	55.7	9.8
Norwich	10.4	19.2	63.2	9.5
Truro	10.9	18.1	71	9.6

* figures for Bovey Tracey

| | 10 15 20 | 50 100 | 5 10 15 |

Sustainable gardening

Conserving water supplies

Most garden plants currently receive enough moisture from rainfall to thrive, tapping into winter rain stored in the soil during dry periods. However, our changing climate is becoming warmer all year, and scientists predict that rainfall in the UK will continue to be highly variable, with more wet days, especially in winter, and longer dry periods, particularly in summer, which will stress garden plants.

These factors, together with rising populations, put pressure on water supplies and increase prices, but we can employ strategies to preserve precious resources that will benefit both the planet and our wallets.

Twin water butts are a good idea if you have space.

WASTE NOT, WANT NOT

The first strategy is to only water plants that need extra moisture. Established trees and shrubs seldom need watering, and while lawns may turn brown in a drought, they usually green up once rains return. Most garden plants will also cope with a lack of water during the summer, with those from dry climates, such as *Artemisia*, *Ceanothus*, *Cistus*, *Hylotelephium spectabile*, *Lavandula*, *Salvia* and *Stachys* sailing through droughts unscathed. These variously have waxy, grey, hairy, small, narrow or succulent leaves that inhibit water loss, and they are excellent choices for dry, sunny areas that may otherwise need repeated watering.

Instead, save your water for seedlings and new plants that are still establishing in the soil, and those in containers, both of which will need watering during dry periods from spring to early autumn.

WATER HARVESTING

Installing water butts that harvest water from house roofs and outbuildings will offer a good source earlier in the year, but stores often run dry in the summer, at a time when water companies may also impose hosepipe bans during prolonged droughts. While butts may be topped up during summer storms which, in a normal year, make a valuable contribution, you will probably still need other solutions to avoid using tap water.

Salvias flourish in dry soil conditions.

In theory, installing large tanks that store winter rainfall can help, but finding space in an average-sized garden or on an allotment can be a challenge.

GREY MATTERS
Another idea is to use the wastewater from the kitchen, bath and shower, known as 'grey water', which can be safely used in Britain to irrigate plants. The quality ranges from very clean – used to wash fruit and vegetables, for example – to quite rich in soap and detergents, but even this can be used in small amounts on your garden, where any soapy residues will be broken down by soil organisms and may contribute some plant nutrients, too.

Use grey water on ornamental plants, but only apply it to edibles that are cooked before they are eaten, and do not use water containing bleaches, disinfectants, dishwasher salt or strong cleaning products, which harm plants and the soil.

Practically speaking, it is easy to carry water from the kitchen to the garden, but bath water may be trickier to collect, as in many houses the drainage pipe is indoors and inaccessible, and hiking full cans down flights of stairs is not easy. One option is to install a grey water irrigation system, which collects water from your washing facilities and filters it, ready for garden use. These systems can be expensive, however, and need to be installed by a specialist plumber.

BOOSTING SOIL WATER
Improving the water-holding capacity of the soil is another way to preserve supplies. It is usually saturated by spring, with plants drawing up the water in summer, but by late summer it is often dry. Applying a 5cm (2in) deep mulch (layer) of organic matter such as well-rotted manure or homemade compost over the soil surface in spring will help to trap the water for use by plants over a longer period.

Edible garden

Nothing beats the taste of new potatoes, which will be ready to harvest this month, while glistening currants will be colouring up and ripe for picking, too. Keep on top of the many crops you can sow directly in June for harvests later in the year.

Vegetables

SOW INDOORS Calabrese; cucumbers to plant in the greenhouse in July; spring cauliflowers.

SOW OUTDOORS Beetroots; carrots; chicory and endive; Chinese cabbage; courgettes; cucumbers including gherkins; Florence fennel; French beans; herbs including coriander, basil, parsley; kohlrabi, lettuce; mustard greens; pak choi; peas; pumpkins; radishes; rocket; runner beans; salad crops; spinach; spring onions; sprouting broccoli; turnips; winter squash.

PLANT OUT Plants sown indoors in April and May, including artichokes, Brussels sprouts, cabbages, cauliflowers, celeriac, celery, courgettes, kohlrabi, lettuce ❶, marrows, outdoor cucumbers, outdoor tomatoes, squash, sweetcorn.

HARVEST NOW Broad beans ❷; chard; first early potatoes; herbs; lettuce; peas; radishes; spinach; spring cabbages; spring cauliflowers ❸; spring onions; turnips.

HERB OF THE MONTH: SWEET BASIL
(*Ocimum basilicum*)
Sweet basil is a versatile herb, used to spice up a range of pasta dishes, salads and sauces. This tender annual is relatively easy to grow, and you can experiment with different cultivars, including those with cinnamon, lemon or lime flavours, available as seed. The bright green leaves of sweet basil are joined in summer by spikes of white- or pink-tinged flowers. Sow the seed in pots or trays under cover in spring, and plant outside in free-draining soil and a sunny location when all risk of frost has passed in late May or early June.

TOP TIP
Harvesting rainwater
Plants prefer rainwater, and it is most essential for crops that like acid soil, such as blueberries and cranberries. Water is a precious resource and needs to be preserved, especially in dry periods, so it makes sense to install water butts to harvest rainwater (see p.114). However, these can run out during long, dry periods, and while summer downpours help to replenish them, placing buckets and other vessels around the garden will top up your supplies. Store them in a cool spot with netting over the top to prevent wildlife falling in.

Fruit

PLANT NOW Potted fruit trees and shrubs such as blueberries; strawberry plants.

HARVEST Black, red and white currants; gooseberries; rhubarb; strawberries.

Recipe

ROAST BEETROOT, PINK GRAPEFRUIT AND FETA CHEESE SALAD

This tasty, nutritious salad will make the most of an early crop of beetroots and lettuce – we suggest baby gems here, but you can use whatever leaves you are growing. You can also substitute the grapefruit for oranges if you would prefer a sweeter dish.

1   Preheat the oven to 180°C/160°C fan/gas 4. Place the beetroots, maple syrup, sherry vinegar, and 4 tbsp of water in a roasting tray. Cover with foil and roast until the beetroots are tender. This takes approximately 1–1½ hours.

2   Meanwhile, cook two beetroots in water for about 30 minutes to make the candied beets. Leave to cool, then peel and cut into cubes. Heat the unsalted butter and brown sugar in a pan, stirring until syrupy. Add the beetroot cubes and cook for a further five minutes, stirring regularly so they don't burn, then transfer to a bowl and leave to cool.

3   While still warm, peel the roasted beetroots and cut them into wedges. Peel and segment the pink grapefruit, crumble the feta cheese, and wash the baby gem lettuce leaves. Slice the candied beetroot into slim sections.

4   To make the dressing, combine all the dressing ingredients in a glass jar with a lid, shake, taste, and add a pinch of salt, if needed. This can be made while the beetroot is cooking.

5   Assemble the dish and drizzle the dressing over the top before serving.

INGREDIENTS

For the salad
4 large beetroots
2 tbsp sherry vinegar
2 tbsp maple syrup
2 pink grapefruit
300g feta cheese
2 whole baby gem leaf lettuce
2 candied beetroots (for a garnish)

For the candied beets
2 beetroots
3 tbsp unsalted butter
4 tbsp brown sugar
Salt to taste

For the dressing
60ml balsamic vinegar
30ml maple syrup
1 tsp Dijon mustard
120ml extra-virgin olive oil
Salt to taste

Challenges this month

Continue to be vigilant and check regularly for fast-spreading plants that may overwhelm your ornamentals and crops. Oak processionary moth may also be detected on trees this month and will require immediate action if you spot the caterpillars.

OAK PROCESSIONARY MOTH can defoliate oak trees and check their growth, but it is the caterpillars' white hairs, which cause skin rashes, eye irritation and breathing difficulties if inhaled, that cause most concern. A native to southern Europe, the moth is now established in parts of London and the South-East. It lays its eggs high up in oak trees, and the caterpillars that hatch in spring initially feed in the treetops. In early summer, they move down the tree in processionary lines, hence the name, and construct white webbing nests on trucks and branches, which they leave in processions to feed at dawn and dusk. If you see these caterpillars on a tree in your garden or elsewhere, submit a Tree Alert via the website treealert.forestresearch. gov.uk and you will be contacted with the action you need to take.

STINGING NETTLES include perennial nettles (*Urtica dioica*) and annuals (*Urtica urens*), both of which are covered with stinging hairs. While these fast-spreading plants provide food for butterflies, moths and birds, they are best limited to a quiet spot and controlled in beds and borders. Simply don a pair of sturdy gloves and dig or pull out any mature plants or hoe off the seedlings, and smother emerging nettles in spring with a layer of cardboard topped with a deep 20cm (8in) mulch of bark or wood chips.

BLACKFLY, also known as the black bean aphid (pictured), forms dense colonies on broad beans and other plants in spring and summer. They suck sap from young shoot tips, flower stems and young leaves, causing distorted or stunted growth and reducing broad bean crops. While blackfly can be a nuisance, they rarely kill plants and provide a vital food source for a wide range of wildlife, so small groups are best tolerated. To limit their numbers, gently squash them with your fingers, and encourage natural predators, such as ladybirds, ground beetles, hoverflies and earwigs, with a selection of plants and habitats. Biological controls are also effective in greenhouses.

Garden benefactors

Wild solitary bees

It is a well-known fact that bees pollinate flowers and crops, but you may not be aware that most of this vital work is carried out not by honeybees, but by an army of wild species that neither live in hives nor make the sweet syrup we spread on our toast.

In fact, the honeybee makes up just one of over 270 species that live in Britain, with solitary bees accounting for over 250 of the total. Solitary wild bees are the heavy lifters and come in all shapes and sizes, but unlike their sociable cousins, the females make their own nests independently, although they may congregate in areas close together.

Mining bees and many other species make their nests in the ground (pictured), while leafcutter and mason bees favour hollow stems or cracks in dead wood or walls. The nests are made from mud, leaves, body secretions or floral oils, and the female lays an egg, together with a ball of nectar and pollen to feed the larva when it emerges, in an individual cell. Eggs that become female bees are often laid first, at the back of the nest, while males are laid at the front and will emerge first in the spring, ready to mate when the females come out. Solitary bees live for just a few weeks, so the females must mate, make a nest and lay their eggs as soon as possible.

Populations of many bee species are in decline, largely due to habitat loss and the use of insecticides, but gardeners can help to reverse this trend. To support these important pollinators, banish all pesticides, and create a range of habitats for them, including areas of long and short grass, piles of decaying wood, walls with areas of loose mortar and a water source that they can access easily, such as bowl with a stone in it.

Bees also require plenty of nectar- and pollen-rich plants throughout the year, but especially in spring and early summer when wild species are emerging from their nests. Good choices include fruit trees, alliums, lungwort (*Pulmonaria officinalis*), hardy geraniums, foxgloves (*Digitalis*), cornflowers (*Centaurea cyanus*), the poached egg plant (*Limnanthes douglasii*), anemones and primroses (*Primula* species).

Design masterclass

Harry Holding

Multi-award-winning garden designer Harry Holding is celebrated for his environmentally conscious gardens that respect nature and wildlife. His work focuses on sustainable, immersive spaces and ranges from tiny courtyard gardens in London to a public botanical garden in the Isle of Man, each offering a mosaic of habitats and biodiverse planting.

In 2024, he designed 'The RHS No Adults Allowed Garden' at the Chelsea Flower Show in collaboration with 30 primary school children. Highlighting the importance of access to nature, this beautiful, immersive garden was later relocated to Sulivan Primary School in London. This show garden followed Harry's debut at Chelsea in 2023 when he designed the 'School Food Matters Garden', which won the People's Choice Award and a silver-gilt medal.

Harry's parents both loved gardening and influenced his love of plants from a young age. After working in Australia and the UK for other designers, landscape firms and nurseries, he set up his own design and maintenance company in 2016.

HOW TO DESIGN A GARDEN FOR KIDS
Tap into children's innate love for the natural world with Harry's advice on creating a magical and engaging garden.

▶ 'Use tactile, natural materials such as stone, timber and water to create a space that stimulates children's curiosity and encourages positive physical and emotional development. Incorporate planting with a variety of colours, textures, and fragrances to engage their senses as they explore.'

▶ 'Provide areas for imaginative play, such as dens or climbing trees, which give children a sense of ownership and adventure. Include natural play elements such as dead wood, wildlife habitats and boulders that allow children to connect with insects and other garden creatures.'

▶ 'For older children where water doesn't pose a risk, add a wildlife pond. These provide endless opportunities for play and also attract wildlife, such as frogs and toads, helping children develop an understanding of natural processes.'

Plants for difficult places

Free-draining, sunny sites

Many gardens are experiencing higher than usual temperatures throughout the year, particularly in summer, and planting can struggle to cope with these increasingly common conditions. For those also gardening on free-draining sandy soils, the problem is exacerbated, and making suitable plant choices is critical if they are to survive.

Choosing plants that have adapted to thrive in hot, dry conditions is the best option. Drought-tolerant plants often have deeper roots or show other adaptations to cope with prolonged dry weather. These include waxy leaf surfaces that protect plants from moisture loss, and small leaves such as those of *Genista* and *Ozothamnus*, which have a reduced surface area, limiting the volume of water lost through tiny pores on the undersides, known as 'stomata'. The silvery, scaly surface of the *Ozothamnus* foliage also reflects heat and reduces moisture loss.

Some plants, including *Cistus*, *Verbena* and *Salvia*, have slightly hairy or bristly foliage, which helps conserve moisture both by creating a protective, insulating layer and holding droplets of water after rainfall that then drip down into the soil. Plants such as the ice plant (*Hylotelephium*) have fleshy foliage that stores moisture within the cells, helping the plant through dry conditions.

However, even drought-tolerant plants will need watering during their first year of growth, while they are establishing, after which they should thrive with minimal or no extra irrigation. Having said that, you may find that some self-seed into gravel or sand and survive with no help from you whatsoever.

Mulching the soil can help it to retain moisture for longer (see p.115), but only apply a mulch after heavy rain, so that the insulating material traps the moisture already in the soil. Many drought-loving plants prefer a dry mulch of gravel or crushed aggregates

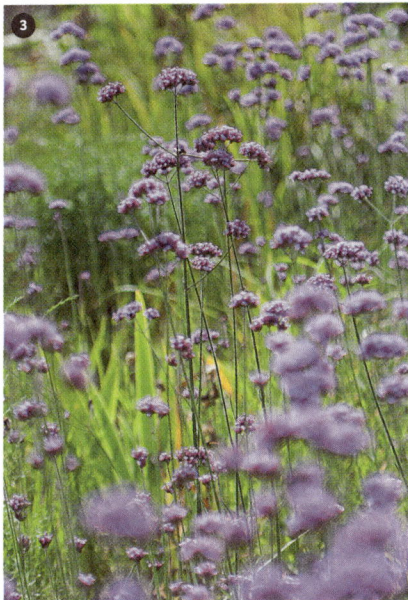

Sea rosemary 'Silver Jubilee'
(*Ozothamnus rosmarinifolius*
'Silver Jubilee')
Linear, silvery-grey leaves clothe the
stems of this medium-sized evergreen
shrub, while compact clusters of
scented white flowerheads open from
red buds for many weeks in summer.
H&S: 2 × 1.5m (6ft 6in × 5ft)

③ Purple top (*Verbena bonariensis*)
An easy-to-grow perennial for dry soils,
it produces tall, square-shaped, slender
stems with small leaves, topped with
dainty pompons of lilac-purple flowers
throughout the summer months.
H&S: 1.5 × 0.45m (5ft × 18in)

Salvia 'Nachtvlinder'
Toothed mid-green leaves cloth the
stems of this evergreen subshrub, while
small, velvety, maroon-purple flowers
appear from summer to autumn.
H&S: 75 × 50cm (30 × 20in)

Ice plant 'Brilliant' (*Hylotelephium
spectabile* 'Brilliant')
Characterized by thick stems and fleshy
grey-green leaves, this hardy perennial
produces flat-topped heads of nectar-
rich, bright pink flowers from late
summer, followed by bronze seedheads.
H&S: 45 × 45cm (18 × 18in)

that will not wet their stems, which may
cause them to rot and die.

DROUGHT-TOLERANT PLANT CHOICES

❶ Broom 'Porlock' (*Genista* 'Porlock')
Semi-evergreen with small green leaves,
this medium-sized shrub is covered with
fragrant, bright yellow flowers in spring.
H&S: 1.5 × 1.5m (5 × 5ft)

❷ Rock rose (*Cistus × purpureus*)
A Mediterranean evergreen shrub with
linear foliage and round, papery,
purplish-pink flowers with dark red
blotches at the centre in summer.
H&S: 90 × 90cm (3 × 3ft)

July

A confection of colours and scents, the midsummer garden delivers a bounty of blooms, some jostling for attention in the bright sunlight, others quietly peeping out of the shade to catch the eye of passing pollinators. Watering plants in pots and deadheading keeps the show going, while harvested pods, leaves and fruits fill our plates, these gardening tasks also erasing the worries of the day.

KEY EVENTS

RHS Badminton Garden Festival, 5–12 July
Battle of the Boyne (Holiday in Northern Ireland), 12 July
St Swithin's Day, 15 July

What to do in July

With most plants and crops already planted out before July, the tasks this month mainly focus on watering. Call in friends or neighbours to help during holiday periods, or try the tips below. Mow lawns regularly, unless the hot weather has caused the grass to stop growing, and plant crops for the months ahead.

In the garden

GROUP POTS to shade one another and reduce watering needs, especially if you are going away. This is also a good idea for plants that like cool roots, such as Japanese maples (*Acer palmatum*), clematis and lilies. Grouping your containers together in a shady spot and setting them on a shallow tray of water when you go on holiday will also help to keep them hydrated for a week or so.

DO NOT WATER LAWNS that have turned brown and parched during hot, dry spells, since they will soon recover when rain returns and irrigating uses up precious supplies in summer.

DIVIDE BEARDED IRIS about six weeks after they have flowered, if their rhizomes have become congested. Dig out a clump and divide up the rhizomes into sections about 15cm (6in) long, each with roots and some leaves, discarding old, withered pieces.

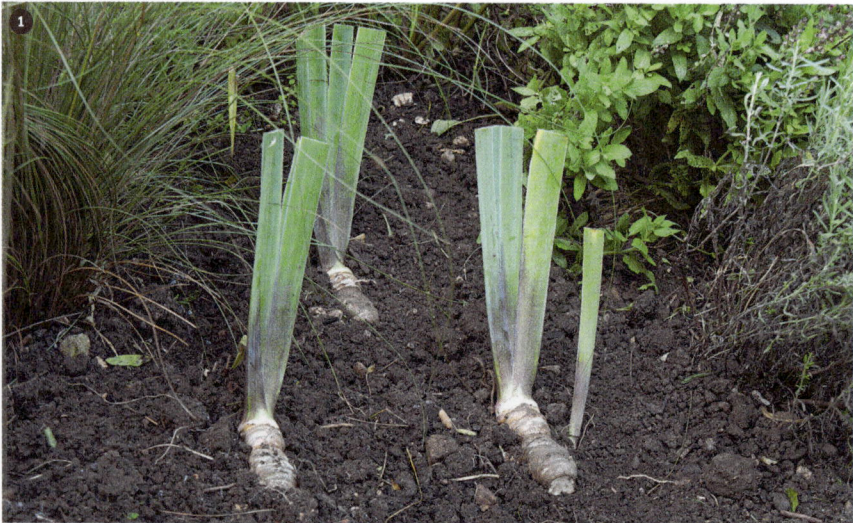

Trim the leaves down by about a third of their length, and replant with the rhizome at the surface on heavy soils or just below on sandy soils, spacing them about 30cm (12in) apart, or a little closer for dwarf varieties. ❶

DEADHEAD FLOWERING PERENNIALS that self-seed prolifically such as *Alchemilla mollis*, *Geranium nodosum* and *Valeriana officinalis* to prevent them spreading throughout the garden.

CUT OFF HOLLYHOCK (*ALCEA ROSEA*) LEAVES that are showing signs of rust, then water and feed plants to help protect them from this disease. ❷

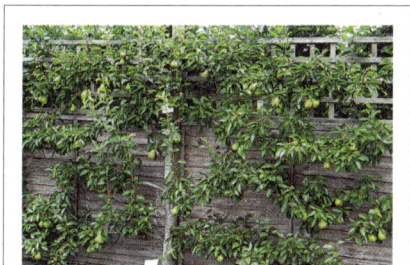

In the fruit & veg patch

FEED POT-GROWN CROPS such as tomatoes, peppers and aubergines every couple of weeks when the fruits start to develop, using a potassium-rich organic-based fertilizer. Those formulated for tomatoes are ideal.

PINCH OUT THE TIPS of cordon tomatoes when outdoor varieties have four trusses (clusters of fruiting stems) per plant, and indoor types have five or six trusses. This prevents them from putting energy into growing taller, rather than producing fruits.

TIE IN LONG NON-FRUITING BLACKBERRY STEMS, which will carry the fruits that form next year. Bring them together and tie them loosely with garden twine to a stake or horizontal wires. This saves them from getting tangled up with this year's fruiting stems, which will need to be cut away after harvesting in autumn.

HARVEST GARLIC and overwintered onions and shallots this month and next when the leaves turn yellow, but before

PRUNING TIP
Apples and pears

Trees grown as espaliers, cordons or fans are pruned in summer to allow light to reach the ripening fruits and to promote a good crop the following year. Prune pears from late July and apples in mid- or late August. Cut back new shoots more than 20cm (8in) long growing from the main stem to three leaves above the leaf cluster at the base. Also prune new shoots on existing sideshoots to one leaf above the basal leaf cluster, and remove long, upright shoots. Cut back pruned stems that continue to grow in September to one leaf beyond the previous cut.

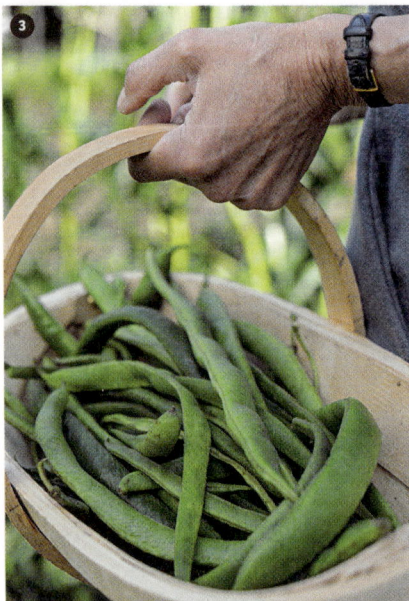

the foliage has died down completely. Gather the crops and leave them until they are 'rustling dry', then store in trays in a cool, light, dry, well-ventilated area indoors. Alternatively, plait the dry foliage into strings to hang up in a suitable storage place.

PICK RUNNER BEANS REGULARLY when young and tender. They not only taste better and tend to be less stringy, but removing them also encourages more flowers and beans. **3**

THIN FRUITS on apple and pear trees. For cooking apples, leave one fruit every 15–23cm (6–9in), and one or two fruits every 10–15cm (4–6in) for dessert apples. For pears, leave one fruit every 10–12cm (4–5in) on trained trees, or two fruits every 10–12cm (4–5in) on a free-standing tree.

Indoors

PLACE HOUSEPLANTS OUTSIDE in a sheltered area on a shallow tray of water if you are going away for a week or two and have no one to care for them. Just make sure they are in pots with drainage holes in the base, allowing the roots to take up the water from below.

BUYING HOUSEPLANTS now gives them time to acclimatize to the conditions in your home before they become dormant or semi-dormant in winter.

MONEY-SAVING IDEA
Weeding with boiling water
A simple and eco-friendly way to remove unwanted plants growing between slabs on a patio or path is to pour the boiling water left in the kettle after making a cup of tea on them. The heat kills them immediately, but take care not to splash the water on ornamentals or crops growing close by. Leave the plants to wither before pulling them up. While very effective on shallow-rooted plants, this probably won't work on dandelions and docks with long tap roots.

Plants of the month

1. African lily (*Agapanthus* 'Oslo' pictured)
2. Plume thistle (*Cirsium rivulare* 'Atropurpureum' pictured)
3. Bloody cranesbill (*Geranium sanguineum* var. *striatum* pictured)
4. Daylily (*Hemerocallis altissima* pictured)
5. Hydrangea (*Hydrangea macrophylla* MAGICAL REVOLUTION pictured)
6. Sweet pea (*Lathyrus odoratus*)
7. Honeysuckle (*Lonicera periclymenum* 'Graham Thomas' pictured)
8. Opium poppy (*Papaver somniferum*)
9. Penstemon (*Penstemon digitalis* DAKOTA BURGUNDY pictured)
10. Wood sage (*Salvia* × *sylvestris* 'Negrito' pictured)
11. Mullein (*Verbascum* 'Moonshadow' pictured)

Project: Plant a sensory walkway

Finding space for more plants that support pollinators can be difficult in a small garden, but one way is to include a few beside and between paving or stepping stones. Perfect for sunny naturalistic and wildlife gardens, this idea is also an option for traditional designs if you take out a whole paving slab and plant creeping thyme or chamomile in the gap. Both plants release a wonderful scent, but take care when thyme is in flower, as it attracts bees that may sting if you step on them.

YOU WILL NEED
Spade or fork
Selection of succulents, such as sedums and houseleeks (*Sempervivum*)
Creeping thyme (*Thymus serpyllum*)
Horticultural sand

1 Remove unwanted plants from the spaces between your stepping stones or pavers. Also remove any large stones and leaf debris.

2 Dig a shallow planting hole and plant either seedlings or small plug plants of your chosen sensory species, filling in around the roots with the excavated soil and a little garden topsoil. Most succulents and thymes are undemanding and will grow happily on the average garden soil, but if yours is heavy clay, add a layer of sand to the bottom of the planting hole and mix some more with the excavated soil to improve drainage.

3 Continue to plant along the walkway with areas of planting. Water the plants in when you have finished.

4 Allow other flowers, such as cat's ears (*Hypochaeris radicata*), Welsh poppies (*Papaver cambricum*) and yellow fumitory (*Corydalis lutea*), to self-seed along the fringes of the walkway.

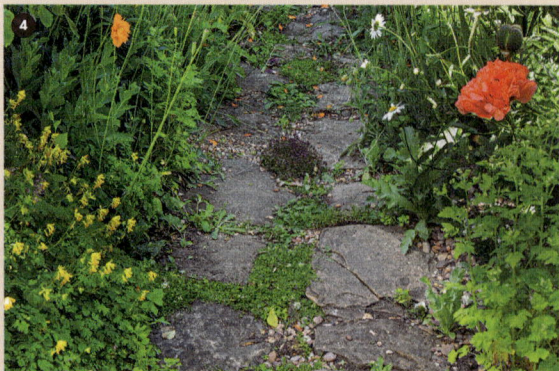

Looking up

Sunrise and sunset

July is generally the warmest month in the UK, driven by long days of intense sun, so keep an eye on pots and new or young plants which can quickly become parched.

DAY	LONDON		EDINBURGH	
	Sunrise	Sunset	Sunrise	Sunset
Wed, 1 Jul	4:45:36 am	9:23:13 pm	4:29:06 am	10:04:17 pm
Thu, 2 Jul	4:46:19 am	9:22:53 pm	4:29:59 am	10:03:47 pm
Fri, 3 Jul	4:47:04 am	9:22:29 pm	4:30:55 am	10:03:13 pm
Sat, 4 Jul	4:47:53 am	9:22:03 pm	4:31:54 am	10:02:35 pm
Sun, 5 Jul	4:48:43 am	9:21:33 pm	4:32:57 am	10:01:54 pm
Mon, 6 Jul	4:49:36 am	9:21:00 pm	4:34:02 am	10:01:08 pm
Tue, 7 Jul	4:50:32 am	9:20:24 pm	4:35:11 am	10:00:19 pm
Wed, 8 Jul	4:51:29 am	9:19:46 pm	4:36:22 am	9:59:27 pm
Thu, 9 Jul	4:52:29 am	9:19:04 pm	4:37:36 am	9:58:30 pm
Fri, 10 Jul	4:53:31 am	9:18:19 pm	4:38:53 am	9:57:31 pm
Sat, 11 Jul	4:54:34 am	9:17:32 pm	4:40:13 am	9:56:27 pm
Sun, 12 Jul	4:55:40 am	9:16:41 pm	4:41:35 am	9:55:21 pm
Mon, 13 Jul	4:56:48 am	9:15:48 pm	4:42:59 am	9:54:11 pm
Tue, 14 Jul	4:57:57 am	9:14:52 pm	4:44:26 am	9:52:57 pm
Wed, 15 Jul	4:59:08 am	9:13:53 pm	4:45:55 am	9:51:41 pm
Thu, 16 Jul	5:00:21 am	9:12:52 pm	4:47:26 am	9:50:21 pm
Fri, 17 Jul	5:01:36 am	9:11:48 pm	4:48:59 am	9:48:59 pm
Sat, 18 Jul	5:02:52 am	9:10:41 pm	4:50:34 am	9:47:33 pm
Sun, 19 Jul	5:04:09 am	9:09:32 pm	4:52:11 am	9:46:05 pm
Mon, 20 Jul	5:05:28 am	9:08:21 pm	4:53:49 am	9:44:33 pm
Tue, 21 Jul	5:06:48 am	9:07:07 pm	4:55:29 am	9:42:59 pm
Wed, 22 Jul	5:08:09 am	9:05:50 pm	4:57:11 am	9:41:23 pm
Thu, 23 Jul	5:09:32 am	9:04:31 pm	4:58:54 am	9:39:43 pm
Fri, 24 Jul	5:10:55 am	9:03:10 pm	5:00:38 am	9:38:01 pm
Sat, 25 Jul	5:12:20 am	9:01:47 pm	5:02:24 am	9:36:17 pm
Sun, 26 Jul	5:13:46 am	9:00:21 pm	5:04:11 am	9:34:30 pm
Mon, 27 Jul	5:15:12 am	8:58:54 pm	5:05:59 am	9:32:41 pm
Tue, 28 Jul	5:16:40 am	8:57:24 pm	5:07:48 am	9:30:50 pm
Wed, 29 Jul	5:18:08 am	8:55:52 pm	5:09:38 am	9:28:57 pm
Thu, 30 Jul	5:19:37 am	8:54:18 pm	5:11:29 am	9:27:01 pm
Fri, 31 Jul	5:21:07 am	8:52:43 pm	5:13:20 am	9:25:04 pm

Moonrise and moonset

Moon phases

◑ **THIRD QUARTER** 7 July   ◐ **FIRST QUARTER** 21 July
● **NEW MOON** 14 July   ○ **FULL MOON** 29 July

DAY	LONDON			EDINBURGH		
	Moonrise	Moonset	Moonrise	Moonrise	Moonset	Moonrise
1 Jul		05:41	22:41		05:22	23:20
2 Jul		06:55	23:00		06:43	23:32
3 Jul		08:10	23:15		08:05	23:40
4 Jul		09:25	23:28		09:27	23:47
5 Jul		10:40	23:39		10:48	23:53
6 Jul		11:56	23:50		12:10	23:59
7 Jul		13:14			13:34	
8 Jul	00:03	14:36		00:06	15:03	
9 Jul	00:19	16:03		00:15	16:38	
10 Jul	00:39	17:33		00:28	18:17	
11 Jul	01:10	19:00		00:50	19:52	
12 Jul	01:55	20:13		01:28	21:07	
13 Jul	03:01	21:07		02:33	21:55	
14 Jul	04:25	21:43		04:04	22:22	
15 Jul	05:58	22:08		05:46	22:39	
16 Jul	07:30	22:26		07:26	22:49	
17 Jul	08:57	22:40		09:01	22:57	
18 Jul	10:20	22:52		10:30	23:03	
19 Jul	11:38	23:03		11:55	23:09	
20 Jul	12:54	23:16		13:17	23:16	
21 Jul	14:10	23:30		14:39	23:24	
22 Jul	15:25	23:48		16:01	23:35	
23 Jul	16:39			17:22	23:52	
24 Jul		00:11	17:48	18:39		
25 Jul		00:43	18:50		00:17	19:44
26 Jul		01:26	19:40		00:57	20:33
27 Jul		02:22	20:18		01:55	21:06
28 Jul		03:29	20:46		03:07	21:27
29 Jul		04:42	21:07		04:28	21:40
30 Jul		05:58	21:23		05:51	21:50
31 Jul		07:14	21:36		07:14	21:57

Average temperature & rainfall

This table shows the average minimum and maximum temperatures, indicated by the blue and red dots, together with the average rainfall and number of rainy days for this month. The horizontal rules show how the figures have varied over the past decade.

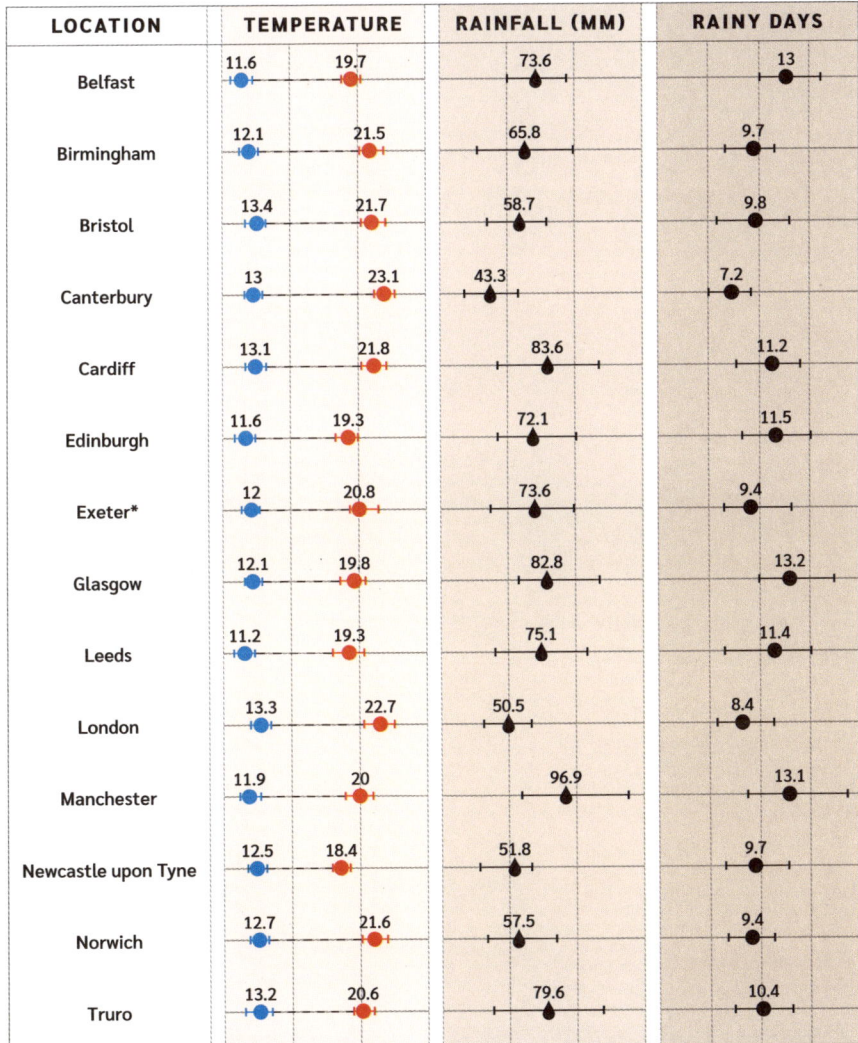

LOCATION	TEMPERATURE	RAINFALL (MM)	RAINY DAYS
Belfast	11.6 — 19.7	73.6	13
Birmingham	12.1 — 21.5	65.8	9.7
Bristol	13.4 — 21.7	58.7	9.8
Canterbury	13 — 23.1	43.3	7.2
Cardiff	13.1 — 21.8	83.6	11.2
Edinburgh	11.6 — 19.3	72.1	11.5
Exeter*	12 — 20.8	73.6	9.4
Glasgow	12.1 — 19.8	82.8	13.2
Leeds	11.2 — 19.3	75.1	11.4
London	13.3 — 22.7	50.5	8.4
Manchester	11.9 — 20	96.9	13.1
Newcastle upon Tyne	12.5 — 18.4	51.8	9.7
Norwich	12.7 — 21.6	57.5	9.4
Truro	13.2 — 20.6	79.6	10.4

* figures for Bovey Tracey

Temperature scale: 10 15 20
Rainfall scale: 50 100
Rainy days scale: 5 10 15

Sustainable gardening

Pesticide-free gardening

The use of pesticides such as weedkillers has a negative impact on the environment, adding to water pollution, while also adversely affecting wildlife populations, so it is important to find ways of reducing or eliminating their use wherever you can.

PAVING THE WAY

Many people resort to weedkillers in paved areas and on gravel drives, where unwanted plants can be difficult to remove by hand. To reduce the growth of unwanted plants, first ensure your paving slabs have good pointing and are laid evenly on a solid surface, so that cracks do not appear.

Mosses and algae also flourish in shade and areas with poor drainage, so removing overhanging branches, and designing a slight fall in levels to ensure water drains into a soakaway will help to limit their growth.

Using self-binding gravel or laying loose chips over a biodegradable weed-proof membrane also helps to minimize problems. For a more informal path, try a 5–10cm (2–4in) layer of natural materials such as woodchips, which will prevent most weed seeds from germinating – plants that do make it through to the light can be scooped up easily and composted.

Self-binding gravel forms a permeable, weed-free surface, ideal for main pathways in the garden.

Eventually, some mosses, algae and unwanted plants will appear and require removing. Pressure washers are effective but use large volumes of water, while brushing and scraping with good weeding tools offer effective control in small areas. For larger spaces, you can hire brushing machines, but be wary of flame weed burners, the fuel for which produces carbon dioxide, the gas largely responsible for climate change.

If all else fails, choose weed control products that cause the least harm to the environment. Look for patio cleaners based on soaps (fatty acids) or acetic or pelargonic acid – the acids leave no residues and quickly degrade and become harmless. Use them during dry weather and remember that they may not kill mature plants.

Clovers feed the grass and the flowers attract bees.

TURF WARS ON WEEDS

Lawn weedkillers selectively eliminate broadleaved plants such as dandelions and daisies, leaving grasses to thrive, but they have both an environmental and financial cost. Alternatively, consider leaving all or part of the lawn untreated, allowing broadleaved plants to grow and flower, adding to the biodiversity of the garden. Some plants – daisies, for example – will arrive of their own accord while others such as clovers can be 'over-seeded' then raked and pressed into the lawn surface. Clovers have many benefits, since they fix nitrogen in the soil, which feeds the grasses, and are drought-tolerant, ensuring a green carpet during hot, dry periods.

THE BIG COVER-UP

Hoeing, digging out plants and mulching are efficient ways of pesticide-free weed control, but perennials such as couch grass, bindweed and ground elder may regrow. Instead of using weedkiller spot treatments, try applying a mulch made up of several layers of cardboard topped with 7cm (3½in) of bark chips to hold them in place. Few weeds can survive a summer smothered in this way.

Edible garden

Summer is in full swing, and many fruits and vegetables are ready to harvest, while seeds sown now will provide crops in autumn and winter. Gluts of vegetables and fruits can be made into delicious chutneys and jams to bring a taste of summer to your winter table.

Vegetables

SOW INDOORS Spring cabbages
(to protect them from slugs).

SOW OUTDOORS Beetroots; carrots;
chard; chicory and endive; cover crops
or green manures to cover any bare
ground; Florence fennel; French beans;
herbs including basil, coriander,
parsley; kohlrabi; lettuce, salad leaves;
mustard greens; pak choi; peas;
perpetual spinach; runner beans;
spinach, spring cabbage; spring onions;
turnips; winter and summer radishes.

PLANT OUT Plants sown indoors in May,
including butternut squash, calabrese,
courgettes, cucumbers, marrows,

> **TOP TIP**
> **The big cover-up**
> Many birds like to sample our crops before
> we have a chance to harvest them, so it's
> best to cover them up to prevent your whole
> harvest disappearing. Covering soft fruits and
> vegetables such as cabbages with bird-proof
> netting is the most effective way to keep them
> at bay. Set out canes, stakes around your crops,
> or use wire hoops over low-growing plants.
> Cover with netting, making sure it is taught,
> and peg it down at ground level. Birds can get
> caught up in loose netting so ensure that you
> pull it tight over and around the supports.

HERB OF THE MONTH: CORIANDER
(*Coriandrum sativum*)
This popular hardy annual herb, with its aromatic, spicy-flavoured leaves and seeds, makes a great addition to a wide variety of savoury dishes. It's easy to grow from seed and can be sown outside in batches from spring to summer for a continuous supply of leaves. Simply sow the seeds in free-draining soil or pots of peat-free compost in a sunny or partly shaded area, where it can be left to grow undisturbed, since it dislikes being transplanted. Keep plants well watered and protect the seedlings from slugs. Harvesting the leafy stems down to about 5cm (2in) above the soil level will encourage a second flush to grow.

pumpkins, peppers ❶, summer and winter squash ❷ and sweetcorn; sprouting broccoli.

HARVEST NOW Beetroots; broccoli; cabbage; calabrese; cauliflowers; chillies; courgettes; cucumbers; French and broad beans; garlic; herbs; lettuce; overwintered onions; peas; radishes; second early and salad potatoes; shallots; spinach; spring onions; small tomatoes.

Fruit

HARVEST Blueberries ❸; cherries ❹; currants; gooseberries; summer raspberries; rhubarb; strawberries.

🍲 Recipe

BEAN SALAD WITH CHIMICHURRI DRESSING

Nothing could be simpler than this quick, refreshing salad, made from the beans that are ripening by the day throughout July, and fresh herbs picked from the garden. Add some shallots and garlic to make a tangy dressing and you have a delicious, healthy combo, ideal for a light lunch or as a side dish.

1   First, make the dressing by combining the garlic cloves, shallot, vinegar and lemon juice in a bowl.

2   Set aside while you blend the fresh herbs and ground spices in a mortar with a pestle. Add the garlic mix to the spices, then drizzle on the olive oil.

3   For the salad, blanch the beans in salted boiling water for 4–6 minutes. Then plunge into ice-cold water to stop the cooking process.

4   Combine the salad ingredients in a bowl and stir through the dressing, mixing well. Serve with crusty bread. This salad can also be stored in the refrigerator for two or three days.

INGREDIENTS
For the dressing
3 garlic cloves, finely chopped
1 medium shallot, finely chopped
1 tbsp each red wine vinegar and lemon juice
½ bunch each flat leaf parsley, basil & coriander
8 tbsp extra-virgin olive oil
½ tsp each ground coriander, ground cumin and salt

For the salad
2 handfuls each: runner and French beans, topped and tailed
½ 400g can butter beans
100g can of Roquito chilli pepper pearls
1 red chilli, sliced (optional)

Challenges this month

Many crops will need some barrier protection to prevent flying insects from laying their eggs next to them and hungry caterpillars devouring your produce. Also keep unwanted plants in check and your eyes peeled for plant diseases that may need your attention.

FAT HEN (*Chenopodium album*), also known as white goosefoot, is a tall, fast-growing annual plant, with silvery green leaves that are pale beneath and resemble a goose's or hen's foot, hence the name. Spikes of small green flowers produce thousands of seed from each plant, which is why it is often considered a weed. However, it is also attractive to butterflies and the edible leaves can be eaten in salads or steamed like spinach. The flowers are also edible. With this in mind, tolerate a few plants but hoe off seedlings, deadhead the flowers before they set seed and dig out mature plants.

ROSE SUCKERS are shoots that develop below ground level from the rootstock and produce stems that are often more vigorous than the others on the plant. The leaves may also be a different colour or have more leaflets. Suckers steal water and nutrients from the main plant and can weaken your rose, so remove any you spot as soon as possible. They often develop if roots are injured, so avoid digging or hoeing close to the plant. To remove a sucker, scrape back the soil to expose its origin on the root, and then pull it away at this point – if you cut it off at soil level, it will regrow.

WESTERN FLOWER THRIP (*Frankliniella occidentalis*) hails from North America and has been in Britain since 1986. This tiny insect feeds on the foliage and/or flowers of many glasshouse plants, especially tomatoes, cucumbers, *Streptocarpus*, African violets (*Saintpaulia*), fuchsias, pelargoniums, and chrysanthemums, causing silvery leaves (pictured), stunted growth, and the flowers to drop. To prevent bringing thrips into your garden or home, check houseplants carefully before buying and avoid any showing the damage described above. Also check indoor plants you own from spring onwards, and set up sticky traps above or among susceptible plants or use biological controls if the damage is severe. Outside, thrips do little harm to mature plants and should be tolerated. Never use sticky traps in the garden, as they will also catch beneficial insects.

Garden benefactors

Social wasps

It's easy to dismiss wasps as pests when they sting us or disrupt our summer garden parties in pursuit of sugary treats, so you may be surprised to find them on a list of garden benefactors. The truth is that these yellow and black striped insects are amazing predators that help to reduce populations of aphids and other unwanted insects, and in doing so, maintain a healthy ecosystem. In fact, researchers estimate that each summer, they eat 14 million kilogrammes (over 30 million pounds) of insect prey in the UK, including aphids, caterpillars and spiders, as well as carrion, consuming carcasses and recycling the nutrients.

The adults feed on nectar and pollen and help to pollinate plants, although their diet consists mainly of sugary foods, including fruit, aphid honeydew, cakes and anything else they find that takes their fancy. The larvae are the insect-eating carnivores, which the adult parent wasps catch, chew and partially digest before regurgitating them to feed to their young.

Social wasps build large elaborate nests underground or in dark cavities, such as lofts, or among the branches of trees or shrubs, depending on the species. Queen wasps emerge from their hibernation sites in spring, and start to build a nest from wood fibres mixed with saliva to form a paste to create a comb of hexagonal cells. The eggs she lays in them hatch into larvae before emerging as infertile females, who then help to build the nest further and feed the young. By midsummer, many nests are the size of a football and are home to about 400–500 worker wasps. Males and fertile females are then produced and mate to form next year's queens. By autumn, the old queen, female workers and male wasps have died out and the new queens hibernate in sheltered areas and animal burrows.

The nasty sting wasps dispatch when threatened is painful, admittedly, but contrary to popular belief, these insects are not especially aggressive if you leave them alone. For this reason, tolerate nests if possible, as they will fade away in late summer. Although wasps eat fruit crops, the damage is limited and it is a small price to pay for the benefits they offer earlier in the year.

Design masterclass

Juliet Sargeant

As the first black woman to exhibit at RHS Chelsea Flower Show in 2016 with 'The Modern Slavery Garden', and the first to create a campaigning garden, Juliet Sargeant is a leading light of the garden design world. Her garden won a gold and People's Choice award, and she then went on to create 'The New Blue Peter Garden' in 2022.

Juliet says her background in medicine and psychology informs her plant-rich designs, which help people to connect with nature, while supporting their mental and physical health.

Born in Tanzania, she spent most of her childhood in the UK, absorbing the natural world around her. She initially studied medicine and worked as an NHS doctor, but wanted a more creative career that would also enhance wellbeing.

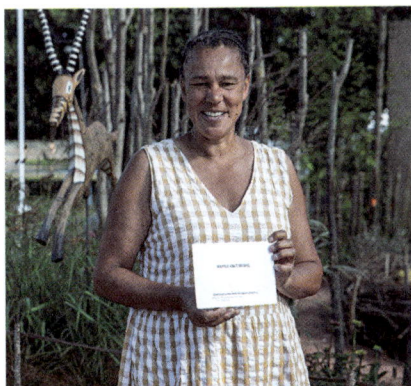

After completing a degree in Garden Design, she set up her company in 1994 and now runs that alongside her garden design school in Sussex.

HOW TO DESIGN A WELLBEING GARDEN
Juliet's gardens deliver a range of mental health benefits, and these tips will help you to create a haven of happiness.

▶ 'It's important that you enjoy your time in the garden, so include plants and features that will make you happy. For example, if you feel refreshed by inhaling wonderful floral fragrances, then include scented roses, jasmine and lavender. Or, if eating the fruits of your labours appeals, grow some easy vegetables and fruits.'

▶ 'Exercise is good for your mental as well as your physical health, and the great thing about gardening is that you can work at your own pace, while using different muscle groups. Sowing seeds, taking cuttings and potting up small plants work your fingers and fine motor skills, while digging raises your heartbeat and makes you breathless enough to be good "cardio" exercise.'

▶ 'Flower-filled gardens, balconies and window boxes hold our attention and help us unwind. Set up a seat near your favourite plants, breathe in deeply, breathe out and *relax*!'

Plants for difficult places

Dry shade

Mature trees or shrubs whose roots suck the moisture from the soil, or buildings and walls that act as rain shadows, can all create a combination of dry soil and shade.

The low levels of moisture and light in these areas make it difficult for many plants to grow and develop, unless they have adapted to survive these inhospitable conditions, so make some smart choices if you want this part of your garden to thrive. Plants without the right adaptations may become stunted, and fail to flower or fruit, and even plants that naturally prefer dry shade may need careful monitoring and watering during their first spring and summer if they are to establish well.

Survivors of dry shade include the Japanese laurel (*Aucuba*), its large leaves offering a greater surface area to absorb as much light as possible, while the waxy coating also helps to reduce moisture loss. *Cotoneaster* foliage also has a waxy surface with a slightly hairy underside, which is another adaptation that reduces moisture loss from the plant. *Epimedium* and hardy geraniums provide some groundcover and help to prevent soil erosion, while their leafy canopies also reduce evaporation from the soil surface. Applying a mulch of organic matter, such as homemade compost or bark chippings, will lock moisture in the soil, too, but these products can rot the stems of woody plants so leave a gap around trees and shrubs.

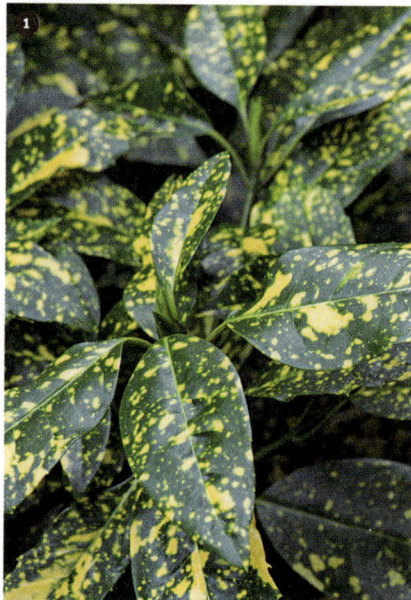

CHOOSING PLANTS FOR DRY SHADE

Cotoneaster (*Cotoneaster lacteus*)
An evergreen shrub or small tree, with leathery, dark green leaves and clusters of small white spring flowers, followed by red berries, loved by birds, in autumn. **H&S:** 4 × 4m (13 × 13ft)

❶ Japanese laurel 'Mr Goldstrike'
(*Aucuba japonica* 'Mr Goldstrike')
Grown for its large, leathery leaves, with yellow spots and botches, this evergreen shrub also produces small purple flowers in the spring, followed by red berries when the flowers are pollinated. **H&S:** 2.5 × 2.5m (8 × 8ft)

2 Copper shield fern 'Brilliance'
(*Dryopteris erythrosora* 'Brilliance')
An evergreen fern with red new fronds
in spring, which then turn coppery
pink and dark green as the seasons
turn. Orange spores appear on the
undersides of the fronds in autumn.
H&S: 60 × 60cm (2 × 2ft)

3 Wood spurge (*Euphorbia
amygdaloides* var. *robbiae*)
A vigorous evergreen perennial, with
rosettes of glossy, dark green leaves and
tall stems bearing long-lasting, lime-
green flowers in late spring and
summer. **H&S:** 50 × 90cm (20 × 36in)

Cranesbill 'Ingwersen's Variety'
(*Geranium macrorrhizum*
'Ingwersen's Variety')
The green, deeply lobed, aromatic
foliage of this evergreen perennial turns
orange and red in the autumn, while
pale pink flowers appear in early
summer. **H&S:** 30 × 60cm (12 × 24in)

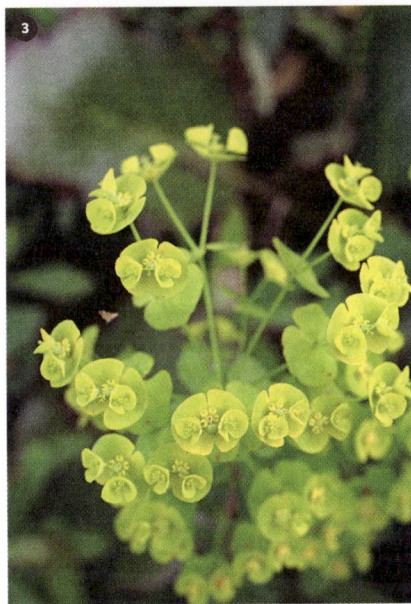

4 Barrenwort 'Cupreum'
(*Epimedium* × *versicolor* 'Cupreum')
An evergreen perennial that produces
a clump of red-tinted, green leaves and
dainty coral-pink and pale yellow
flowers on slender stems in spring.
H&S: 30 × 50cm (12 × 20in)

August

While we take a holiday, the garden bobs along like petals floating on calm waters. Mature plants' roots are buried deep enough in the soil to survive periods of drought, but containers and crops will need our attention. Earlier flowers may have gone to seed, but a new chorus is assembling in the wings, with viticella clematis, rudbeckias, asters and Michaelmas daisies bursting into bloom as the days gradually shorten.

KEY EVENTS
Bank Holiday (Scotland), 3 August
Solar Eclipse (*Partial eclipse in the UK*), 12 August
Summer Bank Holiday (England and Wales), 31 August

What to do in August

The end of summer is a busy time, as fruits, including blackberries, strawberries, tomatoes, courgettes and peppers are ripe for picking. Many flower seeds can be harvested now and sown in the next few weeks or in spring for blooms next year, all for free. Continue watering and feeding potted plants, and deadheading, too.

In the garden

PRUNE RAMBLING ROSES NOW, if they they are too large and need to be kept in check. Remove dead and diseased stems, and limit growth by removing one in three of the oldest stems at the base. Then shorten the side shoots on remaining stems by one third.

HARVEST SEEDS from annual and perennial plants in paper bags or envelopes on a dry day. The seed will be ripe when the cases are dry and brown, and the seed is dark in colour and hard. Remember that only seed from plant species will produce offspring that look like the parents – those from hybrids and cultivars will be more varied.

DEADHEAD DAHLIAS regularly for longer flower displays. The old, spent flowerheads are cone-shaped, while the buds are round and firm. **1**

TOP UP PONDS, water features and bird baths. Use water from a butt for ponds and water features, and tap water for birds, as harvested water may harbour diseases that could harm them.

APPLY AN ORGANIC-BASED FERTILIZER such as seaweed feed to potted plants every fortnight, to boost growth and keep them flowering.

TRIM LAVENDER BUSHES and hedges after flowering. Use shears to cut the old flowering growth down to the new shoots further down the stems.

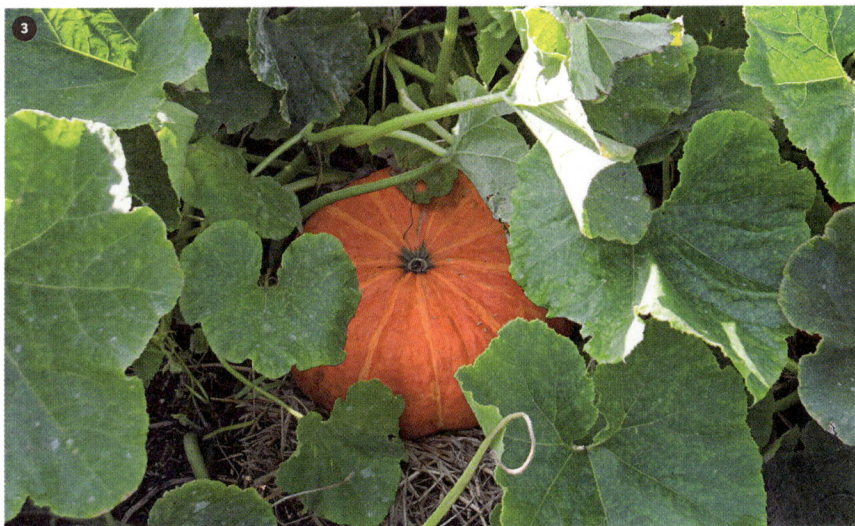

TAKE SOFTWOOD CUTTINGS of tender plants such as fuchsias and pelargoniums and store them indoors over winter (see p.106–7 for cuttings method). This is a cheap and easy way of propagating expensive bedding plants. Check them periodically during the colder months and water sparingly, keeping the leaves dry, when the compost feels dry to the touch. Increase watering next spring and repot the young, rooted plantlets into individual containers to grow on. **2**

In the fruit & veg patch

SOW OVERWINTERING or autumn harvested green manures. These plants suppress weeds and some help to enrich soils when dug in before planting a new crop. Crimson clover (*Trifolium incarnatum*) and the poached egg plant (*Limnanthes douglasii*) are good options for light soils – chop the foliage and leave it to wilt before incorporating it into the soil after flowering in autumn. Or try buckwheat (*Fagopyrum esculentum*), a pollinator- and bird-friendly plant that is reduced to mulch by frosts, ready for spring planting.

WATER SQUASHES AND PUMPKINS as the fruits start to swell to keep plants growing well and to help fend off powdery mildew, a fungal disease that often attacks these plants. **3**

MULCH WINTER BRASSICAS, such as cabbages and Brussels sprouts, spreading a 5–8cm (2–3in) layer of well-rotted homemade compost or manure to protect the soil from compaction during harvest, support wildlife, and leave the soil in good condition for the follow-on crops.

HARVEST COURGETTES regularly before they get too big. The young, tender crops are delicious and picking them regularly encourages more fruits to form, keeping the harvest going.

ORDER STRAWBERRY RUNNERS of new varieties that you haven't tried before, and plant the bare-root plants as soon as they arrive. If you already have strawberry plants, you can propagate them to make new plants for free (see right).

Indoors

OPEN WINDOWS to raise humidity levels for tropical plants such as elephant's ear (*Alocasia*), zebra plants (*Aphelandra squarrosa*) and the bird's nest fern (*Asplenium nidus*), or set those that will tolerate cool nights outside in pots with drainage holes in the base, setting them in a sheltered, shady spot.

CHECK PLANTS FOR DISEASES and unwelcome visitors such as mealybugs, which look like tiny woodlice (pictured). Wash off insects and their eggs, and remove diseased leaves promptly to keep them in check. **4**

REMOVE FALLEN LEAVES AND FLOWERS of houseplants from the surface of the potting compost, especially if they show signs of mould, which may lead to the spread of fungal diseases that could infect your plants.

MONEY-SAVING IDEA
Make new strawberry plants for free
In summer, strawberries send out runners (long stems) with small plantlets at the ends, which will form roots when they are in contact with the soil. Either leave them to do this in the bed in which they are growing or, if raising plants in pots, rest the plantlet on some compost in a separate pot and pin down the stem with wire to keep it in place. When roots develop, sever the stem and detach it from the parent plant.

Plants of the month

1. Tickseed (*Coreopsis verticillata* CRÈME BRÛLÉE pictured)
2. Dahlia (*Dahlia* 'Cornel Brons' pictured)
3. Culver's root (*Veronicastrum virginicum* 'Apollo' pictured)
4. Aster (*Aster × frikartii* 'Mönch' pictured)
5. Japanese anemone (*Anemone × hybrida* 'Honorine Jobert' pictured)
6. Shasta daisy (*Leucanthemum × superbum* 'Becky' pictured)
7. Spanish flag (*Ipomoea lobata*)
8. Cosmos (*Cosmos bipinnatus* 'Cosimo Red-White' pictured)
9. Purple top (*Verbena bonariensis*)
10. Persicaria (*Bistorta amplexicaulis* 'Red Baron' pictured)
11. Butterfly bush (*Buddleja davidii* PEACOCK pictured)

Project: Create a succulent cascade

Nothing could be easier than growing hardy houseleeks (*Sempervivum*) on a patio, and with just a few terracotta pots, you can elevate these humble little succulents into a dramatic, colourful, year-round display. Buy packs of small houseleeks from specialist nurseries or garden centres and if you can't find larger plants such as the one at the top of this display, plant a few in the ground and you will be amazed how big they will grow after a year or two. Remember that houseleeks come in a wide range of shapes, colours and textures, so choose a selection of contrasting species and cultivars.

YOU WILL NEED
3 terracotta pots of different sizes
Alpine or cacti potting compost, or a mix of peat-free multipurpose, loam-based compost and horticultural sand
Selection of houseleeks (*Sempervivum*)

1 Place the largest pot on the ground and add a 5cm (2in) layer of compost on the bottom. Place the second largest pot on top of the compost layer and add more compost in the gap between the two pots so the largest one is full, up to about 5cm (2in) below the rim.

2 Add a 5cm (2in) layer of compost to the middle pot, and place the smallest pot on top of it. Now fill the gap between the middle and smaller pot with more compost, so that the former is filled to about 5cm (2in) below the rim. Finally, fill the smallest pot with compost, to about 5cm (2in) below the rim.

3 Plant the houseleeks around the edges of the large and mid-sized pots, and finally add them to the container at the top, finishing it off with your largest plant. Fill in around each of the rootballs with more compost, and firm in gently. The plants will soon knit together to fill the pots as pictured.

4 Place in a sunny or partly shaded, sheltered area. Water every few days while the houseleeks establish, then water about once a week, even in summer. Treat with nematodes if vine weevil are a problem and, in winter, set the pot in a spot protected from heavy rain.

Looking up

Sunrise and sunset

While the days are gradually shortening, the sun is still high in the sky and shining brightly for many hours, fuelling the growth of both cultivated and unwanted plants.

DAY	LONDON		EDINBURGH	
	Sunrise	Sunset	Sunrise	Sunset
Sat, 1 Aug	5:22:38 am	8:51:05 pm	5:15:13 am	9:23:04 pm
Sun, 2 Aug	5:24:09 am	8:49:26 pm	5:17:06 am	9:21:03 pm
Mon, 3 Aug	5:25:40 am	8:47:45 pm	5:19:00 am	9:18:59 pm
Tue, 4 Aug	5:27:13 am	8:46:02 pm	5:20:54 am	9:16:54 pm
Wed, 5 Aug	5:28:45 am	8:44:17 pm	5:22:49 am	9:14:47 pm
Thu, 6 Aug	5:30:18 am	8:42:31 pm	5:24:44 am	9:12:39 pm
Fri, 7 Aug	5:31:52 am	8:40:43 pm	5:26:40 am	9:10:29 pm
Sat, 8 Aug	5:33:26 am	8:38:54 pm	5:28:36 am	9:08:17 pm
Sun, 9 Aug	5:35:00 am	8:37:03 pm	5:30:33 am	9:06:04 pm
Mon, 10 Aug	5:36:34 am	8:35:11 pm	5:32:30 am	9:03:49 pm
Tue, 11 Aug	5:38:09 am	8:33:17 pm	5:34:27 am	9:01:33 pm
Wed, 12 Aug	5:39:44 am	8:31:22 pm	5:36:24 am	8:59:16 pm
Thu, 13 Aug	5:41:19 am	8:29:26 pm	5:38:22 am	8:56:57 pm
Fri, 14 Aug	5:42:55 am	8:27:28 pm	5:40:19 am	8:54:37 pm
Sat, 15 Aug	5:44:30 am	8:25:29 pm	5:42:17 am	8:52:16 pm
Sun, 16 Aug	5:46:06 am	8:23:29 pm	5:44:15 am	8:49:54 pm
Mon, 17 Aug	5:47:41 am	8:21:28 pm	5:46:13 am	8:47:31 pm
Tue, 18 Aug	5:49:17 am	8:19:26 pm	5:48:10 am	8:45:06 pm
Wed, 19 Aug	5:50:53 am	8:17:23 pm	5:50:08 am	8:42:41 pm
Thu, 20 Aug	5:52:29 am	8:15:18 pm	5:52:06 am	8:40:14 pm
Fri, 21 Aug	5:54:05 am	8:13:13 pm	5:54:04 am	8:37:47 pm
Sat, 22 Aug	5:55:41 am	8:11:07 pm	5:56:02 am	8:35:19 pm
Sun, 23 Aug	5:57:17 am	8:08:59 pm	5:58:00 am	8:32:50 pm
Mon, 24 Aug	5:58:53 am	8:06:51 pm	5:59:58 am	8:30:20 pm
Tue, 25 Aug	6:00:29 am	8:04:43 pm	6:01:56 am	8:27:49 pm
Wed, 26 Aug	6:02:05 am	8:02:33 pm	6:03:53 am	8:25:18 pm
Thu, 27 Aug	6:03:40 am	8:00:23 pm	6:05:51 am	8:22:46 pm
Fri, 28 Aug	6:05:16 am	7:58:11 pm	6:07:48 am	8:20:13 pm
Sat, 29 Aug	6:06:52 am	7:56:00 pm	6:09:46 am	8:17:40 pm
Sun, 30 Aug	6:08:28 am	7:53:47 pm	6:11:43 am	8:15:06 pm
Mon, 31 Aug	6:10:04 am	7:51:34 pm	6:13:41 am	8:12:31 pm

Moonrise and moonset

Moon phases

◑ **THIRD QUARTER** 6 August ◐ **FIRST QUARTER** 20 August
● **NEW MOON** 12 August ○ **FULL MOON** 28 August

DAY	LONDON			EDINBURGH		
	Moonrise	Moonset	Moonrise	Moonrise	Moonset	Moonrise
1 Aug		08:30	21:47		08:36	22:03
2 Aug		09:46	21:59		09:58	22:09
3 Aug		11:03	22:11		11:21	22:15
4 Aug		12:23	22:25		12:48	22:23
5 Aug		13:46	22:43		14:19	22:34
6 Aug		15:13	23:08		15:54	22:52
7 Aug		16:39	23:46		17:29	23:21
8 Aug		17:57			18:51	
9 Aug	00:41	18:57		00:12	19:49	
10 Aug	01:55	19:40		01:30	20:23	
11 Aug	03:24	20:09		03:07	20:44	
12 Aug	04:56	20:29		04:48	20:56	
13 Aug	06:26	20:45		06:26	21:05	
14 Aug	07:52	20:57		07:59	21:12	
15 Aug	09:14	21:09		09:28	21:18	
16 Aug	10:33	21:22		10:53	21:25	
17 Aug	11:50	21:35		12:17	21:32	
18 Aug	13:07	21:52		13:41	21:42	
19 Aug	14:23	22:13		15:04	21:56	
20 Aug	15:35	22:41		16:24	22:18	
21 Aug	16:41	23:20		17:34	22:52	
22 Aug	17:36			18:30	23:43	
23 Aug		00:12	18:18	19:08		
24 Aug		01:15	18:49		00:51	19:33
25 Aug		02:26	19:12		02:09	19:49
26 Aug		03:42	19:30		03:32	19:59
27 Aug		04:59	19:44		04:56	20:07
28 Aug		06:15	19:56		06:19	20:14
29 Aug		07:32	20:07		07:43	20:19
30 Aug		08:50	20:19		09:07	20:26
31 Aug		10:10	20:33		10:33	20:33

Average temperature & rainfall

This table shows the average minimum and maximum temperatures, indicated by the blue and red dots, together with the average rainfall and number of rainy days for this month. The horizontal rules show how the figures have varied over the past decade.

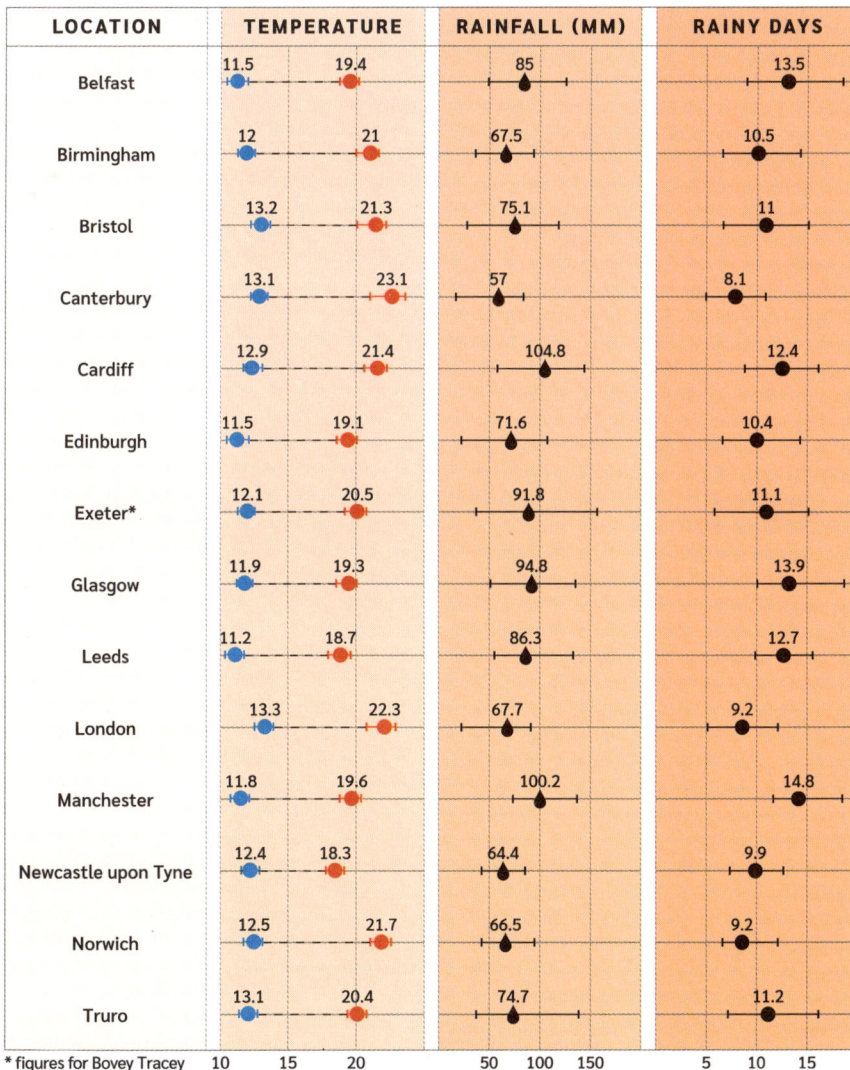

LOCATION	TEMPERATURE		RAINFALL (MM)	RAINY DAYS
Belfast	11.5	19.4	85	13.5
Birmingham	12	21	67.5	10.5
Bristol	13.2	21.3	75.1	11
Canterbury	13.1	23.1	57	8.1
Cardiff	12.9	21.4	104.8	12.4
Edinburgh	11.5	19.1	71.6	10.4
Exeter*	12.1	20.5	91.8	11.1
Glasgow	11.9	19.3	94.8	13.9
Leeds	11.2	18.7	86.3	12.7
London	13.3	22.3	67.7	9.2
Manchester	11.8	19.6	100.2	14.8
Newcastle upon Tyne	12.4	18.3	64.4	9.9
Norwich	12.5	21.7	66.5	9.2
Truro	13.1	20.4	74.7	11.2

* figures for Bovey Tracey

Temperature scale: 10 15 20
Rainfall scale: 50 100 150
Rainy days scale: 5 10 15

Sustainable gardening

Reusing materials

There are many ways gardeners can recycle and repurpose items, rather than buying new, and thereby reduce their carbon footprint. The ultimate goal is to make gardening 'circular', which means generating what we use in our outdoor spaces in the garden itself, with nothing going to waste (see p.94).

REUSABLE PACKAGING
Inevitably, we all buy some products to grow our plants, but before purchasing, think about how you can make some carbon savings. For example, larger packages of potting compost tend to be more sustainable than smaller ones, since the latter require more materials and energy, gramme for gramme, to make. Remember that while fertilizers have a very long shelf life if kept dry, potting compost is best used within one year. Once empty, the sacks can also be repurposed and used to grow potatoes, herbs or dwarf beans, for example.

Purchasing just one large pack of general-purpose fertilizer is preferable to buying lots of products for different

This garden includes an old bin lid bird bath, crushed bricks for the path and a seat made from reused planks.

plant groups, too. Plants are unable to read labels and these general formulas are effective across the board, with a few exceptions such as those formulated for orchids. Try also to limit your use of liquid fertilizers, which are heavier and therefore less sustainable than solid materials, requiring more energy to transport. You can, of course, make your own by steeping compost or other organic manures in water, which have a higher nutrient content than fertilizers made from plants such as comfrey.

RECYCLING PLASTIC

All gardeners accumulate plastic plant pots, many of which can be reused over many years, but problems can arise when disposing of surpluses. Coloured plastic can be recycled, but most black plastic requires specialist treatment and often finds its way into landfill. To prevent this, many garden centres now offer a recycling service that accepts black pots and trays, and you can either dispose of your old ones, or, if you're new to gardening, pick up some for free. Alternatively, grow young plants in used yoghurt pots and food trays, or sow seeds in paper- and coir-based pots and module cells if you have to buy new.

Carpets have long been used to suppress weeds but they contain glues that can leach into and harm the soil.

Those made of synthetic fibres also release tiny plastic particles as they decay, and once they have reached the end of their life they must go to landfill. Synthetic plastic mulches are no better. Cardboard seems a safer bet, as it rots down into organic matter over time if you remove the packing tape and labels first. Layers of cardboard topped with an organic material or grass mowings to hold them in place make highly effective weed-suppressing, soil-improving mulches (see p.135), that disappear into the ground or can be composted.

TOOL EXCHANGE

When buying tools, opt for the best quality products you can afford, which should last for many years, or search for second-hand items. Fitting new wooden handles or plastic grips on spades and forks, or seeking the help of a welder for metal tools, will extend their lives.

Replace wooden handles on otherwise usable tools.

Edible garden

The summer harvest continues throughout this month, with an abundance of climbing beans, courgettes, peppers and tomatoes ripe for picking, to name but a few. Also continue to sow small batches of fast-maturing vegetables for autumn harvests.

Vegetables

SOW INDOORS Herbs for autumn crops.

SOW OUTDOORS Carrots; chard; chicory and endive; dwarf French beans; kohlrabi; lettuce; onions; pak choi; perpetual spinach; radishes; rocket; spring cabbages; spring onion; turnips.

PLANT OUT Plants sown in pots or trays earlier in the year, including autumn and winter cabbages, kale, spring cauliflowers.

HARVEST NOW Aubergines (in greenhouse); beetroots; broad beans; broccoli; calabrese; carrots; cauliflowers; chard; chicory and endive; chillies; courgettes; cucumbers; French and runner beans; globe artichokes; herbs; lettuce; maincrop potatoes; marrows; onions; peas; peppers; radishes; spring onions; summer squash; sweetcorn; tomatoes.

Fruit

HARVEST Early apples; blackberries ❶; currants; blueberries; gooseberries; raspberries; strawberries; nectarines; early pears; peaches; plums.

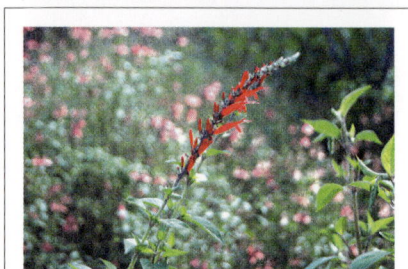

HERB OF THE MONTH:
PINEAPPLE SAGE (*Salvia elegans* 'Scarlet Pineapple')
A tender subshrub, this tall sage doubles as a beautiful garden plant, bearing hooded, bright scarlet, edible flowers in late summer and early autumn. The blooms rise up on tall spikes among the pineapple-scented leaves, which are perfect for adding to cocktails and savoury dishes. Grow this sage in a pot in a sheltered spot in full sun, and bring it indoors over winter.

Challenges this month

Blights abound as summer progresses and gardeners must be vigilant to prevent them spreading to susceptible crops such as tomatoes and potatoes. Also protect brassica crops from moths and butterflies whose hungry larvae will feast on the foliage.

TOMATO BLIGHT is a disease that rots the foliage and fruits of tomato plants. Those grown outside are most susceptible but tomatoes raised in greenhouses may also succumb. Initial symptoms include discoloured leaves that then shrivel and turn brown. You may also see a white fungus-like growth on the undersides of the foliage. Brown marks appear on the stems and on the fruits before they begin to rot. There is no cure for the disease and even if you pick off affected leaves quickly, the plant may still die, with a loss of the crop – harvest the green fruits at this stage and use them immediately to save them.

To help prevent blight, chose a resistant cultivar and keep the leaves of plants grown indoors as dry as possible. Never reuse compost or soil in which tomatoes have been grown and don't replant tomatoes (or potatoes, which are affected by the same disease) in the same spot for at least four years. Also use a disinfectant such as Jeyes Fluid to clean plant supports and other equipment that has come into contact with blight.

DANDELIONS (*Taraxacum officinale*) (pictured) are loved by children for their delicate seedheads or 'clocks' that blow apart in a breeze, and by pollinators that visit the nectar-rich flowers, but they are often considered a weed, as they spread rapidly by seed. Plants also have long tap roots that are difficult to remove and will regenerate from tiny fragments. While it's best to leave some for wildlife, remove young plants growing close to crops or ornamentals. In other areas, deadhead the flowers promptly.

CABBAGE MOTH and cabbage white butterfly larvae feast on brassica plant leaves. Both small white and large white butterflies lay yellow eggs which hatch into plain green or black speckled caterpillars, while the moth has round white eggs and yellowish or brownish-green caterpillars. Caterpillars provide food for birds, so protect most of your plants with 4mm mesh butterfly netting or fleece – ensuring it is not touching the leaves – while leaving a few uncovered to support wildlife.

Garden benefactors

Lacewings

Known as 'aphid lions' or 'aphid wolves', the delicate appearance of lacewings belies their killer instinct and voracious appetite for other insects that can harm our plants and crops.

The UK is home to 14 species of the green lacewing (pictured top right) and 29 species of the brown type (pictured right), and both the adults and larvae eat a range of aphids, mites, thrips, scale insects and whiteflies. The adults of many species also eat nectar and pollen and help pollinate the flowers they visit.

Lacewings provide benefits in other ways, too, their graceful, translucent wings and colourful bodies decorating the garden and helping to increase our mental wellbeing as we watch them fly around at dusk. They also provide food for birds, bats and other wildlife, contributing to a healthy ecosystem, rich in biodiversity, although they are not easy prey, avoiding attack by releasing an unpleasant odour. They can detect bat echolocation signals, too, allowing them to close their wings to appear smaller and avoid detection.

Lacewings produce several generations in one year, starting in spring when mated females emerge from hibernation and locate suitable prey for their offspring. They then lay eggs nearby, each suspended on a mucus thread to prevent the emerging larvae from eating one another. Fifteen to twenty days after hatching, the larvae pupate and the adults emerge two weeks after that.

Like many insects, lacewing populations are under pressure due to habitat loss, pesticide use and climate change, so take steps to protect them by avoiding pesticides, leaving perennials intact and beds undisturbed in autumn to provide overwintering sites, turning off outside lights at night to protect these nocturnal creatures, and planting a range of nectar-rich flowers to feed the adults.

Design masterclass

Andy Sturgeon

Internationally acclaimed garden designer Andy Sturgeon is known for his award-winning contemporary designs, which range from large-scale public realm projects to small urban gardens and country estates.

Fusing traditional materials, innovative planting and architectural features, his design prowess has earned him nine RHS Chelsea Flower Show gold medals and three coveted 'Best in Show' awards.

Andy began his career as a landscaper but soon realized that design was his true calling. After studying at the Welsh College of Horticulture, working with the eminent garden designer David Stevens, and spending three years travelling the world, he returned to set up his own business in 1994. A succession of RHS Chelsea medals catapulted him into the

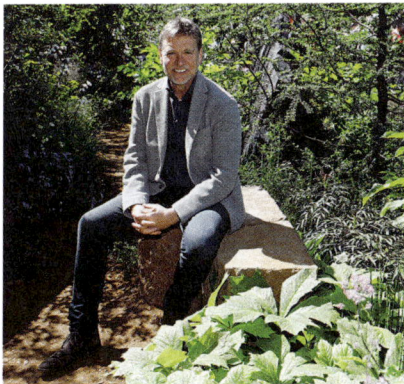

limelight and secured his place among the great designers of our time.

HOW TO DESIGN A HOT, DRY GARDEN
Having designed for all soil types and climates, Andy offers his tips on planting a hot, dry garden.

▶ 'You can opt for the Mediterranean classics – olives, lavender and rosemary, with a few *Trachycarpus* palms – but I also mix in Australasian shrubs with Californian natives, such as *Grevillea*, *Baccharis* and *Arctostaphylos manzanita*. These enjoy similar conditions and look quite comfortable together.'

▶ 'In the UK, a garden can be hot and dry in summer, but also experience winter wet and flash flooding, the enemies of Mediterranean-climate plants. To protect them, plant into a mound of free-draining soil set over a layer of crushed hardcore, or directly into a deep layer of sand.'

▶ 'Create some shade to improve the atmosphere and help future-proof your garden as the planet warms. Light canopy trees that cast dappled shade are best. Try the Mount Etna broom (*Genista aetnensis*) or an evergreen cork oak (*Quercus suber*), which lends an arid quality but is not as dense as the holm oak. In smaller spaces, the strawberry tree (*Arbutus × andrachnoides*) is perfect.'

Plants for difficult places

Slopes and hillsides

Sloping gardens are often exposed to wind and the sun for long periods each day, while the soil may be unstable and subject to erosion, especially after heavy rain. These conditions make some plants vulnerable to drying out and damage due to root disturbance.

Plants growing on sunny slopes will be exposed to long hours of daylight and rapid drainage as water runs down the hill, often taking the top layer of soil with it. On a shadier slope, moisture may last slightly longer but drainage will still be sharp and the soil unstable.

On a steep slope, try temporarily clearing it of vegetation and then pegging coarse coconut matting or a similar material over the soil to keep it in place. You can then plant into the soil on the slope through slits cut into the matting.

Another idea is to carve out shallow shelves on the slope before putting the matting in place. This will help to hold the water around the roots for a little longer and give them a better chance of establishing. Once established, the plants will also then help to secure the soil as the matting decays.

The spreading habit of plants such as shrubby *Ceanothus* and *Mahonia* are particularly effective in protecting the soil surface from erosion, securing the ground as the matting decays. The shallow but expansive roots of *Crocosmia*, *Agastache*, *Euphorbia* and *Bergenia* will also knit the soil particles together, while low-growing thyme makes good groundcover, reducing soil erosion and protecting the surface from the drying effects of wind on exposed hillsides.

CHOOSING PLANTS FOR SLOPES

Giant hyssop 'Blue Fortune'
(*Agastache* 'Blue Fortune')
Spikes of small, violet-blue flowers, loved by bees, appear over a long period from summer to early autumn among this perennial's tall stems of aromatic green leaves. **H&S:** 90 × 40cm (36 × 16in)

Oregon grape 'Apollo'
(*Mahonia aquifolium* 'Apollo')
This compact, spreading, hardy evergreen shrub produces glossy green spiny leaves that are purplish-bronze in winter. Clusters of yellow flowers appear in spring, followed by blue-black berries. **H&S:** 60 × 90cm (24 × 36in)

① Californian lilac 'Blue Mound'
(*Ceanothus* 'Blue Mound')
A mound-forming evergreen shrub
with glossy, dark green leaves and round
clusters of small, bright blue flowers
in late spring and again in late summer.
H&S: 1.5 × 2m wide (5ft × 6ft 6in)

② Elephant's ears 'Eroica'
(*Bergenia* 'Eroica')
Spikes of small, bright purple-pink
flowers on red stems appear on this
hardy evergreen perennial in spring.
The bronze-green rounded leaves
are infused with red in winter.
H&S: 50 × 50cm (20 × 20in)

Golden thyme
(*Thymus pulegioides* 'Aureus')
Also known as lemon thyme, this
spreading evergreen subshrub produces
small, bright yellow, lemon-scented
leaves and short spikes of tiny pale lilac
flowers in spring and summer.
H&S: 20 × 60cm (8 × 24in)

③ Montbretia 'Carmin Brilliant'
(*Crocosmia* × *crocosmiiflora*
'Carmin Brilliant')
Arching stems of dark orange, tubular
flowers push up between this hardy
perennial's green, sword-shaped
foliage from mid- to late summer.
H&S: 60 × 90cm (24 × 36in)

September

Warm soil and returning rain provide the perfect conditions for new life as summer moves into autumn. Gardeners can make the most of this time by planting seasonal flowers for instant colour and spring bulbs, with their promise of beautiful blooms next year. Hardy crops can be sown now to overwinter, while sweet raspberries and tomatoes are ripe and ready to be picked.

KEY EVENTS

Janmashtami, 4 September
Yom Kippur, 20–21 September
International Day of Peace, 21 September
Autumn Equinox, 22 September
Michaelmas Day (*Last day of the harvest season*), 29 September

What to do in September

Warmth from the early autumn sun and return of rain in September offer the perfect conditions for planting and sowing before winter sets in. It's also a good time aerate a lawn by plunging a fork into the soil at regular intervals and filling the gaps with a 3:6:1 mix of loam-based compost, horticultural sand and peat-free potting compost.

In the garden

SOW HARDY ANNUALS such as the laceflower (*Orlaya*) and California poppy (*Eschscholzia californica*) in pots or trays and protect them in a cold frame over winter for earlier blooms next year. You can also sow tougher types, including love-in-a-mist (*Nigella*), pot marigolds (*Calendula*), opium poppies (*Papaver somniferum*) and cornflowers (*Centaurea cyanus*) directly in the ground if you have free-draining soil that's not prone to waterlogging in winter.

PLANT POT-GROWN SHRUBS, climbers and perennials, which will also get off to a flying start when planted in early autumn. Make sure you plant them at the same depth they were growing at in their original pots, apart from large-flowered clematis, the rootballs of which need to be 5–7.5cm (2–3in) below the soil surface, while the top of the rootballs of other clematis should be buried just below the surface.

PLANT OUT SPRING-FLOWERING BIENNIALS such as forget-me-nots (*Myosotis sylvatica)* and wallflowers (*Erysimum cheiri*) – the latter are now available as bare-root plants from the garden centre or online nurseries, and are cheaper than those grown in pots.

START PLANTING SPRING BULBS such as daffodils (*Narcissus*), grape hyacinths (*Muscari*), crocuses and hyacinths. Plant them at a depth equal to three times the length of the bulb in a sunny or partly shaded site. For example, if your daffodil bulbs measure 5cm (2in) from tip to base, plant them 15cm (6in) deep, with the pointed ends facing up. ●❶

MONEY-SAVING IDEA
Bulk buy spring bulbs
Wholesalers and online nurseries usually offer sizeable discounts for large orders of spring bulbs, so buying a hundred, for example, will be much cheaper per bulb than buying just ten. You can then share the bulbs and the cost with other gardeners to reap the benefits.

DIVIDE HARDY PERENNIALS that have underperformed due to congested roots or have outgrown their allotted space. (see also p.47). ❷

SOW OR TURF NEW LAWNS Autumn is the perfect time to install a new lawn, when the soil is warm and damp. Choose an appropriate seed mix and remember that newly sown lawns should not be used for about eight months when sown in autumn; leave a newly turfed lawn to settle for a few weeks before walking on it. Visit the RHS website at rhs.org.uk for detailed instructions of how to sow grass seed or lay new turf.

In the fruit & veg patch

CUT BACK THE FRUITED STEMS of blackberry bushes once the berries have been harvested. Tie in the non-fruiting stems (see p.127) to their supports to replace them, as these will produce blackberries next summer. ❸

HARVEST PUMPKINS and squash over the next few weeks, before the frosts return, when the stalks have become woody and the fruits ring hollow when you tap them. Cut them when dry weather is forecast and lay them out in the sun for a week to allow the skins to harden – if rain is on the cards, set them in a greenhouse, cold frame or cool room indoors. Then store them in a well-ventilated place at 10–15°C (50–60°F), and check them regularly every few weeks for signs of rot.

REMOVE TRUSSES OF UNRIPE TOMATOES at the end of the month and ripen them indoors. Pop them in a paper bag with a banana and place them in a drawer to continue ripening – the banana releases ethylene, a hormone that helps to speed up the ripening process. Check the fruit regularly and remove the tomatoes as soon as they are ripe.

SOW SPINACH in a prepared bed for a winter or early spring crop.

REMOVE FOLIAGE from maincrop potato crops if you spot signs of blight (see p.157 for symptoms on top growth). Cut the stems down to ground level to prevent blight spores infecting the tubers, harvesting two weeks later once the tubers have developed hard skins and spores lose viability.

Indoors

RETURN SUN-LOVING PLANTS such as cacti and succulents to the brightest areas in your home as the sun strength and light levels fall in the autumn. ❹

STOP FEEDING INDOOR PLANTS at the end of the month, when growth slows and they do not require additional nutrients.

BRING IN ANY HOUSEPLANTS that you placed outside in the garden before the colder nights set in. Check them for slugs, snails and any other unwanted creatures before bringing them indoors.

Plants of the month

1. White snakeroot (*Ageratina altissima*)
2. Fuchsia (*Fuchsia magellanica* 'Logan Woods' pictured)
3. Prickly heath (*Gaultheria mucronata* 'Mulberry Wine' pictured)
4. Sneezeweed (*Helenium autumnale* 'Fuego' pictured)
5. Perennial sunflower (*Helianthus* 'Lemon Queen' pictured)
6. Panicled hydrangea (*Hydrangea paniculata* 'Savill Lace' pictured)
7. Stonecrop (*Hylotelephium* 'Abbey Dore', synonym *Sedum* 'Abbey Dore')
8. Himalayan honeysuckle (*Leycesteria formosa* GOLDEN LANTERNS pictured)
9. Eulalia (*Miscanthus sinensis* 'Yakushima Dwarf' pictured)
10. Bowden lily (*Nerine bowdenii*)
11. Aster (*Symphyotrichum laeve* 'Nightshade' pictured)

Project: Make a turf seat

This naturalistic seat will suit any garden style and is easy to make with a few pallets, some soil and a roll of turf or grass seed. You will find pallets for sale or free online, or ask your local garden centre if they have some to spare. Look for pallets with closely spaced planks, which are the sturdiest types, and set the seat on a flat surface in sun or part shade, where the grass will grow well. If using seed, rather than turf, do not sit on the grass until next spring. Trim the seat with shears.

YOU WILL NEED
Pallets
Tape measure
Saw and electric drill
12 long screws
Sandpaper
Old compost bags
Drawing pins
Topsoil
Spade

1 Prise off the lower planks from the pallet to leave the deck, then saw in half to create the two longer sides of the bench. Measure and cut six short planks from those you removed to make the shorter ends, three for each side. Drill guide holes and screw the sides together. Sand the edges of the bench so they feel smooth.

3 Fill the bench with topsoil – you can start with a bottom layer of rubble if you have some to hand. Do not use compost, which will shrink over time. Compact it with the back of a spade, and level it.

4 Roll the turf out over the soil and cut it to fit. Pat down to ensure the roots are in good contact with the soil and water.

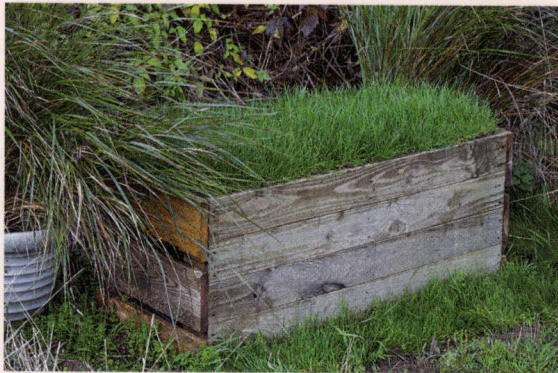

2 Rake the soil and tread to compact so the ground is level before putting the bench on top. Line the inside of the bench with plastic (we used old compost bags) to prevent soil seeping out, fixing it in place with drawing pins.

Looking up

Sunrise and sunset

As the nights draw in and hours of daylight are more limited, look out for late-season plants that burst into bloom now to decorate your early autumn garden.

DAY	LONDON		EDINBURGH	
	Sunrise	Sunset	Sunrise	Sunset
Tue, 1 Sep	6:11:39 am	7:49:21 pm	6:15:38 am	8:09:56 pm
Wed, 2 Sep	6:13:15 am	7:47:06 pm	6:17:35 am	8:07:20 pm
Thu, 3 Sep	6:14:51 am	7:44:52 pm	6:19:32 am	8:04:44 pm
Fri, 4 Sep	6:16:26 am	7:42:36 pm	6:21:29 am	8:02:08 pm
Sat, 5 Sep	6:18:02 am	7:40:21 pm	6:23:26 am	7:59:31 pm
Sun, 6 Sep	6:19:38 am	7:38:05 pm	6:25:22 am	7:56:53 pm
Mon, 7 Sep	6:21:13 am	7:35:48 pm	6:27:19 am	7:54:16 pm
Tue, 8 Sep	6:22:49 am	7:33:31 pm	6:29:16 am	7:51:38 pm
Wed, 9 Sep	6:24:24 am	7:31:14 pm	6:31:13 am	7:49:00 pm
Thu, 10 Sep	6:26:00 am	7:28:57 pm	6:33:09 am	7:46:21 pm
Fri, 11 Sep	6:27:35 am	7:26:39 pm	6:35:06 am	7:43:42 pm
Sat, 12 Sep	6:29:11 am	7:24:21 pm	6:37:02 am	7:41:03 pm
Sun, 13 Sep	6:30:46 am	7:22:03 pm	6:38:59 am	7:38:24 pm
Mon, 14 Sep	6:32:22 am	7:19:45 pm	6:40:55 am	7:35:45 pm
Tue, 15 Sep	6:33:58 am	7:17:26 pm	6:42:52 am	7:33:06 pm
Wed, 16 Sep	6:35:33 am	7:15:08 pm	6:44:49 am	7:30:26 pm
Thu, 17 Sep	6:37:09 am	7:12:49 pm	6:46:45 am	7:27:47 pm
Fri, 18 Sep	6:38:45 am	7:10:30 pm	6:48:42 am	7:25:07 pm
Sat, 19 Sep	6:40:21 am	7:08:11 pm	6:50:39 am	7:22:27 pm
Sun, 20 Sep	6:41:57 am	7:05:53 pm	6:52:35 am	7:19:48 pm
Mon, 21 Sep	6:43:33 am	7:03:34 pm	6:54:32 am	7:17:08 pm
Tue, 22 Sep	6:45:09 am	7:01:15 pm	6:56:29 am	7:14:29 pm
Wed, 23 Sep	6:46:46 am	6:58:57 pm	6:58:27 am	7:11:49 pm
Thu, 24 Sep	6:48:22 am	6:56:38 pm	7:00:24 am	7:09:10 pm
Fri, 25 Sep	6:49:59 am	6:54:20 pm	7:02:21 am	7:06:31 pm
Sat, 26 Sep	6:51:36 am	6:52:02 pm	7:04:19 am	7:03:52 pm
Sun, 27 Sep	6:53:13 am	6:49:44 pm	7:06:17 am	7:01:13 pm
Mon, 28 Sep	6:54:50 am	6:47:26 pm	7:08:15 am	6:58:35 pm
Tue, 29 Sep	6:56:27 am	6:45:09 pm	7:10:13 am	6:55:57 pm
Wed, 30 Sep	6:58:05 am	6:42:52 pm	7:12:11 am	6:53:19 pm

Moonrise and moonset

Moon phases

◑ **THIRD QUARTER** 4 September   ◐ **FIRST QUARTER** 18 September
● **NEW MOON** 11 September   ○ **FULL MOON** 26 September

DAY	LONDON			EDINBURGH		
	Moonrise	Moonset	Moonrise	Moonrise	Moonset	Moonrise
1 Sep		11:34	20:50		12:04	20:43
2 Sep		13:00	21:12		13:38	20:58
3 Sep		14:26	21:45		15:13	21:22
4 Sep		15:45	22:32		16:39	22:04
5 Sep		16:51	23:38		17:44	23:11
6 Sep		17:38			18:25	
7 Sep	01:00	18:10		00:40	18:49	
8 Sep	02:29	18:33		02:17	19:03	
9 Sep	03:58	18:50		03:55	19:13	
10 Sep	05:24	19:04		05:29	19:21	
11 Sep	06:47	19:16		06:58	19:27	
12 Sep	08:08	19:28		08:25	19:34	
13 Sep	09:27	19:41		09:50	19:41	
14 Sep	10:45	19:56		11:15	19:50	
15 Sep	12:03	20:15		12:40	20:02	
16 Sep	13:18	20:41		14:03	20:20	
17 Sep	14:27	21:16		15:19	20:49	
18 Sep	15:27	22:02		16:21	21:33	
19 Sep	16:14	23:01		17:06	22:34	
20 Sep	16:49			17:36	23:49	
21 Sep		00:09	17:15	17:54		
22 Sep		01:22	17:35		01:10	18:07
23 Sep		02:38	17:50		02:33	18:16
24 Sep		03:55	18:03		03:57	18:23
25 Sep		05:12	18:15		05:20	18:29
26 Sep		06:31	18:27		06:45	18:36
27 Sep		07:52	18:40		08:12	18:43
28 Sep		09:16	18:56		09:43	18:52
29 Sep		10:43	19:17		11:18	19:06
30 Sep		12:11	19:47		12:55	19:27

Average temperature & rainfall

This table shows the average minimum and maximum temperatures, indicated by the blue and red dots, together with the average rainfall and number of rainy days for this month. The horizontal rules show how the figures have varied over the past decade.

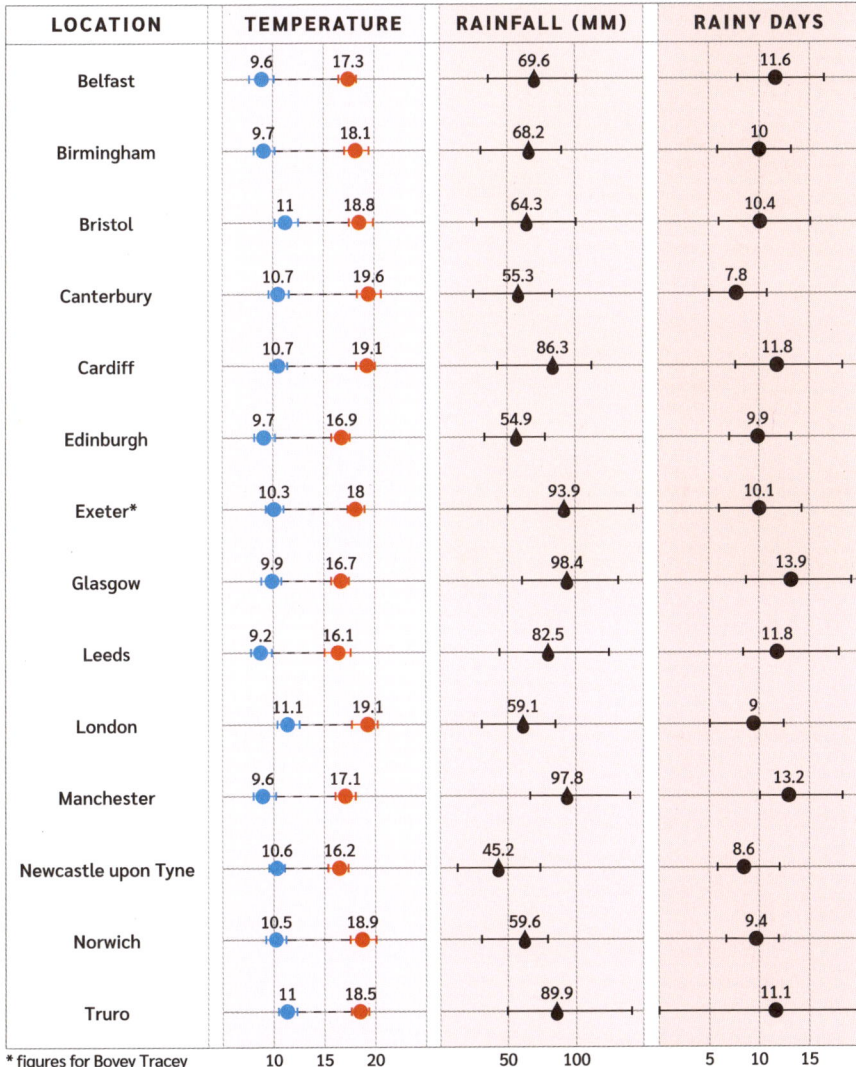

LOCATION	TEMPERATURE		RAINFALL (MM)	RAINY DAYS
Belfast	9.6	17.3	69.6	11.6
Birmingham	9.7	18.1	68.2	10
Bristol	11	18.8	64.3	10.4
Canterbury	10.7	19.6	55.3	7.8
Cardiff	10.7	19.1	86.3	11.8
Edinburgh	9.7	16.9	54.9	9.9
Exeter*	10.3	18	93.9	10.1
Glasgow	9.9	16.7	98.4	13.9
Leeds	9.2	16.1	82.5	11.8
London	11.1	19.1	59.1	9
Manchester	9.6	17.1	97.8	13.2
Newcastle upon Tyne	10.6	16.2	45.2	8.6
Norwich	10.5	18.9	59.6	9.4
Truro	11	18.5	89.9	11.1

* figures for Bovey Tracey

Temperature scale: 10 15 20
Rainfall scale: 50 100
Rainy days scale: 5 10 15

Sustainable gardening

Zinnias provide late-season nectar for pollinators.

Increasing biodiversity

Gardens offer many benefits, including a space to play, grow food and flowers, and relax, but they also enhance a wide variety of living organisms that create a healthy ecosystem. These mutually dependent organisms, from microscopic fungi to large mammals, each play an essential role, and the loss of any of them affects our future and that of the planet. Scientific studies show that we are currently in a biodiversity crisis, with an estimated one million species under threat of extinction worldwide, including 45 per cent of all known flowering plant species, so anything we gardeners can do to help reverse that trend is a step in the right direction.

BOOST BIODIVERSITY

One way we can increase biodiversity is to grow food. Gardeners usually add compost and other organic matter to the soil, which in turn increases the number of soil-borne organisms, while sowing winter cover crops such as clover in late summer helps support overwintering birds, worms and other garden creatures. In spring, you can go a step further and leave some leeks and cabbages to bloom and feed pollinators; after flowering, clear the plants before establishing new crops to prevent problems such as allium leaf miner from spreading.

The blossom of fruit trees such as apples, pears and plums is also a great resource for bees and other pollinators, while the trees themselves promote biodiversity by supporting algae, lichens, and mosses, and a rich fauna of mites, insects and spiders that, in turn, feed birds. In fact, most garden trees have high biodiversity value and retaining them wherever possible is especially worthwhile, since the bigger and older they are, the more benefits they offer.

In small gardens, large shrubs and hedges act as good tree substitutes, while the flowers of more compact soft fruit plants offer pollinators similar benefits to tree blossom.

GO WILD

Commercial soft fruit growers often sow wild flowers alongside their plantations to support native insects, many of which are parasitic and help to control the unwanted bugs that attack their crops. Take these farmers' cue and try growing small patches of wild flowers, such as clovers (*Trifolium*), cornflowers (*Centaurea cyanus*), dandelions (*Taraxacum*), kidney vetch (*Anthyllis vulneraria*), mint (*Mentha*) and yarrow (*Achillea millefolium*), next to your soft fruits. However, do not grow them too close, as these crops, unlike mature fruit trees, are very sensitive to competition from other plants.

Bees are sustained by apple blossom in spring.

Lawns provide habitats for many more insects if at least some of the grass is left to grow during the summer, then cut once the seeds of native plants such as clovers and daisies have fallen. Adding low-growing clover seeds to lawns in spring can also make conventionally mown swards more biodiverse.

BEAUTY WITH BENEFITS

Ornamental gardens typically contain a wide variety of plants that boost biodiversity. Make an audit of your beds and borders, and add plants that fill any gaps in the availability of pollen and nectar. For example, many native plants finish flowering by late summer but tender non-native types, including single-flowered dahlias, cosmos, fuchsias and zinnias, for example, plug the shortfall, often blooming up to the frosts in autumn. Late winter flowers – crocuses, snowdrops and mahonias, for example – also help when many pollinator foods are scarce.

Providing water for birds, mammals and amphibians is as valuable to biodiversity as including trees in the garden. Ponds, ideally spanning a width of 2m (6ft 6in), or child-safe bubble features and birdbaths are all very helpful. A muddy landing place adjacent to the water provides material for nest-building insects and birds, too.

Edible garden

As temperatures cool, especially at night, sow crops indoors or under cover to overwinter, unless your plants are fully hardy and will the tolerate frosts that begin next month. Also finish harvesting tender crops such as tomatoes, aubergines, peppers, courgettes and cucumbers, and bring tender herbs such as basil indoors.

Vegetables

SOW INDOORS OR UNDER CLOCHES
Herbs; pak choi; spring cabbages.

SOW OUTDOORS Salad leaves; spinach; turnips; winter-hardy spring onions; winter lettuce.

PLANT OUT Onion sets; spring cabbage sown in summer.

HERB OF THE MONTH: FRENCH MARJORAM (*Origanum* 'French')
Very easy to grow, French marjoram is a hardy, evergreen subshrub with spicy leaves that add piquancy to many savoury dishes. It's a pretty plant, too, with green leaves in winter that turn golden yellow in summer, and little tubular pink flowers that are loved by bees and other pollinating insects. Grow it in free-draining soil and full sun or part shade.

HARVEST NOW Aubergines ❶; beetroots; broccoli; calabrese; carrots; cauliflowers; celery; chicory and endive; Chinese cabbage, chillies; courgettes ❷; cucumbers; French and runner beans; globe artichokes; herbs; lettuce; maincrop potatoes ❸; marrows, pumpkins; parsnips; peas; peppers; radishes; spring onions; summer squash; sweetcorn; tomatoes; winter squash.

Fruit

PLANT NOW Strawberry plants.

HARVEST Apples ❹; autumn raspberries; blackberries; blueberries; late-season strawberries; medlars; pears; quinces.

TOP TIP
Perfect pumpkins
Pumpkin season is almost upon us and care needs to be taken to ensure the growth of plants is not checked by dry spells, and the fruits don't rot if the weather turns unseasonably wet. If plants succumb to powdery mildew, pick off heavily affected leaves but retain sound foliage – sugars produced in the leaves increase the pumpkins' quality and they should not be removed to allow sun to fall on the fruits to ripen them. Dew and rain will not harm the fruits but might delay maturity slightly. It is well worth supporting ripening pumpkins on bricks, wooden blocks or tiles to get perfectly finished skin and fruit shape, but not essential.

Recipe

TOMATO TART TATIN

This delicious savoury tart offers a great way to use up a glut of tomatoes at this time of year. Surprisingly easy to make, it would make an eye-catching starter for a dinner party and looks especially pretty if you use a selection of different coloured varieties.

INGREDIENTS

25g unsalted butter
1 tbsp olive oil
2kg fresh, ripe homegrown tomatoes
1 tsp soft brown sugar
2 tbsp balsamic vinegar
1 tbsp honey
Sea salt to taste
Freshly ground black pepper to taste
1 tbsp chopped fresh thyme
1 sheet puff pastry

1   Preheat the oven to 200°C/180°C fan/gas 6.

2   Cut the tomatoes into halves and wedges depending on their size. Melt the butter and olive oil in an ovenproof heavy-based frying pan and add the tomatoes, skin side up, in a single layer. Cook over a low heat until they release their juices. Remove the tomatoes, leaving the juices in the pan.

3   Add the sugar, balsamic vinegar and honey to the pan and reduce to create a syrupy consistency. Transfer to a flameproof ceramic or metal tatin dish if your frying pan isn't ovenproof.

4   Return the tomatoes to the pan or dish in an even layer, skin side down, and season with salt and pepper and add the thyme.

5   Roll out the pastry on a lightly floured surface until it is a little larger than the top of your pan or dish. Lay the pastry on top of the tomatoes and prick holes in it with a fork to allow the steam to escape.

6   Place the tart in the oven and bake for 30 minutes or until the pastry is golden brown. Remove from oven and let the tart rest for ten minutes. Then run a knife around the edge and carefully flip the tart over on to a serving plate or board.

Challenges this month

You may notice the symptoms of fungal diseases that established earlier in the year start to appear in early autumn, while many insects regarded as pests are yet to be killed off by wintry weather, so keep your eyes peeled for any damage they may cause.

SWEETCORN SMUT (*Ustilago maydis*) is a fungal disease that can mark, stunt, blister and distort the leaves, stems, flowers and, most noticeably, the cobs. Some kernels may become swollen and grey in colour – when cooked this grey mass is actually a Mexican delicacy. The infected grains eventually rupture, releasing clouds of black spores that resemble soot or smut, hence the name. There is no cure for the disease and plants should be buried deeply or burnt. Avoid planting sweetcorn in the same place for at least four years.

SOUTHERN GREEN SHIELD BUGS arrived in Britain in 2003 from mainland Europe and look very similar to our native common green shield bug (pictured). There are about fifty species of shield bug in the UK, named after the adults' shield-like shape. While all shield bugs suck sap from plants, most do very little damage and should be encouraged in gardens, since they also provide food for other wildlife. The southern species can distort runner and French bean pods, but the evidence so far suggests that the bugs do not become numerous until late summer or early autumn, by which time beans are coming to the end of their cropping season, making control unnecessary.

THE BROADLEAVED DOCK (*Rumex obtusifolius*) and smaller curled dock (*R. crispus*) are tall perennials with large green leaves, rusty-brown seedheads and deep taproots, which can grow up to 1.2m (4ft) deep in the soil. These UK natives provide food for butterflies and other insects, as well as birds, but they spread rapidly via seed and are on the Weeds Act 1959 (see p.99). While a few docks are beneficial in the garden, if they threaten to outcompete your plants, deadhead mature plants before they set seed, hoe off seedlings, and dig out young plants before the deep taproots develop. Cutting back the new growth of mature plants regularly will weaken and eventually kill them, too. If making a new bed where docks are growing, try laying a cardboard and bark chip mulch over it (see p.135) to exclude the light and kill them.

Garden benefactors

Mycorrhizal fungi

Fungi in the form of brightly coloured toadstools or mushrooms will be a familiar sight when you're out on an autumn walk in the woods or they pop up in your lawn or borders. While some are famously toxic to humans and can cause diseases in plants, of the 15,000 known species in the UK, the vast majority are beneficial to gardens, plants and ecosystems.

Neither plant nor animal, fungi are a kingdom of their own, and play essential roles in recycling nutrients from decaying vegetation and enabling plants to absorb water.

Fungi that form mycorrhizal relationships with plant roots are of special importance to gardeners and farmers. These form a symbiotic relationship with plants, creating an interdependence essential to both parties, without which neither could survive in many environments.

Beneath the soil the fungi grow as networks of microscopic tubes, and some produce fruiting bodies (pictured), which can be seen above the surface growing around trees in the form of toadstools, or as truffles and chanterelles in ancient woodlands.

Some mycorrhizal fungi form sheaths around plant roots, while others penetrate the roots themselves, creating a mass and thickening them. In exchange for sugars they derive from the plants, the fungi offer a number of key benefits, extending the reach of the roots, while absorbing and supplying water and nutrients to them. This in turn makes plants more resilient to drought and helps them to outcompete weeds. Fungi can also protect plants against nematodes and root diseases.

These amazing organisms are present in almost all soils, but they are partially suppressed in cultivated soils enriched with manures and fertilizers, and where brassicas are grown. Brassicas are one of the very few non-mycorrhizal plants. While manuring is valuable for edible crops to obtain good yields of high quality produce, ornamental and other plants are best manured as lightly as possible to encourage these fungi to colonize their roots and deliver their package of benefits.

Design masterclass

Helen Elks-Smith

Multi-award-winning garden designer, Helen Elks-Smith is renowned for her contemporary gardens and subtle, textured planting style. Her work is informed by natural landscapes and an intuitive understanding of the positive way gardens make us feel.

Helen holds two gold medals for her RHS Chelsea Flower Show and RHS Hampton Court Palace Garden Festival show gardens, and became a household name when she appeared on the BBC TV series, *Your Garden Made Perfect*, creating many beautiful designs for a range of clients. She also lectures widely on soil and tree health.

Helen read mathematics at university and worked in IT before a love of plants and gardens led her to retrain as a designer. She studied horticulture at evening classes and took a degree in Landscape and Garden Design at Writtle University College before setting up her Hampshire-based studio in 2005.

HOW TO DESIGN A COUNTRY GARDEN
Helen has won numerous awards for her country gardens, and offers advice on contemporary designs for rural settings.

► 'Make a connection between your garden and the wider landscape by placing pathways and seating areas to take advantage of the views of the countryside and trees beyond the boundaries. Remember, too, that seating and dining spaces do not need to be directly next to the house and by surrounding them with planting you can create immersive green spaces that draw you outside.'

► 'Tall boundary hedges and walls can make a garden feel "caged", so create breakpoints with gaps or gates that take the gaze out to the landscape. Emphasize a gap with a great view by flanking it with a pair of trees, and repeating the shape of a tree outside the garden with one inside also brings a connection to the borrowed landscape.'

► 'Leave hedges unclipped for a more organic, free-flowing boundary that will also provide a mosaic of wildlife habitats, or opt for a more formal look with a clipped single species.'

Plants for difficult places

Heavy clay soils

Clay soils can be extremely heavy and sticky in winter when saturated with rainwater, and then form wide cracks as the surface bakes into a hard crust during the summer months. However, clay-rich soils have some benefits: they tend to be rich in nutrients and hold on to moisture well, providing the conditions that many plants enjoy.

Choosing species that will thrive in your heavy clay soil is essential, but your list of options will be wider, and the ground easier to cultivate, if you improve it a little. Spreading a mulch (layer) of organic matter over the surface each year in autumn will pay dividends, opening up channels between the clay particles to allow water to drain through, while offering better moisture retention during dry periods (see also pp.36–7 for advice on using mulches).

When planting, use a fork to break up the soil at the bottom and sides of the planting hole to loosen it and prevent a sump from forming – this would collect water that may then rot the roots of even some clay-tolerant plants.

Shrubs such as *Garrya, Deutzia, Cornus* and *Hydrangea* grow well on clay soils, as they tolerate fluctuating moisture levels and benefit from the high level of nutrients available in many clay soils. Herbaceous perennials such as

Sanguisorba, Bergenia and *Ajuga* will also thrive and provide valuable groundcover to help reduce moisture loss from exposed soils in the summer.

Choosing the right plant for the right place in this way will create a robust, long-lived scheme that benefits soil health and garden biodiversity.

CHOOSING PLANTS FOR CLAY

1 **Silk tassel 'James Roof'**
(*Garrya elliptica* 'James Roof')
This bushy evergreen wall shrub is clothed in leathery, dark green leaves all year round and eye-catching grey-green catkins that hang from the branches throughout winter. **H&S:** 4 × 4m (13 × 13ft)

Oak-leaved hydrangea SNOWFLAKE
(*Hydrangea quercifolia* SNOWFLAKE)
The lobed oak-like leaves of this elegant hydrangea turn red in autumn, just as the white conical flowerheads fade to pink. It prefers an acid or neutral soil. **H&S:** 2 × 2m (6ft 6in × 6ft 6in)

2 Dogwood 'Magic Flame'
(*Cornus sanguinea* 'Magic Flame')
A lovely shrub for autumn and winter
colour, the green leaves turn yellow,
orange and red in the autumn, while the
bare winter stems are orange-yellow
with bright red tips. Creamy-white
summer flowers are followed by
blue-black fruit. **H&S:** 1.5 × 1.5m (5 × 5ft)

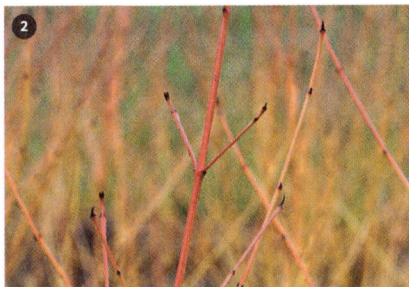

3 Burnet 'Little Angel'
(*Sanguisorba* 'Little Angel')
The slim flower stems of this hardy
perennial are topped with small
burgundy drumsticks in late summer,
which appear over a skirt of white-
edged, blue-green leaves.
H&S: 40 × 30cm (16 × 12in)

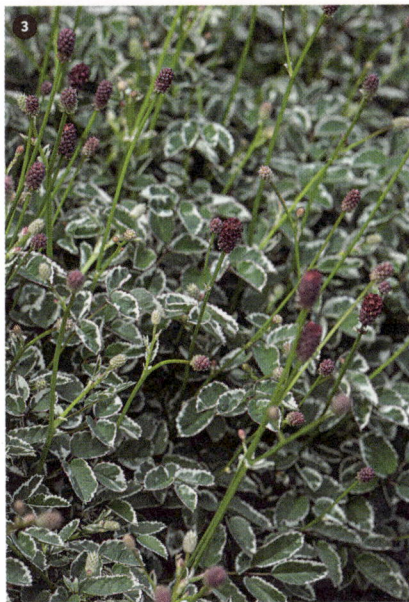

Bugle 'Catlin's Giant'
(*Ajuga reptans* 'Catlin's Giant')
A creeping, evergreen perennial that
forms a mat of glossy, dark bronze-
purple leaves and spikes of bright blue
flowers in late spring and summer.
H&S: 30 × 60cm (12 × 24in)

4 *Astilbe* 'Bronze Elegance'
Divided dark green leaves flushed
bronze when young adorn this hardy,
moisture-loving perennial from spring
to autumn. The feathery plumes of
salmon-pink flowers appear in late
summer. **H&S:** 40 × 40cm (16 × 16in)

October

Autumn marks the end of the growing season as the days shorten and temperatures fall, but as many plants start to fade, others leave their best performance till last. Acers, winged spindles and smoke bushes light up the garden, their foliage blazing in shades of red, orange and gold, while glossy berries are ripening and wands of starry flowers sparkle on Japanese saxifrages as the nights draw in.

KEY EVENTS
Apple Day (*Celebration of British apples*), 21 October
British Summer Time ends, 25 October
Halloween, 31 October

What to do in October

Sowing and planting continue throughout October when the weather allows and soils are not waterlogged or frozen. Spring bulbs and hardy pot-grown plants will all establish well, but for cheaper shrubs and trees, wait until next month when bare-root plants become available. Also bring all tender plants under cover before frost strikes.

In the garden

TAKE SEMI-RIPE CUTTINGS OF EVERGREEN HOLLIES and other evergreen plants in mid-autumn. Using clean, sharp secateurs, cut healthy stems with hard bases and soft tips, removing about 10–15cm (4–6in). Trim each cutting to just below a leaf node (bud) and remove the lower leaves, so that about four are remaining. For plants with large foliage, cut these leaves in half to reduce water loss. Gently push the cuttings into a pot of cuttings compost, then label and place in a propagator or cover with a used, clear plastic bag, removing it when the seeds germinate. Keep the cuttings under cover over winter, making sure that the compost is just moist but not wet.

BRING IN HALF-HARDY PLANTS for the winter. Take cuttings (see above) if you don't have space for large plants.

LIFT DAHLIA TUBERS Wait until the foliage has been blackened by frost, cut back the stems to about 10cm (4in) and then dig up the tubers. Turn them upside down, place in a tray and leave in a frost-free place for a couple of weeks to allow moisture to drain out before storing them in a cool but frost-free shed or room in a shallow tray of dry compost or horticultural sand. Don't water and keep them in the dark. ❶

CLEAR UP FALLEN ROSE LEAVES to prevent diseases such as black spot from overwintering on them. Bury the collected leaves in a hole in ground in the vegetable patch or at some distance away from other roses.

PILE UP FALLEN LEAVES and old, pruned branches in a quiet corner of the garden to make a hibernation area for wildlife. ❷

In the fruit & veg patch

PLANT ONION SETS at the beginning of the month. Look out for overwintering or Japanese onions that will withstand the cold, and plant in a sunny area and free-draining soil, with the pointed tip just showing above the surface.

AFTER HARVESTING beans and peas, cut plants down to the ground, leaving the roots in the soil to decompose. Compost the stalks and stems, too, as both are rich in nitrogen, a key plant nutrient (see also p.195).

CUT BACK THE FRUITED CANES of your summer-fruiting raspberries, leaving the new green canes for next year's crop. Tie in next year's raspberry canes to plant support wires or fencing.

REMOVE NETTING from fruit cages to allow birds such as blue tits and blackbirds to catch and eat any pests that are lurking among the plants. ❸

Indoors

GUARD AGAINST OVERWATERING
your houseplants, now light levels and
temperatures are falling and growth is
slowing (see p.18 for watering tips).

FORCE HYACINTH BULBS in the first
week of October for Christmas flowers.
Buy prepared bulbs and place a layer
of bulb fibre in a pot. Set the bulbs close
together, but not touching, on top. Add
more compost around the bulbs, so the
tips are just showing above the surface.
Store in a cool, dark place. When roots
develop and the shoots are 4–5cm
(1½–2in) long, bring the pots into a cool
room indoors. After the leaves green
up, move to a warmer room to
encourage the flowers to open. **4**

MONEY-SAVING IDEA
Organize a plant swap with friends
Decide who wants what and then dig up and
divide perennials and pot-up self-sown plants
to share. You can also collect seed from species
flowers and some crops (see p.54) to swap.
Free plants are a great benefit, of course, and
the social aspect of working with others can
do wonders for your mental wellbeing, too.

Plants of the month

1. Japanese maple (*Acer japonicum* 'Aconitifolium' pictured)
2. Beautyberry (*Callicarpa bodinieri* var. *giraldii* 'Profusion' pictured)
3. Plumbago (*Ceratostigma plumbaginoides*)
4. Chrysanthemum (*Chrysanthemum* 'Bronze Elegance' pictured)
5. Spindle (*Euonymus europaeus* 'Red Cascade' pictured)
6. Maidenhair tree (*Ginkgo biloba*)
7. Rose hips (*Rosa rugosa* 'Rubra' pictured)
8. Coneflower (*Rudbeckia subtomentosa* 'Henry Eilers' pictured)
9. Japanese saxifrage (*Saxifraga* 'Rubrifolia' pictured)
10. New York ironweed (*Vernonia noveboracensis* 'White Lightning' pictured)
11. Japanese snowball (*Viburnum plicatum* f. *tomentosum* 'Pink Beauty' pictured)

Project: Plant an autumn basket

Replanting a summer hanging basket with winter-interest plants will liven up your outdoor space for many months as the temperatures fall. You can even extend the display into the night by adding a festive string of solar fairy lights. The best winter displays focus on hardy evergreens with different leaf shapes and berries, partnered with winter flowers such as hellebores and heathers. The cyclamens in this arrangement are not hardy and can be replaced as winter progresses with hardy pansies (*Viola*) or more evergreens. Once completed, hang your basket on a supporting wall bracket above other pots filled with larger evergreens such as *Sarcococca*, *Euonymus* and daphnes.

1 Line the basket with a compostable fabric liner or a piece of an old plastic or compost bag with holes snipped in the base for drainage. Fill with peat-free multipurpose compost mixed with a handful of horticultural grit.

2 Stand your basket on top of a pot or bucket to keep it level, then loosen the plants from their pots by gently squeezing the sides and turning them out. Carefully tease out any congested roots. Place the largest plant in the centre of the basket, with the smaller ones around it, and trailing stems tumbling over the sides.

3 Firm compost around the plants with your fingertips, filling in any gaps, and leave a space between the surface and rim of the basket for water to collect. Water the plants, before fixing your solar fairy lights in place, ensuring the panel is facing the sun.

Looking up

Sunrise and sunset

As the days shorten, spend as much time as you can outside to keep your spirits up as the light dwindles. The clocks turn back by one hour at the end of the month.

DAY	LONDON		EDINBURGH	
	Sunrise	Sunset	Sunrise	Sunset
Thu, 1 Oct	6:59:43 am	6:40:35 pm	7:14:10 am	6:50:41 pm
Fri, 2 Oct	7:01:21 am	6:38:19 pm	7:16:09 am	6:48:04 pm
Sat, 3 Oct	7:02:59 am	6:36:03 pm	7:18:08 am	6:45:27 pm
Sun, 4 Oct	7:04:37 am	6:33:47 pm	7:20:07 am	6:42:51 pm
Mon, 5 Oct	7:06:16 am	6:31:32 pm	7:22:07 am	6:40:15 pm
Tue, 6 Oct	7:07:55 am	6:29:17 pm	7:24:07 am	6:37:39 pm
Wed, 7 Oct	7:09:35 am	6:27:03 pm	7:26:07 am	6:35:04 pm
Thu, 8 Oct	7:11:14 am	6:24:49 pm	7:28:07 am	6:32:30 pm
Fri, 9 Oct	7:12:54 am	6:22:36 pm	7:30:08 am	6:29:56 pm
Sat, 10 Oct	7:14:34 am	6:20:24 pm	7:32:09 am	6:27:23 pm
Sun, 11 Oct	7:16:14 am	6:18:12 pm	7:34:11 am	6:24:50 pm
Mon, 12 Oct	7:17:55 am	6:16:01 pm	7:36:12 am	6:22:18 pm
Tue, 13 Oct	7:19:36 am	6:13:51 pm	7:38:14 am	6:19:47 pm
Wed, 14 Oct	7:21:17 am	6:11:41 pm	7:40:17 am	6:17:16 pm
Thu, 15 Oct	7:22:59 am	6:09:33 pm	7:42:19 am	6:14:46 pm
Fri, 16 Oct	7:24:41 am	6:07:25 pm	7:44:22 am	6:12:17 pm
Sat, 17 Oct	7:26:23 am	6:05:18 pm	7:46:26 am	6:09:49 pm
Sun, 18 Oct	7:28:06 am	6:03:12 pm	7:48:29 am	6:07:22 pm
Mon, 19 Oct	7:29:48 am	6:01:06 pm	7:50:33 am	6:04:55 pm
Tue, 20 Oct	7:31:31 am	5:59:02 pm	7:52:38 am	6:02:30 pm
Wed, 21 Oct	7:33:15 am	5:56:59 pm	7:54:42 am	6:00:05 pm
Thu, 22 Oct	7:34:58 am	5:54:57 pm	7:56:47 am	5:57:42 pm
Fri, 23 Oct	7:36:42 am	5:52:56 pm	7:58:52 am	5:55:20 pm
Sat, 24 Oct	7:38:26 am	5:50:56 pm	8:00:57 am	5:52:59 pm
Sun, 25 Oct*	6:40:10 am	4:48:58 pm	7:03:03 am	4:50:39 pm
Mon, 26 Oct	6:41:55 am	4:47:00 pm	7:05:09 am	4:48:20 pm
Tue, 27 Oct	6:43:39 am	4:45:04 pm	7:07:15 am	4:46:02 pm
Wed, 28 Oct	6:45:24 am	4:43:09 pm	7:09:21 am	4:43:46 pm
Thu, 29 Oct	6:47:09 am	4:41:16 pm	7:11:28 am	4:41:31 pm
Fri, 30 Oct	6:48:54 am	4:39:24 pm	7:13:34 am	4:39:18 pm
Sat, 31 Oct	6:50:40 am	4:37:33 pm	7:15:41 am	4:37:06 pm

*Note: clocks go backward by 1 hour.

Moonrise and moonset

Moon phases

- ◑ **THIRD QUARTER** 3 October
- ● **NEW MOON** 10 October
- ◐ **FIRST QUARTER** 18 October
- ○ **FULL MOON** 26 October

DAY	LONDON			EDINBURGH		
	Moonrise	Moonset	Moonrise	Moonrise	Moonset	Moonrise
1 Oct		13:34	20:30		14:26	20:03
2 Oct		14:45	21:30		15:38	21:02
3 Oct		15:37	22:47		16:26	22:24
4 Oct		16:13			16:54	23:58
5 Oct	00:12	16:38			17:11	
6 Oct	01:40	16:56		01:34	17:22	
7 Oct	03:05	17:11		03:06	17:30	
8 Oct	04:27	17:23		04:35	17:37	
9 Oct	05:46	17:35		06:01	17:43	
10 Oct	07:05	17:48		07:26	17:50	
11 Oct	08:23	18:02		08:50	17:58	
12 Oct	09:41	18:20		10:15	18:09	
13 Oct	10:58	18:42		11:39	18:25	
14 Oct	12:10	19:13		12:59	18:50	
15 Oct	13:14	19:55		14:08	19:27	
16 Oct	14:07	20:49		15:00	20:22	
17 Oct	14:47	21:53		15:35	21:31	
18 Oct	15:16	23:04		15:58	22:49	
19 Oct	15:38			16:13		
20 Oct		00:18	15:55		00:10	16:23
21 Oct		01:33	16:09		01:32	16:31
22 Oct		02:49	16:21		02:54	16:38
23 Oct		04:06	16:33		04:17	16:44
24 Oct		05:25	16:46		05:43	16:51
25 Oct*		05:49	16:01		06:13	16:00
26 Oct		07:16	16:20		07:48	16:12
27 Oct		08:46	16:47		09:27	16:31
28 Oct		10:15	17:26		11:04	17:02
29 Oct		11:33	18:22		12:26	17:55
30 Oct		12:33	19:36		13:23	19:12
31 Oct		13:14	21:00		13:57	20:44

*Note: clocks go backward by 1 hour.

Average temperature & rainfall

This table shows the average minimum and maximum temperatures, indicated by the blue and red dots, together with the average rainfall and number of rainy days for this month. The horizontal rules show how the figures have varied over the past decade.

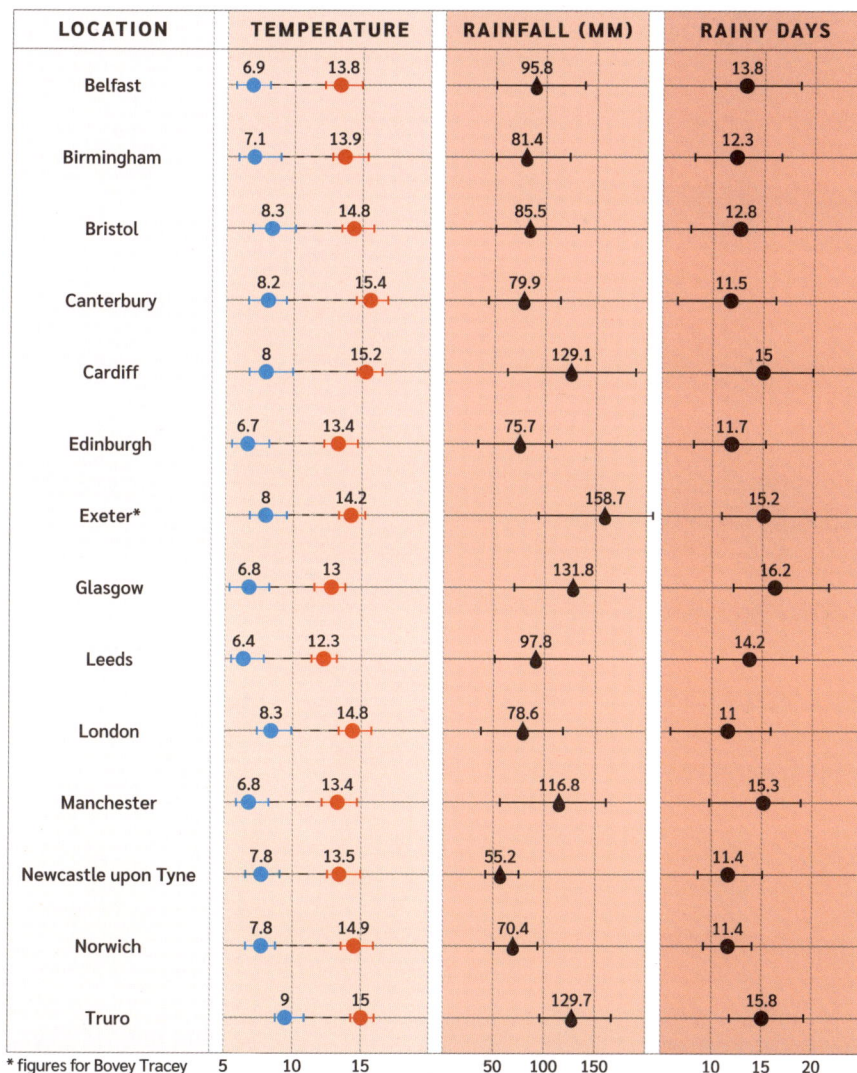

LOCATION	TEMPERATURE	RAINFALL (MM)	RAINY DAYS
Belfast	6.9　13.8	95.8	13.8
Birmingham	7.1　13.9	81.4	12.3
Bristol	8.3　14.8	85.5	12.8
Canterbury	8.2　15.4	79.9	11.5
Cardiff	8　15.2	129.1	15
Edinburgh	6.7　13.4	75.7	11.7
Exeter*	8　14.2	158.7	15.2
Glasgow	6.8　13	131.8	16.2
Leeds	6.4　12.3	97.8	14.2
London	8.3　14.8	78.6	11
Manchester	6.8　13.4	116.8	15.3
Newcastle upon Tyne	7.8　13.5	55.2	11.4
Norwich	7.8　14.9	70.4	11.4
Truro	9　15	129.7	15.8

* figures for Bovey Tracey

Temperature scale: 5　10　15
Rainfall scale: 50　100　150
Rainy days scale: 10　15　20

Sustainable gardening

Planting for birds

Birds eat a varied diet of fauna and flora, and, depending on the species, consume spiders, insects, worms, seeds, berries, and plants such as cabbages and crocus flowers. A well-planted garden will offer a rich larder for birds, while those that include evergreens for winter cover and trees and shrubs for nesting and roosting also provide a secure habitat.

Many of us put out food for birds, and enjoy watching them flock to our feeders, but growing plants they eat or that provide food for their prey also sustains them. Plants also add diversity to the garden – in general, the wider the range, the better for wildlife. The more birds roaming the garden the more unwanted plant seeds and insect eggs are likely to be hoovered up, too.

QUICK FIXES
A quick and easy way to support birds is to sow the annual flowers they love, such as phacelia and sunflowers, the seedheads of which provide high-energy food for goldfinches, blackbirds, robins and thrushes. The flowers also feed moths and butterflies, whose larvae sustain baby birds in spring – boosting insect numbers by growing a range of plants, offering water and retaining mature trees also supports birds.

If you have some spare ground, try growing crops from packets of bird seed – autumn-sown flax or linseed and wheat are good choices. Buckwheat, sold as green manure, is another option, flowering and then setting seed that provides energy and protein in autumn.

Grass seeds are a favourite winter food of birds, and lawns can play their part. Most domestic lawns include grasses that shed seeds, although immaculate, closely mown lawns are less bird-friendly. Where feasible, allow at least some of the lawn to grow uncut until late summer so that the grass and other lawn plants can flower and set seed.

NUTS AND BERRIES
Trees are very important to birds as roosts and nesting sites, with many also supplying berries and nuts. The fruits of the mountain ash (*Sorbus*) are loved by

Goldfinches are drawn to gardens offering seeds.

Fruiting shrubs that feed birds include ornamental currants (*Ribes sanguineum*), *Berberis*, snowberries (*Symphoricarpos*) and elder (*Sambucus*). In smaller gardens, try lining your boundaries with berry-rich wall shrubs such as *Pyracantha* and climbing native ivy (*Hedera helix*) and honeysuckle (*Lonicera periclymenum*) that take up very little ground space. The seeds of compact border plants such as lavender, lemon balm (*Melissa officinalis*) and *Verbena bonariensis* are also loved by birds.

HEDGEROW FOODS

Tightly clipped hedges rarely produce many berries and nuts, but they do still support insects that feed birds. Native beech (*Fagus*) and hornbeam (*Carpinus*) make fine clipped hedges. Less formal hedges composed of native dog rose (*Rosa canina*), hawthorn (*Crataegus*), spindle (*Euonymus*) and hazel (*Corylus*) produce fruits and nuts and berries, when cut every three years, as well as providing secure nesting sites.

Evergreen hedging plants that offer shelter, protection and nesting sites include cotoneaster (avoid the invasive *Cotoneaster horizontalis*), Portugal laurel (*Prunus lusitanica*) and semi-evergreen privet (*Ligustrum ovalifolium*). If some brambles can be tolerated, so much the better, as their fruits are loved by birds.

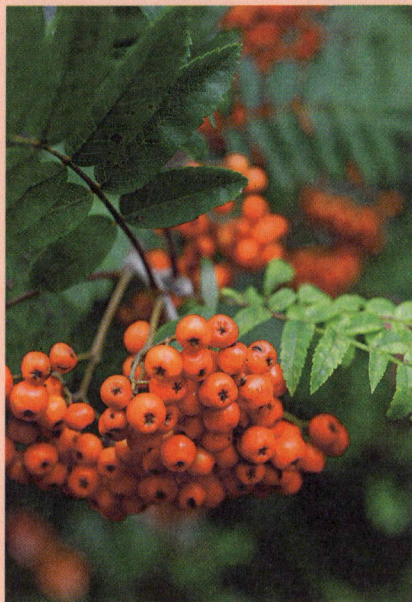

The mountain ash produces autumn berries for birds.

birds, or try *Sorbus aucuparia* 'Beissneri' or the snowy mespilus (*Amelanchier lamarckii*) in a smaller garden. Nut-producing hazel (*Corylus*) and berrying holly (*Ilex*) are two native trees that suit larger gardens, and both have attractive garden selections, such as the purple-leaved *Corylus maxima* 'Red Filbert' and the self-fertile *Ilex aquifolium* 'J.C. van Tol'. New trees take years to grow big enough to offer a full range of benefits for birds and wildlife, so try to retain existing specimens where possible.

Edible garden

Sharing gluts of fruits and vegetables with neighbours is a great way to reach out to your local community, or invite them round for a home-grown, home-cooked meal. Also try sowing broad beans and peas in mild areas this month.

Vegetables

SOW INDOORS OR UNDER CLOCHES
Herbs; pak choi; spring onions; winter lettuce; winter salad leaves.

SOW OUTDOORS Broad beans; overwintering peas (in mild areas).

PLANT OUT Garlic sets; onion sets; spring cabbages and pak choi sown in summer.

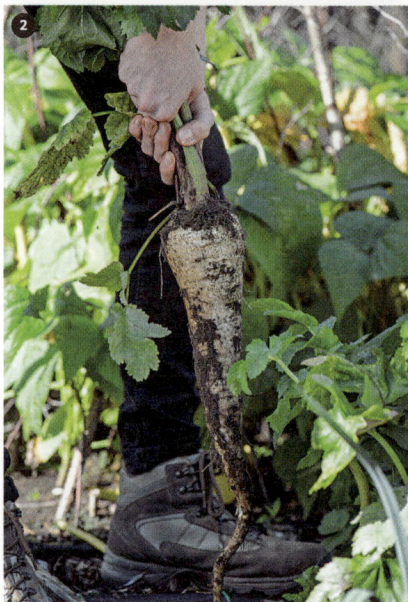

HERB OF THE MONTH: LOVAGE
(*Levisticum officinale*)
This hardy relative of celery and parsley is not often available in supermarkets, but it is a great herb to grow in your garden. The leaves can be harvested from spring to midsummer to add flavour to savoury dishes, while the tall stems of nectar-rich summer flowers are followed by tasty edible seeds used in baking. Grow it from seed or young plants in any soil, except waterlogged, and in light shade. It may self-seed, too, offering more plants for free.

HARVEST NOW Beetroots **1**; cabbages, including storing and red cabbage, and savoys; calabrese; carrots; cauliflowers; celery; celeriac; chicory and endive; Florence fennel; French beans; greenhouse-grown chillies; herbs; kohlrabi; lettuce; maincrop potatoes; pak choi, parsnips **2**; peppers; pumpkins; winter radishes, winter squash; tomatoes **3**; turnips.

Fruit

PLANT NOW Pot-grown fruit trees and bushes; rhubarb crowns.

HARVEST Apples; autumn raspberries; medlars **4**; pears; quinces.

> **TOP TIP**
> **Leave legumes to fertilize the soil**
> Peas and beans belong to a group of plants called legumes, which perform a clever trick to store nitrogen, one of the key plant nutrients. Nodules on their roots are able to convert nitrogen gas from the air and make it into a usable form that benefits plant growth. If left in the ground over winter, the roots of these crops will naturally decompose and release that nitrogen into the soil, making it available to crops sown the following spring. The nutrient-rich top growth can also be added to the compost heap.

Recipe

AUTUMN VEGETABLE SOUP

Nothing beats a hearty vegetable soup made from fresh produce picked from the veg patch as the long nights draw in. You may have to wait until November for some of the ingredients, including parsnips and carrots, to sweeten after a frost.

INGREDIENTS
6 carrots
3 parsnips
2 sweet potatoes
1 butternut squash
2 large onions
4 celery sticks
1 large leek
3 cloves of garlic
10 sprigs of thyme
2tbsp vegetable oil
25g unsalted butter
Splash of olive oil
1.5l good chicken or
   vegetable stock
Sea salt and ground
   pepper to taste

1   Pre-heat oven to 200°C/180°C fan/gas 6.

2   Peel and roughly chop the carrots, parsnips, sweet potato and butternut squash. Place in a roasting tray with the vegetable oil, sprigs of thyme and seasoning, toss thoroughly and roast for 25–30 minutes until all the vegetables are tender.

3   Meanwhile, finely dice the onions, celery, leek and garlic. Add the olive oil and butter to a large saucepan and sweat the vegetables until soft but not coloured.

4   Add the roasted vegetables and stock to the saucepan and simmer for 10–15 minutes.

5   Using a hand blender or food processor, blitz the soup until smooth, then add seasoning to taste and serve with crusty bread.

Challenges this month

Many diseases that affect trees become more apparent in the autumn as the foliage falls to reveal dying branches, but on a more positive note, the numbers of plant-eating insects are on the decline as temperatures decrease this month.

CHRYSANTHEMUM WHITE RUST is a serious fungal disease that can devastate these plants, causing shrivelled leaves and stunted growth. It spreads via airborne spores and is most commonly found on plants in autumn, when cool, wet weather returns. Symptoms include pale yellow spots on the upper leaf surfaces (pictured) that become sunken and brown, while beige pustules develop on the undersides of the leaf, which then release spores. White rust is difficult to eliminate and you will have to dispose of heavily affected plants and buy new ones. Also, keep any new plants separate from others for a few weeks until you are sure they are disease-free.

WIREWORMS are the larvae of click beetles and feed on plant roots, but they usually only cause problems when the grassy areas that they favour are converted to vegetable beds, and they bore into root crops. The yellowish-brown larvae are up to 25mm (1in) in length and usually decline in numbers over a couple of years, as digging exposes them to birds and other natural predators. Since the damage from wireworms is usually fleeting, it is best to tolerate them, although in severe cases you could use a biological control.

SILVER LEAF is a fungal disease that causes the foliage of *Malus* and *Prunus* tree species, including apples, cherries and plums, to turn a silvery colour, hence the name. The affected branches then die. Fungal growths with whitish woolly upper surfaces, purple-brown below, may also occur from late summer, and cut stems reveal irregular dark stains on the inner wood. To prevent the disease, prune susceptible plants in summer when fewer fungal spores are around and wounds heal quickly. If trees become infected, remove diseased stems before the fungal growths appear, cutting branches 10–15cm (4-6in) beyond the area of infection to wood that shows no sign of the dark staining. Sterilize cutting tools between each cut to prevent reinfection and burn the diseased stems or take them to a recycling centre.

Garden benefactors

Woodlice

Known affectionately as pillbugs, wood-pigs and cheesey-bugs, we often overlook woodlice in the garden, especially as they do our plants little or no harm and only come to our attention when we lift a pot and they scuttle out.

However, these little terrestrial crustaceans work for our benefit by processing dead and decaying plant material and helping to recycle the nutrients for use by plants. They are also pollution busters, removing heavy metals such as lead, arsenic and cadmium from the soil and preventing them from leaching into groundwater and rivers and oceans.

Woodlice also provide food for garden predators, including spiders, frogs, toads, hedgehogs and birds, thereby helping to increase biodiversity and maintain a healthy ecosystem.

These little creatures are not insects but crustaceans and closely related to crabs, lobsters and shrimps, and they breathe through gills on the underside of their bodies. Active throughout the year, mostly at night, they can be found during the day under stones, garden pots, and logs.

Woodlice live for between one and four years and breed during the summer months, producing between 200 and 600 young in one season. The females carry their fertilized eggs in a pouch under their bodies and the young remain there for a few days after they have hatched, before being released to live independently. Newly hatched woodlice, known as mancas, are white but otherwise look like adults. They shed their skins as they grow and mature before the autumn, after which they overwinter in sheltered areas.

To support these nutrient recyclers, plant densely, make wood piles at the back of your borders, create compost heaps, and leave fallen autumn foliage on the soil to provide them with suitable habitats. Do not use insecticides, which may harm them and their predators.

Design masterclass

Ann-Marie Powell

A powerhouse of the garden design world, Ann-Marie Powell's visionary landscapes and exuberant plant style have elevated her to become one of the UK's most highly respected designers. Her extensive portfolio includes the Wildlife and World Food Gardens at RHS Garden Wisley, and a string of show gardens, including a feature garden highlighting the benefits of gardening in cities for the 2016 RHS Chelsea Flower Show, and her 2024 'The Octavia Hill Garden by Blue Diamond with the National Trust' which won the inaugural Children's Choice Award, the People's Choice Award and a silver-gilt medal.

Ann-Marie's grandfather's garden and allotment first inspired her love of horticulture, and offered a respite from the utilitarian army bases where she spent her childhood. A gap year travelling the world opened her eyes to the beauty of nature and, on her return, she signed up for a garden design course at Capel Manor College. Subsequent television presenting roles threw her into the limelight, and she opened her own design practice in 1998.

HOW TO DESIGN A RESILIENT GARDEN
Passionate about the environment, Ann-Marie offers her advice on plants and design ideas that make gardens and wildlife more resilient to our changing climate.

▶ 'Mix native and non-native plants with diverse root systems that offer resilience to weather extremes. Try the crape myrtle tree (*Lagerstroemia* 'Natchez'), which shrugs off wet winters and hot summers, and the Chinese hackberry (*Celtis sinensis*).'

▶ 'Don't worry about the odd nibbled leaf or a few aphids – they're signs a garden will be attracting beneficial insects. I add *Tagetes* to my vegetable beds, which bring in pollinators and actually improve my harvest.'

▶ 'Some seemingly tricky soils are exactly what you need for climate resilience. Many sun-loving plants develop deep roots in pure sand, while the 'no-dig' approach (see p.37) preserves beneficial fungi that help plants access water. Also try 'chop and drop' mulches, using chopped prunings to cover the soil.'

Plants for difficult places

Paved courtyards

A courtyard or patio garden offers a sheltered enclave in a town or city, decorated with an array of plants that are happy in containers or thrive when their roots are restricted to narrow beds or gaps between pavers.

By definition, courtyards have a high proportion of paved surfaces, which reflect the heat and make them warmer than more exposed sites. Building waste and sandy pointing between the cobbles or slabs often mix with the underlying soil to create free-draining and nutrient-poor conditions, so if you want to plant into the ground, you will need species that tolerate drought. Plants that thrive in pots tend to also prefer drier conditions, while the additional warmth and shelter offer opportunities to include species that are not fully hardy in other areas of the country.

If your courtyard is entirely paved, consider removing some slabs and improving the soil beneath with well-rotted garden compost to create pockets of planting.

You can also include raised beds filled with a mix of composted organic matter and topsoil to increase your planting spaces. These beds hold more water than pots and will therefore not need watering as frequently.

Hardy palms such as *Trachycarpus* cope well in poor soils or large containers and provide height and some shade. Spiky cordylines or even a yucca, if you have enough space to avoid its sharp leaf tips, will also lend a tropical note to a sunny courtyard. For seasonal flower colour, try *Agapanthus* or a hardy fuchsia, both of which grow well in pockets of soil or containers. Alternatively, opt for scented lavender and catmint (*Nepeta*) to introduce a Mediterranean flavour – their long-lasting, nectar-rich flowers also support pollinating insects.

Ornamental grasses such as *Pennisetum* provide structural interest and movement as they sway in the breeze, while groundcover plants, such as thyme (see p.161), squeezed into the gaps between the paving help to soften the hard edges. Thyme is quite forgiving and can be walked on occasionally without coming to harm.

CHOOSING PLANTS FOR PATIOS

1 **Chusan palm**
(*Trachycarpus fortunei*)
An evergreen palm with a stout, fibre-covered trunk and deeply divided, fan-shaped, dark green leaves. Large, arching sprays of small, light yellow flowers may appear in a hot summer.
H&S: up to 5 × 3m (16 × 10ft)

Needle palm 'Golden Sword'
(*Yucca flaccida* 'Golden Sword')
Relatively hardy, this evergreen shrub forms a fountain of variegated blue-green and creamy-yellow leaves with sharp tips. Bell-shaped, creamy-white flowers in may appear in late summer. **H&S:** 1 × 1m (39 × 39in)

French lavender 'Victory'
(*Lavandula stoechas* 'Victory')
Forms of French lavender flower over a long period from late spring and produce scented, dark purple flowers, topped by decorative bracts, over grey-green, needle-like foliage. **H&S:** 60 × 75cm (24 × 30in)

② African lily 'Midnight Star'
(*Agapanthus* 'Midnight Star')
This perennial produces narrow, strap-shaped leaves and stout stems topped with spherical heads of dark blue flowers from mid- to late summer. **H&S:** 80 × 40cm (32 × 16in)

③ Fountain grass 'Rubrum'
(*Pennisetum advena* 'Rubrum')
Dark-red foliage emerges in spring, followed in late summer by red-purple, bottlebrush-shaped flowers that fade to brown. **H&S:** 1.2 × 0.6m (4 × 2ft)

Fuchsia 'Mrs Popple'
Large, single, bright red and purple flowers adorn this hardy fuchsia throughout summer and autumn. **H&S:** up to 90 × 60cm (36 × 24in)

November

Daylight is in short supply as winter approaches, making moments spent outside more precious than ever. Despite the cold, nature continues to deliver its treasures, as violet *Callicarpa* berries, tiny crab apples and scarlet viburnum fruits twinkle in the gloom. Fallen leaves offer more gifts, protecting the soil from wintry weather and rotting down to feed hungry roots.

KEY EVENTS

Guy Fawkes Night, 5 November
Diwali/Deepavali, 8 November
Remembrance Sunday, 9 November
St Andrew's Day, 30 November
National Tree Week, 28 November–6 December

What to do in November

As light levels and temperatures fall, work in the garden slows, but there are still jobs to keep us busy. Collect leaves from paths and patios in old compost bags with holes punched in the base, where they will rot down to make leaf mulch, a valuable soil conditioner. Also order and plant bare-root plants from November to March.

In the garden

PLANT BARE-ROOT TREES as soon as they arrive, if the ground is neither frozen nor waterlogged – store them in a pot of compost if conditions are unfavourable. Dig a large, square hole, three times as wide and no deeper than the root ball, checking the depth so that the dark soil line on the tree's stem will be level with or just proud of the surface once planted. Soak the tree roots for thirty minutes before planting, then water thoroughly. Tall or top-heavy trees will also need staking – check the RHS website at rhs.org.uk for instructions on how to do this.

TAKE HARDWOOD CUTTINGS of roses and other deciduous shrubs after leaf fall. Select healthy stems that have grown this year, and remove the soft tip before cutting into sections 15–30cm (6–12in) long. Make a sloping cut just above a bud at the top, so water will drain away from it, and a straight cut just below a bud at the bottom of each cutting. Prepare a narrow trench in well-drained soil in the garden and add a layer of sand to the base. Insert the cuttings with the slanted end at the top, and two-thirds

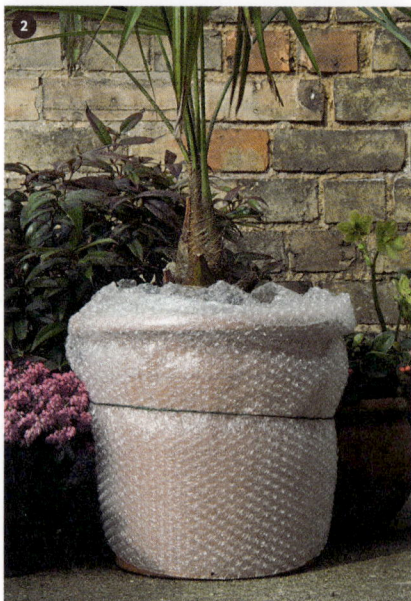

buried below the surface, spacing them 15cm (6in) apart. Firm in the cuttings, adding more soil if needed. Leave until next autumn and replant the rooted cuttings in their final positions. **1**

PLANT WINTER FRAGRANCE SHRUBS such as witch hazel (*Hamamelis*), sweet box (*Sarcococca*) and wintersweet (*Chimonanthus*) to bring cheer to the garden next January and February.

WRAP OUTDOOR TERRACOTTA POTS in recycled bubble plastic to prevent frost cracking them. Alternatively, use chicken wire to make a cage around your pots and fill with autumn leaves to insulate them. **2**

PLANT TULIP BULBS These can be left until now, and there is evidence that tulips and hyacinths do better when planted later in autumn.

PROTECT ROSES FROM WIND-ROCK by pruning the stems by one-third to a half in length. Both climbers and tall shrubs will benefit from this autumn cut.

INSTALL WATER BUTTS to capture rain from house roofs and outbuildings. If you have a large roof, consider two butts linked with flexible pipes.

In the fruit & veg patch

PLANT GARLIC varieties, such as 'Early Wight', 'Purple Wight', 'Solent Wight', 'Arno', 'Germidour' and 'Cristo', in a sunny site and free-draining soil – plant

MONEY-SAVING IDEA
Plant a fruit garden
This is a good time now that cheaper, bare-root trees and plants are available. Fruits such as raspberries, blackcurrants and blackberries are expensive to buy because they don't transport or store well, but they are easy to grow and plants will produce fruit year after year, although you may have to initially wait 12 months after planting for a crop. Visit the RHS website at rhs.org.uk for instructions on how to plant and care for your chosen fruits.

in a raised bed or pots of gritty compost if you have heavy clay. Dig a shallow trench and set the individual cloves with the pointed end upwards and the tip 2.5cm (1in) below the surface, spacing them 15cm (6in) apart in rows 30cm (12in) apart. The garlic will be ready to harvest from June next year.

LIFT PARSNIPS AFTER THE FIRST FROSTS, when their flavour will have been sweetened by the cold weather. Turnips and carrots also taste sweeter when harvested after a cold snap.

MAKE NEW BEDS for spring sowing and planting. Remove all the plants – you can leave grass *in situ* – and then cover the soil with newspaper or cardboard. Add a thick layer of well-rotted organic matter such as homemade compost or soil improver from the garden centre, and leave to rot down over winter before planting into the compost when the weather warms up.

DIVIDE MATURE CLUMPS OF RHUBARB after the leaves have died down. Dig up the clump and, using a spade or kitchen knife, slice the rhizomes into sections, each with a portion of rhizome and at least one growing point or bud. Discard any weak or dead sections from the middle of the plant. Replant the divided sections immediately.

Indoors

PLANT AMARYLLIS (*Hippeastrum*) bulbs now for blooms in December and January. Select a pot just wider than the bulb and add a layer of peat-free multipurpose compost, setting the amaryllis on top. Fill in around it, so that two-thirds of the bulb is above the surface, then place in a warm, light room. Water sparingly until new leaves develop and then water more regularly, so that the compost is moist but not wet. Turn the pot every couple of days to prevent the flower stalk growing towards the light, and stake varieties with large flowers. When flowers appear, move the plant to a cooler place, about 15–18°C (60–65°F), to extend the display.

BUY FLOWERING PLANTS such as moth orchids (*Phalaenopsis*) (pictured) and peace lilies (*Spathiphyllum wallisii*) that flower through winter to bring colour and interest to your indoor displays. ❸

Plants of the month

1. Slender sweet flag (*Acorus gramineus*)
2. Japanese cedar (*Cryptomeria japonica* 'Little Champion' pictured)
3. Yunnan liquorice (*Glycyrrhiza yunnanensis*)
4. Mahonia (*Mahonia × media* 'Winter Sun' pictured)
5. Ornamental cabbage (*Brassica oleracea*)
6. Tibetan cherry (*Prunus serrula*)
7. Coral bark willow (*Salix alba* var. *vitellina* 'Britzensis' pictured)
8. Japanese skimmia (*Skimmia japonica*)
9. Winter daffodil (*Sternbergia lutea*)
10. David viburnum (*Viburnum davidii*)
11. Chinese lantern (*Physalis alkekengi* var. *franchetii*)

Project: Create a pebble mosaic

Mosaic features are easy to make and can decorate a path, patio or quiet corner of the garden that needs a little colour and interest. This project shows the basic method but you can expand it to cover a larger area, and use pebbles found in the garden, as we did, or shells, coloured glass or broken clay pot pieces. Just make sure they are frostproof before you start. You can also buy mosaic materials if you don't have any at home.

1 Create the foundation for your mosaic by screwing together a frame made from four wooden battens, and set it on a flat surface in the garden. Alternatively, dig out a shallow hole in the ground with straight sides to contain the mortar for the mosaic.

2 Mix the mortar according to the instructions on the packaging and pour a 10cm (4in) deep layer into your wooden frame or hole in the ground.

3 Draw a design for the mosaic before you start. Then push pebbles half-deep into the mortar to create the pattern. Lay a plank over the finished mosaic and push gently to achieve an even top.

4 Top up areas of mortar if necessary. A fine spray of water will smooth the mortar surface. Also use water to clean the surfaces of the pebbles. Leave the mortar to set before walking on the mosaic.

Looking up

Sunrise and sunset

Daylight is limited now, triggering the top growth of many herbaceous plants to die down or dry out. Leave these stems and seedheads intact to provide wildlife habitats.

DAY	LONDON		EDINBURGH	
	Sunrise	Sunset	Sunrise	Sunset
Sun, 1 Nov	6:52:25 am	4:35:44 pm	7:17:47 am	4:34:55 pm
Mon, 2 Nov	6:54:10 am	4:33:56 pm	7:19:54 am	4:32:47 pm
Tue, 3 Nov	6:55:56 am	4:32:11 pm	7:22:01 am	4:30:39 pm
Wed, 4 Nov	6:57:41 am	4:30:26 pm	7:24:07 am	4:28:34 pm
Thu, 5 Nov	6:59:26 am	4:28:44 pm	7:26:14 am	4:26:30 pm
Fri, 6 Nov	7:01:11 am	4:27:03 pm	7:28:20 am	4:24:28 pm
Sat, 7 Nov	7:02:56 am	4:25:24 pm	7:30:27 am	4:22:28 pm
Sun, 8 Nov	7:04:41 am	4:23:47 pm	7:32:33 am	4:20:30 pm
Mon, 9 Nov	7:06:26 am	4:22:12 pm	7:34:38 am	4:18:33 pm
Tue, 10 Nov	7:08:10 am	4:20:38 pm	7:36:44 am	4:16:39 pm
Wed, 11 Nov	7:09:54 am	4:19:07 pm	7:38:49 am	4:14:47 pm
Thu, 12 Nov	7:11:38 am	4:17:38 pm	7:40:53 am	4:12:57 pm
Fri, 13 Nov	7:13:21 am	4:16:11 pm	7:42:57 am	4:11:09 pm
Sat, 14 Nov	7:15:04 am	4:14:46 pm	7:45:00 am	4:09:24 pm
Sun, 15 Nov	7:16:46 am	4:13:24 pm	7:47:03 am	4:07:41 pm
Mon, 16 Nov	7:18:28 am	4:12:03 pm	7:49:05 am	4:06:01 pm
Tue, 17 Nov	7:20:09 am	4:10:45 pm	7:51:06 am	4:04:23 pm
Wed, 18 Nov	7:21:49 am	4:09:30 pm	7:53:06 am	4:02:47 pm
Thu, 19 Nov	7:23:28 am	4:08:17 pm	7:55:05 am	4:01:14 pm
Fri, 20 Nov	7:25:07 am	4:07:06 pm	7:57:02 am	3:59:45 pm
Sat, 21 Nov	7:26:44 am	4:05:58 pm	7:58:59 am	3:58:17 pm
Sun, 22 Nov	7:28:21 am	4:04:53 pm	8:00:55 am	3:56:53 pm
Mon, 23 Nov	7:29:56 am	4:03:50 pm	8:02:49 am	3:55:32 pm
Tue, 24 Nov	7:31:30 am	4:02:50 pm	8:04:41 am	3:54:14 pm
Wed, 25 Nov	7:33:03 am	4:01:53 pm	8:06:32 am	3:52:59 pm
Thu, 26 Nov	7:34:35 am	4:00:59 pm	8:08:21 am	3:51:47 pm
Fri, 27 Nov	7:36:05 am	4:00:07 pm	8:10:08 am	3:50:38 pm
Sat, 28 Nov	7:37:34 am	3:59:19 pm	8:11:54 am	3:49:33 pm
Sun, 29 Nov	7:39:01 am	3:58:33 pm	8:13:37 am	3:48:31 pm
Mon, 30 Nov	7:40:27 am	3:57:51 pm	8:15:19 am	3:47:33 pm

Moonrise and moonset

Moon phases

◗ **THIRD QUARTER** 1 November ◖ **FIRST QUARTER** 17 November
● **NEW MOON** 9 November ○ **FULL MOON** 24 November

DAY	LONDON			EDINBURGH		
	Moonrise	Moonset	Moonrise	Moonrise	Moonset	Moonrise
1 Nov		13:42	22:28		14:17	22:20
2 Nov		14:02	23:53		14:30	23:52
3 Nov		14:18			14:39	
4 Nov	01:14	14:31		01:21	14:46	
5 Nov	02:33	14:43		02:45	14:53	
6 Nov	03:50	14:55		04:08	14:59	
7 Nov	05:07	15:09		05:31	15:07	
8 Nov	06:23	15:25		06:55	15:17	
9 Nov	07:40	15:46		08:19	15:31	
10 Nov	08:54	16:14		09:40	15:52	
11 Nov	10:02	16:51		10:53	16:25	
12 Nov	10:59	17:41		11:52	17:13	
13 Nov	11:43	18:41		12:33	18:18	
14 Nov	12:16	19:50		13:00	19:32	
15 Nov	12:40	21:02		13:17	20:51	
16 Nov	12:59	22:15		13:29	22:11	
17 Nov	13:13	23:29		13:38	23:31	
18 Nov	13:26			13:45		
19 Nov		00:43	13:38		00:51	13:51
20 Nov		01:59	13:50		02:13	13:58
21 Nov		03:18	14:04		03:39	14:06
22 Nov		04:43	14:21		05:10	14:16
23 Nov		06:12	14:44		06:48	14:32
24 Nov		07:43	15:17		08:28	14:57
25 Nov		09:09	16:07		10:00	15:41
26 Nov		10:19	17:16		11:11	16:50
27 Nov		11:09	18:40		11:55	18:21
28 Nov		11:43	20:11		12:21	20:00
29 Nov		12:07	21:39		12:36	21:37
30 Nov		12:24	23:03		12:47	23:08

Average temperature & rainfall

This table shows the average minimum and maximum temperatures, indicated by the blue and red dots, together with the average rainfall and number of rainy days for this month. The horizontal rules show how the figures have varied over the past decade.

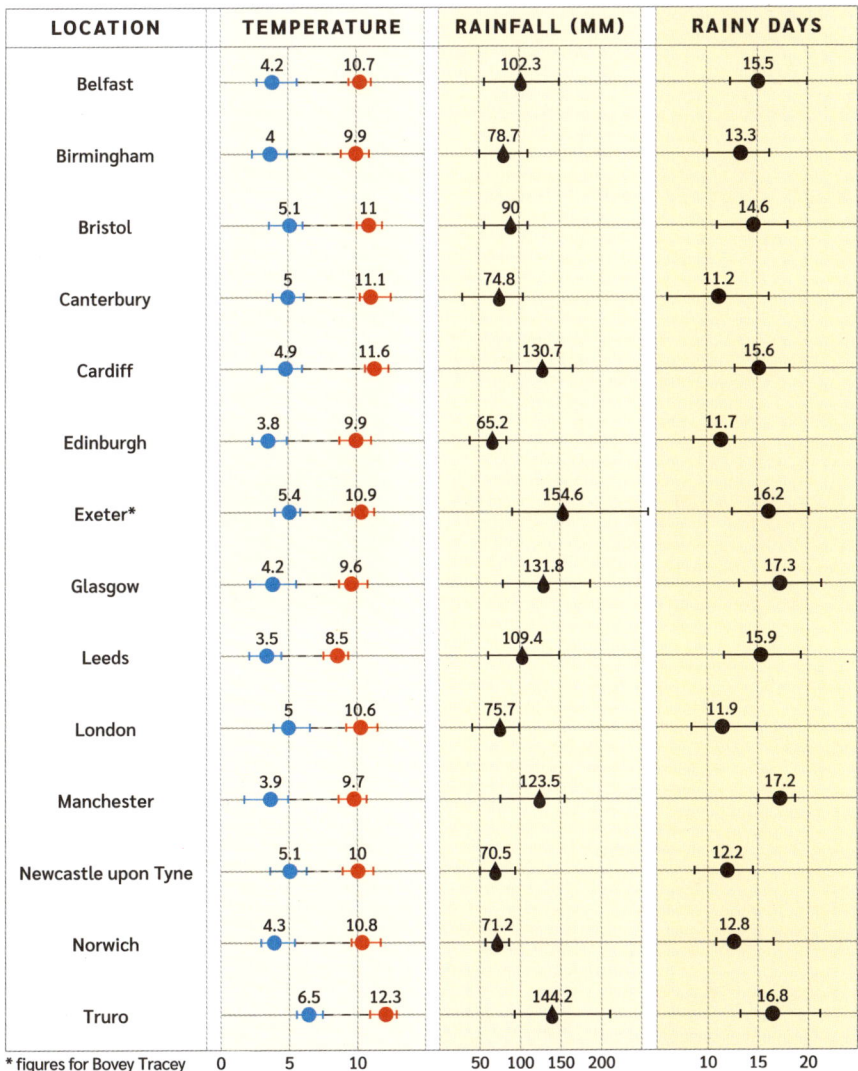

LOCATION	TEMPERATURE		RAINFALL (MM)	RAINY DAYS
Belfast	4.2	10.7	102.3	15.5
Birmingham	4	9.9	78.7	13.3
Bristol	5.1	11	90	14.6
Canterbury	5	11.1	74.8	11.2
Cardiff	4.9	11.6	130.7	15.6
Edinburgh	3.8	9.9	65.2	11.7
Exeter*	5.4	10.9	154.6	16.2
Glasgow	4.2	9.6	131.8	17.3
Leeds	3.5	8.5	109.4	15.9
London	5	10.6	75.7	11.9
Manchester	3.9	9.7	123.5	17.2
Newcastle upon Tyne	5.1	10	70.5	12.2
Norwich	4.3	10.8	71.2	12.8
Truro	6.5	12.3	144.2	16.8

* figures for Bovey Tracey

Temperature scale: 0 5 10
Rainfall scale: 50 100 150 200
Rainy days scale: 10 15 20

Edible garden

The autumn harvest is well under way, with cool season crops such as parsnips, carrots and turnips becoming sweeter after the first frosts, while herbs and leafy crops grown under cover add fresh greens to the table during the winter.

Vegetables

SOW INDOORS OR UNDER CLOCHES
Herbs such as basil, chives, dill and parsley for overwintering indoors; pak choi; pea shoots; spring onions; winter salad leaves.

SOW OUTDOORS Broad beans.

PLANT OUT Asparagus crowns; garlic sets; shallots; spring cabbages (at the beginning of the month) and pak choi sown in summer.

HARVEST NOW Beetroots; Brussels sprouts ❶; carrots; cauliflowers; celeriac; chicory and endive; Chinese artichokes; Florence fennel; hardy salad leaves; kale; leeks; pak choi; parsnips; perpetual spinach; spring-sown cabbages; swedes; turnips.

Fruit

PLANT NOW Bare-root fruit trees and bushes such as blackberries, currants, and gooseberries; potted blueberry plants; potted patio fruits; raspberry canes; rhubarb; strawberry runners.

HARVEST Apples; medlars; pears; quinces.

HERB OF THE MONTH: SWEET CICELY (*Myrrhis odorata*)
Perfect for a shady garden, sweet cicely's tall stems provide a plentiful crop of sweet, aniseed-flavoured ferny foliage from spring to late autumn. The herb's tiny white flowers are held in flat-topped umbels and appear from late spring to summer. They are followed by spindle-shaped seedheads full of large edible seeds that can be added to salads and baked goods. Grow this easy perennial in any soil, except waterlogged, and some shade – it will even tolerate quite deep shade but may not produce as many flowers.

Challenges this month

Some fungal diseases are prevalent all year round and can be exacerbated by the wet soil conditions in November, while flooding after heavy autumn rain and storms can kill many plants if they are submerged for long periods.

GREY MOULD is a fungal disease that rots the buds, flowers and other plant parts of many ornamentals and soft fruit plants (pictured). It normally enters through a wound or infects plants under stress, but sometimes affects healthy plants, and spreads rapidly in humid conditions throughout the year. Symptoms include a fuzzy grey-brown mould and the affected areas will start to decay, then shrivel and die. To prevent it, remove infected leaves, buds and flowers from the soil or compost and increase ventilation around plants by spacing them apart more widely and opening greenhouse windows. Do not use fungicides since they will have little effect on the disease and pose a risk to the environment.

IVY (*Hedera*) is a self-clinging climber, native to the UK, that provides a valuable source of food and shelter for a wide range of wildlife. It can also help keep buildings cooler in summer and warmer in winter. However, it may cause problems when growing up old trees, where its additional weight makes them unsound. The leafy stems can also clog drains and gutters, and grow over windows, while the aerial roots may damage old or unsound brickwork. To remove problematic plants, cut through the stems at ground level and dig out as much of the woody stump as possible, and any subsequent growth. Aerial roots that persist on surfaces can be removed with a hard brush.

FLOODED GROUND can kill garden plants if they are submerged for long periods. Unable to take up oxygen or diffuse carbon dioxide, roots literally drown, causing yellow leaves, root rot, and stunted growth. Flooding may be due to heavy rain, compacted soils, or overwhelmed drains. The water often carries pollutants, so wear gloves to wash down hard surfaces and collect up any debris after it subsides, and don't eat crops affected by flooding or use the soil for crops for a further two years. Keep off the soil until it is dry and remove any damaged plants. In the longer term, break up compacted soils, add mulches to improve drainage (see p.24) and, if you have a high water table, consider installing drains, if practical.

Garden benefactors

Centipedes

Noted for their many legs and scuttling crawl, members of this group of invertebrates are predators and help to keep unwanted insects that feed on plants and crops in check.

Similar in appearance to millipedes, which are vegetarians and eat decaying organic matter, centipedes have just one pair of legs per body segment, while their cousins have two pairs per segment, although few produce hundreds of legs, as their common name implies.

There are over 50 species of centipede in Britain and most are orange-brown in colour and adults grow to about 3cm (1¼in) in length. They live in the soil or under stones and logs, and come out at night to feed on slugs, flies, spiders and worms, paralysing their prey with an injection of venom, emitted from specially adapted, pincer-like front legs. They also use this approach to ward off predators, such as birds, mice and beetles, although centipede species found in Britain do not harm humans.

Centipedes are active in our gardens all year round, and reproduce during the warmer months, when the females lay between 20 and 100 eggs, depending on the species, in dark, damp places. The eggs hatch into nymphs that resemble the adults, and then moult a few times as they grow – some species accumulate more legs during this process. An adult centipede can live for several years.

To protect this army of useful predators, refrain from using pesticides, which may kill them and their prey. Also provide suitable habitats, such as leaf and log piles, compost heaps, stones and uncultivated areas of the garden.

Design masterclass

Dave Green

Horticulturist, landscape architect and garden designer, Dave Green is passionate about plants and uses them in imaginative ways to create accessible, sustainable, tranquil outdoor spaces that help to improve wellbeing. Accolades include his 2025 RHS Chelsea Flower Show 'The London Square Chelsea Pensioners Garden', and the 2023 'RHS Garden of Royal Reflection and Celebration', a tribute to the late Queen Elizabeth and King Charles. He also won a gold, 'Best in Category' and 'Best Construction' for his 'Stop and Pause Garden' at the 2019 RHS Hampton Court Palace Garden Festival.

After initially studying management and working in business and IT, Dave changed careers to pursue his love of horticulture. He studied at Pershore College and went on to work as an apprentice at Birmingham Botanical Gardens.

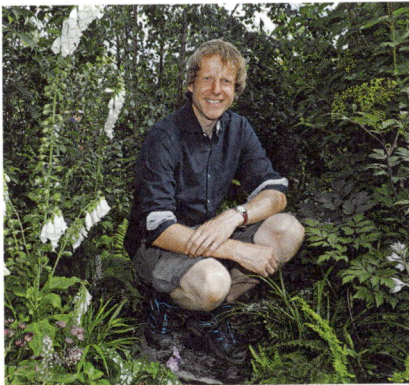

Dave then moved to work and study at RHS Wisley, and later became Show Manager for the RHS Hampton Court Palace Flower Show. In 2017 he left to set up his own studio and take a Masters degree in Landscape Architecture at Birmingham City University.

DESIGNING A SUSTAINABLE GARDEN

Dave designed the new Greener Skills Garden at RHS Garden Wisley, which includes the following sustainable ideas.

▶ 'Habitat towers for wildlife can be made by stacking small prunings and leaves inside a tepee made from timber posts (tree and shrub stems are ideal). The contents will rot down after a year or two to make a valuable soil improver, too.'

▶ 'When choosing plants, always look at those thriving nearby to identify what will grow well in your garden. From your observations, identify some plants to grow from seed or cuttings and enjoy the process of nurturing them as they grow.'

▶ 'Made objects for the garden add a personal touch and can be very sustainable. Try plant labels made from timber offcuts, bird feeders from teacups, and paper pots using old newspapers. Including friends and family in a communal activity can be fun, too, and will make memories as well as artefacts.'

Plants for difficult places

Coastal gardens

The dual effects of strong winds (see pp.42–3) and salt spray can make coastal gardens very challenging and these conditions will limit your plant choices. However, maritime climates also tend to be mild and less prone to frost and snow, allowing tender plants that would struggle in cold, inland areas to thrive.

If you have space, consider planting a hedge to create some shelter for you and your plants. *Elaeagnus* (see p.43), *Cotoneaster lacteus* (see p.142) and *Griselinia littoralis* are all good options for a coastal hedge. First, erect a brushwood screen in the path of the oncoming wind and then plant your hedge behind it. The screen will protect your hedging plants while they are establishing. For a more immediate solution, try a slatted fence that allows some wind to pass through, but avoid solid structures such as walls, which can create wind turbulence behind them and exacerbate the problem.

Plants such as *Phormium*, *Griselinia* and *Crambe* have thick, waxy foliage that helps protect the plant and reduces stress caused by coastal weather. If you are looking for a tree, the tamarisk is a popular choice for a seaside location, its small, scaly leaves and lax branches coping well in windy sites. The perennial sea holly (*Eryngium*) is also tolerant of coastal winds and salt spray, its silvery leaves reflecting strong light in sunny

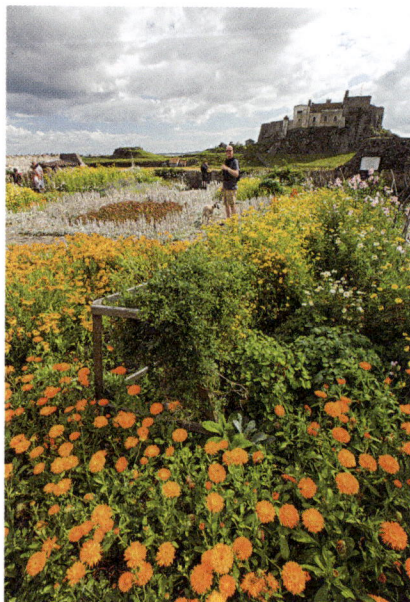

The plants in Gertrude Jekyll's garden at Holy Island in Northumberland all tolerate salt-laden wind.

gardens, while the little ground-hugging Mexican fleabane (*Erigeron karvinskianus*) helps to protect and cover bare soil. It flowers almost all year in mild coastal locations, and will self-seed into cracks in paving and next to houses to create a soft, flowery effect.

Coastal winds whip over the soil, stripping it of moisture, but adding a mulch (see pp.36–7) can help to mitigate the drying effects. Many coastal plants do not like wet stems, however, so opt for gravel or small stones, rather than rotted compost or manure.

CHOOSING PLANTS FOR COASTS

❶ Tamarisk 'Pink Cascade'
(*Tamarix ramosissima* 'Pink Cascade')
A deciduous shrub or small tree with reddish branches, needle-like green foliage and feathery heads of small pink flowers in late summer and autumn.
H&S: 5 × 5m (16 × 16ft)

Phormium 'Sundowner'
An evergreen perennial that forms a fountain of arching, sword-shaped, bronze-green leaves with red and pink stripes. **H&S:** 1 × 1m (39 × 39in)

❷ Globe thistle 'Veitch's Blue'
(*Echinops ritro* 'Veitch's Blue')
Blue spherical flowerheads appear on this tall hardy perennial over a long period in summer. The spiny, dark green leaves are downy white beneath.
H&S: 90 × 45cm (36 × 18in)

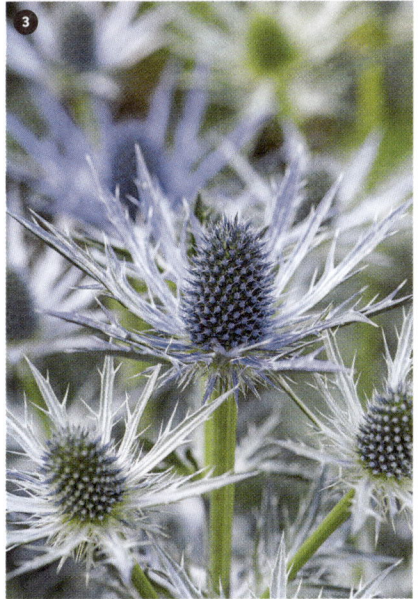

❸ Sea holly 'Big Blue'
(*Eryngium* × *zabelii* 'Big Blue')
This hardy perennial's spiky, silvery-green foliage forms a skirt beneath the large thistle-like flowers with bright blue bracts (petal like structures) that appear in summer. **H&S:** 70 × 60cm (28 × 24in)

Greater sea kale (*Crambe cordifolia*)
A towering hardy perennial, it produces dark green, lobed leaves and airy sprays of small, scented white flowers in summer. **H&S:** 1.8 × 1.2m (6 × 4ft)

December

As winter sets in and the year comes to a close, the sepia landscape crystallized with snow and ice signals a time for rest and reflection. Seasonal celebrations are punctuated with garish glitter, but no tinsel or decoration can compete with the beauty of a polished holly leaf, the spiral pattern on a pine cone, or a robin's red breast – gifts from nature in the darkest of months.

KEY EVENTS
Hanukkah, 4–12 December
Winter Solstice (*Shortest day of the year*), 21 December
Christmas Day, 25 December
New Year's Eve, 31 December

What to do in December

The festive season is upon us and much of the garden is taking a rest. The long nights offer time indoors to make plans for next year and pre-order seeds and plants to arrive in spring. There's still time to plant spring bulbs – up to the third week in December should guarantee a display – while bare-root plants can also be planted this month.

In the garden

PLAN YOUR FLOWER DISPLAYS for next year. Seed catalogues arrive in the post in late autumn, tempting us with new varieties and colourful flowers we have yet to try. Or look online for specialist nurseries for unusual plants – there are so many wonderful independents run by passionate people to support. **1**

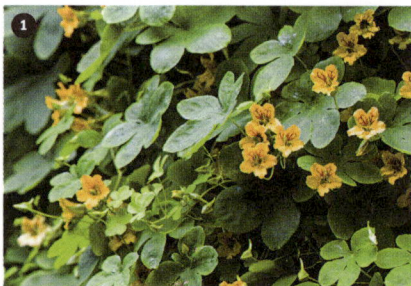

PLANT AN EVERGREEN HEDGE for a permanent boundary or screen, and to offer safe nesting sites for birds, too. Wildlife-friendly options include yew (*Taxus baccata*), *Cotoneaster lacteus*, holly (*Ilex aquifolium*) and *Viburnum tinus* 'Eve Price'. Plants from specialist retailers are usually cheaper than those from garden centres and will be delivered to your door. Just remember that evergreens will need pruning once or twice a year. **2**

LEAVE THE FADED FLOWERHEADS on mophead hydrangeas to protect the swelling buds further down the stems from frost. You can then cut them back to healthy buds in spring.

PRUNING TIP
Apple and pear trees
Remove no more than 10–20 per cent of the tree canopy and aim for a balanced shape. Start by taking out dead, diseased and crossing stems, then thin congested growth. Also remove strong stems growing towards the centre of the tree and those growing downwards. Any strong vertical stems should be shortened to a side shoot, while new stems on each of the main branches can be cut back by one-third to an outward-facing bud. On tip-bearing fruit trees such as 'Bramley's Seedling' apples, leave some of the new stems uncut – these will bear fruit next year. Instead, prune back older wood by about a quarter.

HARVEST SPRIGS OF HOLLY with berries, twining ivy stems, rose hips, and fluffy clematis seedheads to make natural Christmas garlands and wreaths, or try a more contemporary look with large-leaved evergreens (see p.224). Add more colour with dried orange slices. Cut the fruit into thin slices, place on parchment on a baking tray, and pop in a preheated oven at 100°C/gas ¼ for three hours. Leave to cool before attaching them with wire. ❸

In the fruit & veg patch

REMOVE YELLOWING LEAVES from your winter brassicas such as cabbages, Brussels sprouts and kale to prevent the spread of diseases they may harbour.

daylight, but out of direct sun, and consistent temperatures of 16–21°C (65–70°F). Avoid cold, draughty spots or temperatures below 12°C (54°F), which will cause the leaves and bracts (the colourful flowerlike modified leaves that surround the small flowers) to fall. Water plants sparingly with tepid water when the top of the compost feels dry.

INCREASE HUMIDITY for ferns and other tropical plants. Heating in winter can dry the atmosphere and these plants may suffer, so place them on shallow trays filled with pebbles and water. Also move plants away from radiators.

DIGGING A TRENCH in winter for next year's beans is a traditional practice, but not essential. Fill it with kitchen waste (not cooked food), a little cardboard and scrunched newspaper before replacing the excavated soil. These will rot down by late spring, adding a little fertility and possibly helping to retain moisture.

KEEP AN EYE ON BIRD-PROOF NETTING during the winter, and brush off heavy snow to prevent it breaking. Alternatively, remove netting earlier in the season (see p.185). ❹

Indoors

POINSETTIAS BRING CHEER during the winter seasonal festivities, but to thrive they need a bright room with lots of

MONEY-SAVING IDEA
Decorate presents with natural materials
Save money on shiny bows and tinsel that are difficult to recycle by using a selection of beautiful natural stems that are all compostable and will not damage the environment. Harvest red rose hips, pine cones and evergreen foliage from the garden or forage for them in your local area. Wrap your presents in plain brown paper and secure with natural jute twine or reusable string made from recycled materials. Then simply poke your natural materials under the twine, adding a few cinnamon sticks for fragrance – they can also be added to the compost bin after use.

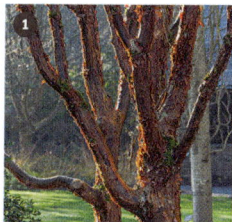

Plants of the month

1. Paperbark maple (*Acer griseum*)
2. Hard fern (*Blechnum spicant)*
3. Evergreen sedge (*Carex* 'Ice Dance' pictured)
4. North America wild oats (*Chasmanthium latifolium*)
5. Golden-twig dogwood (*Cornus sericea* 'Flaviramea')
6. Teasel (*Dipsacus fullonum*)
7. Japanese aralia (*Fatsia japonica* 'Spider's Web' pictured)
8. Leucothoe (*Leucothoe keiskei* 'Royal Ruby' pictured)
9. Winter honeysuckle (*Lonicera × purpusii* 'Winter Beauty' pictured)
10. Japanese spurge (*Pachysandra terminalis* 'Variegata' pictured)
11. Firethorn (*Pyracantha* 'Fiery Cascade' pictured)

Project: Make a foliage wreath

No front door is complete this month without a seasonal wreath, and while traditional holly and ivy are a classic choice, larger and more intricately shaped leaves will create a bolder, more contemporary design. To make this wreath, look around your garden for plants with waxy or glossy leaves such as *Fatsia japonica*, young *Eucalyptus*, *Bergenia cordifolia* or *Magnolia grandiflora*, which won't wilt as quickly as softer foliage. And for a touch of colour, add a few sprigs of berries.

YOU WILL NEED
Wire wreath ring
Ethically sourced
    sphagnum moss or
    lawn moss
Selection of leaves
Garden berry sprigs
Florists' wire

1 Lay down the wreath ring and tie florists' wire to one side. Place a fist-sized clump of moss on top then fix on to the ring by tightly winding florists' wire around it. Repeat until the whole ring is thickly covered.

2 Place the longest sprigs on to the wreath, so that they point outwards. Wind the wire around the stems, anchoring each in place. Then tie off the wire, leaving a loop at the top for hanging.

3 Add the bold, glossy leaves and stems of berries last, poking them through the wires and into the moss. Water the wreath every three days by spritzing it with a mister or submerging in a tray of water and leaving it to drain before rehanging on the door.

4 There are several ways to hang a wreath on your door: the simplest is to attach it to the knocker with thin wire or nail or screw a hook on to a wooden door. Alternatively, use a suction hook on a glass or PVC door.

Looking up

Sunrise and sunset

The day length is limited to about eight hours in December, too little for deciduous plants that have now all shed their leaves and will remain dormant over winter.

	LONDON		EDINBURGH	
DAY	Sunrise	Sunset	Sunrise	Sunset
Tue, 1 Dec	7:41:50 am	3:57:11 pm	8:16:58 am	3:46:38 pm
Wed, 2 Dec	7:43:12 am	3:56:35 pm	8:18:34 am	3:45:47 pm
Thu, 3 Dec	7:44:32 am	3:56:02 pm	8:20:09 am	3:45:00 pm
Fri, 4 Dec	7:45:50 am	3:55:32 pm	8:21:40 am	3:44:16 pm
Sat, 5 Dec	7:47:06 am	3:55:05 pm	8:23:09 am	3:43:36 pm
Sun, 6 Dec	7:48:20 am	3:54:42 pm	8:24:36 am	3:43:00 pm
Mon, 7 Dec	7:49:31 am	3:54:21 pm	8:25:59 am	3:42:28 pm
Tue, 8 Dec	7:50:40 am	3:54:05 pm	8:27:19 am	3:42:00 pm
Wed, 9 Dec	7:51:47 am	3:53:51 pm	8:28:36 am	3:41:36 pm
Thu, 10 Dec	7:52:51 am	3:53:41 pm	8:29:50 am	3:41:16 pm
Fri, 11 Dec	7:53:53 am	3:53:34 pm	8:31:01 am	3:41:01 pm
Sat, 12 Dec	7:54:52 am	3:53:31 pm	8:32:08 am	3:40:49 pm
Sun, 13 Dec	7:55:49 am	3:53:31 pm	8:33:12 am	3:40:42 pm
Mon, 14 Dec	7:56:42 am	3:53:34 pm	8:34:12 am	3:40:38 pm
Tue, 15 Dec	7:57:33 am	3:53:41 pm	8:35:09 am	3:40:39 pm
Wed, 16 Dec	7:58:21 am	3:53:51 pm	8:36:02 am	3:40:44 pm
Thu, 17 Dec	7:59:06 am	3:54:05 pm	8:36:51 am	3:40:54 pm
Fri, 18 Dec	7:59:48 am	3:54:22 pm	8:37:36 am	3:41:08 pm
Sat, 19 Dec	8:00:26 am	3:54:42 pm	8:38:17 am	3:41:25 pm
Sun, 20 Dec	8:01:02 am	3:55:06 pm	8:38:55 am	3:41:47 pm
Mon, 21 Dec	8:01:35 am	3:55:33 pm	8:39:28 am	3:42:14 pm
Tue, 22 Dec	8:02:04 am	3:56:03 pm	8:39:57 am	3:42:44 pm
Wed, 23 Dec	8:02:30 am	3:56:36 pm	8:40:22 am	3:43:19 pm
Thu, 24 Dec	8:02:53 am	3:57:13 pm	8:40:43 am	3:43:57 pm
Fri, 25 Dec	8:03:13 am	3:57:53 pm	8:41:00 am	3:44:40 pm
Sat, 26 Dec	8:03:29 am	3:58:36 pm	8:41:13 am	3:45:27 pm
Sun, 27 Dec	8:03:42 am	3:59:22 pm	8:41:21 am	3:46:17 pm
Mon, 28 Dec	8:03:52 am	4:00:11 pm	8:41:26 am	3:47:12 pm
Tue, 29 Dec	8:03:58 am	4:01:03 pm	8:41:26 am	3:48:10 pm
Wed, 30 Dec	8:04:01 am	4:01:58 pm	8:41:22 am	3:49:12 pm
Thu, 31 Dec	8:04:02 am	4:02:56 pm	8:41:14 am	3:50:18 pm

Moonrise and moonset

Moon phases

◗ **THIRD QUARTER** 1 December   ◑ **FIRST QUARTER** 17 December   ◗ **THIRD QUARTER**
● **NEW MOON** 9 December   ○ **FULL MOON** 24 December   30 December

DAY	LONDON			EDINBURGH		
	Moonrise	Moonset	Moonrise	Moonrise	Moonset	Moonrise
1 Dec		12:38			12:55	
2 Dec	00:23	12:50		00:34	13:02	
3 Dec	01:40	13:03		01:57	13:08	
4 Dec	02:56	13:16		03:19	13:16	
5 Dec	04:12	13:31		04:41	13:25	
6 Dec	05:28	13:50		06:04	13:38	
7 Dec	06:42	14:15		07:25	13:56	
8 Dec	07:51	14:50		08:41	14:25	
9 Dec	08:52	15:35		09:44	15:08	
10 Dec	09:40	16:33		10:31	16:08	
11 Dec	10:16	17:39		11:02	17:19	
12 Dec	10:43	18:50		11:22	18:37	
13 Dec	11:03	20:02		11:36	19:56	
14 Dec	11:19	21:15		11:45	21:15	
15 Dec	11:32	22:27		11:53	22:33	
16 Dec	11:43	23:40		11:59	23:52	
17 Dec	11:55			12:05		
18 Dec		00:55	12:07		01:13	12:12
19 Dec		02:14	12:22		02:38	12:21
20 Dec		03:38	12:41		04:10	12:33
21 Dec		05:07	13:08		05:47	12:53
22 Dec		06:35	13:49		07:24	13:25
23 Dec		07:55	14:48		08:47	14:21
24 Dec		08:56	16:07		09:45	15:45
25 Dec		09:39	17:39		10:20	17:25
26 Dec		10:07	19:13		10:40	19:07
27 Dec		10:28	20:42		10:53	20:44
28 Dec		10:44	22:07		11:03	22:16
29 Dec		10:57	23:27		11:10	23:42
30 Dec		11:09			11:17	
31 Dec	00:45	11:22		01:06	11:24	

Average temperature & rainfall

This table shows the average minimum and maximum temperatures, indicated by the blue and red dots, together with the average rainfall and number of rainy days for this month. The horizontal rules show how the figures have varied over the past decade.

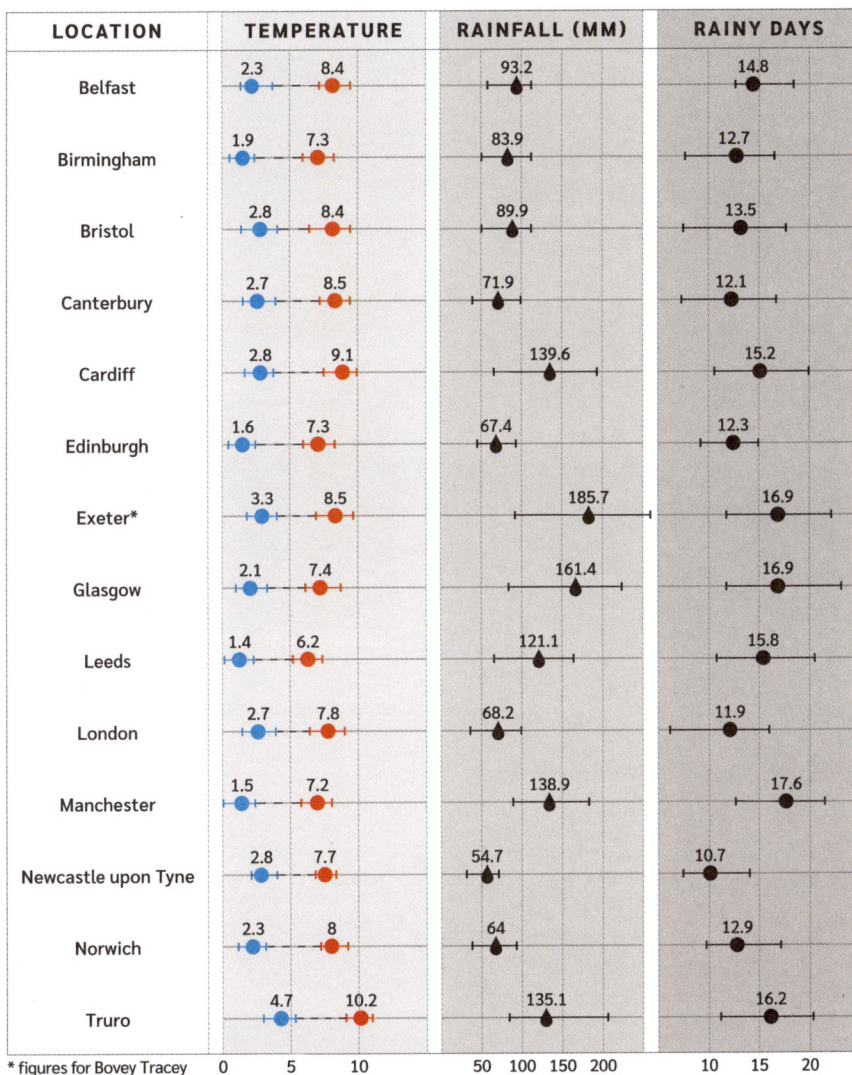

LOCATION	TEMPERATURE		RAINFALL (MM)	RAINY DAYS
Belfast	2.3	8.4	93.2	14.8
Birmingham	1.9	7.3	83.9	12.7
Bristol	2.8	8.4	89.9	13.5
Canterbury	2.7	8.5	71.9	12.1
Cardiff	2.8	9.1	139.6	15.2
Edinburgh	1.6	7.3	67.4	12.3
Exeter*	3.3	8.5	185.7	16.9
Glasgow	2.1	7.4	161.4	16.9
Leeds	1.4	6.2	121.1	15.8
London	2.7	7.8	68.2	11.9
Manchester	1.5	7.2	138.9	17.6
Newcastle upon Tyne	2.8	7.7	54.7	10.7
Norwich	2.3	8	64	12.9
Truro	4.7	10.2	135.1	16.2

* figures for Bovey Tracey	0	5	10	50 100 150 200	10 15 20

Edible garden

Activity in the productive garden slows in winter as the low light levels and cold temperatures limit germination and growth. However, you can still sow some salad leaves and herbs in a heated greenhouse or on a warm windowsill indoors.

Vegetables

SOW INDOORS ON A WINDOWSILL Herbs such as basil, chives, dill and parsley for growing over winter indoors; minigreens such as mustard and cress; pea shoots; winter salad leaves.

HARVEST NOW Brussels sprouts; cabbages including savoys; carrots; celeriac; hardy salad leaves; Jerusalem artichokes; kale; leeks; parsnips; perpetual spinach; swedes; turnips; winter radishes.

Fruit

PLANT NOW Bare-root fruit trees and bushes such as blackberries, currants and gooseberries; potted blueberry plants; raspberry and hybrid berry canes; rhubarb crowns.

HARVEST Citrus grown indoors. **1**

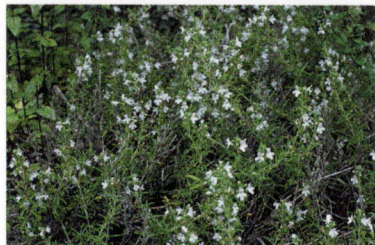

HERB OF THE MONTH: WINTER SAVORY (*Satureja montana*)
As the name suggests, this lesser-known herb is a good choice if you are looking for fresh leaves over winter. Its narrow, lance-shaped dark green or greyish-green leaves are said to aid digestion and soothe bee stings, but they are more often used to add a peppery flavour to savoury dishes and stuffing. Winter savory is a hardy semi-evergreen, compact perennial that prefers a sunny position and moist but well-drained soil. The small pale mauve flowers add to its appeal in summer.

Challenges this month

Unwanted insects can continue to cause a nuisance on houseplants in a warm home, even in the depths of winter, so be vigilant and take action quickly. Birds may also be munching on unprotected winter crops this month.

GLASSHOUSE LEAFHOPPER is a tiny, pale green insect with brown markings (pictured) that causes pale mottling on the upper leaf surfaces of a wide range of plants in the greenhouse and on houseplants. The spots can merge together, giving the leaves a chlorotic appearance that could be mistaken for a nutrient deficiency. You will also notice the adults jumping off the leaves when you brush against them, while their creamy white, wingless nymphs are less active. The immature nymphs also shed white cast skins on the undersides of damaged leaves. Leafhoppers do not affect the growth or vigour of affected plants and are best tolerated. Other species of leafhopper live outside in gardens and these do not affect plant growth either and should be left to feed other wildlife.

RED DEAD NETTLE (*Lamium purpureum*) is a decorative plant with non-stinging, nettle-shaped leaves and pink spring and summer flowers that help to feed bees. It is known as a weed because it spreads rapidly via seed and its stems and roots, and quickly overwhelms other plants. It can also carry the cucumber mosaic and potato leaf-roll viruses. To keep unwanted plants in check, deadhead flowers before they set seed, hoe off seedlings, and dig out mature plants and take them to your municipal green waste site.

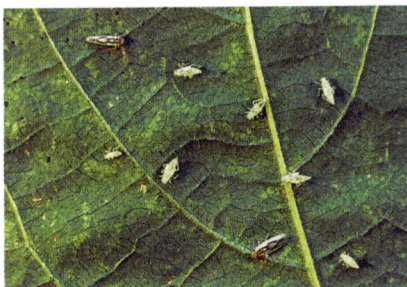

WOOD PIGEONS are large UK-native birds that form part of a garden's ecosystem, but, sadly, they are also partial to crops, such as cabbages, broccoli, and peas, tearing at the foliage and often reducing plants to a few leaf stalks. Rarely deterred by scarecrows or other devices, the best way to keep pigeons off your crops is to cover them with bird-proof netting or a fruit cage. If using nets, make sure they are taut, so these and other birds do not become entangled in them. Spraying crops with deterrent products based on calcium chloride such as Grazers G1 may also give some protection against pigeons.

Garden benefactors

House sparrow

Loved for their chirpy calls and gregarious habits, these sociable little birds have always been cherished by gardeners. They eat seeds, berries, grain and fresh buds, and also catch insect prey, including aphids and caterpillars, in spring and summer to feed to their chicks, thereby helping to keep populations of these plant-eating invertebrates in check.

The males and females look very similar, but the males have a black bib and more defined grey markings on their heads, while the females often sport a pale yellow strip behind their eyes (pictured).

Sparrows nest from April to August in holes or crevices in buildings and ivy-covered walls and fences, as well as in hedges and nest boxes, often congregating in loose colonies. In a good year, they may produce three broods of chicks in one season, laying up to eight eggs in each clutch. Both parents incubate the eggs, which hatch after 11 to 14 days, and the chicks then fledge 14 to 16 days after that.

Reports show that house sparrow numbers have plummeted in recent years, with almost 30 million disappearing from the UK since 1970, although there has been a slight recovery in more recent years in Scotland, Wales and Northern Ireland. Habitat loss and the use of insecticides that kill their prey are thought to be the main causes of the decline, but gardeners can help to protect them by not using chemicals in their gardens and increasing the number of berrying and seed-producing plants, such as holly (*Ilex aquifolium*), hawthorn (*Crataegus*), ivy (*Hedera helix*), teasel (*Dipsacus*), sunflowers (*Helianthus annuus*) and tickseed (*Coreopsis*).

Also provide plenty of nesting sites for colonies of these small birds – planting trees and hedges and leaving ivy to cover a boundary fence are some options, or put up several nesting boxes close together and at least 2m (6ft 6in) above the ground.

Design masterclass

Manoj Malde

Award-winning garden designer Manoj Malde is renowned for his contemporary style and bold use of colour, which he showcased in his spectacular 'RHS Eastern Eye Garden of Unity' Feature Garden for the 2023 RHS Chelsea Flower Show. It celebrated communities from diverse backgrounds with a smorgasbord of colourful materials and sculptural planting, reflecting Manoj's role as RHS Ambassador for inclusivity and diversity, with a remit to ensure the Society is open and appealing to all.

Manoj began his career in the fashion industry, before swapping the jet-setting world of haute couture for the natural beauty of plants and garden design. He studied at the English Gardening School and set up his business in 2011. Manoj has also starred in the popular TV series, *Your Garden Made Perfect*.

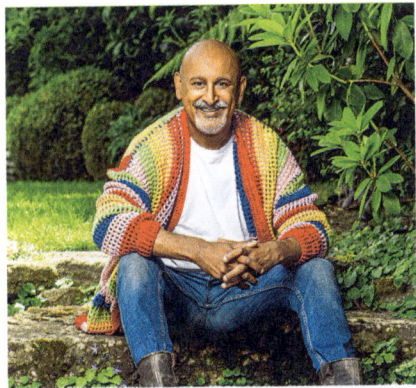

HOW TO DESIGN A VIBRANT GARDEN

If you would like to introduce more colour into your garden, Manoj offers advice on creating a palette of shades to make your design zing.

▶ 'Try basing your colours on a theme. For example, your inspiration could be a work by your favourite artist. Choose five to seven colours used in it, as well as shades and tones of your selection. Creating a scheme in this way will give it cohesion, especially if you repeat the colours throughout your design.'

▶ 'The light in the UK has a cool quality and some colours work better than others in gardens here. Dark backdrops such as anthracite and French navy are good choices, making the plant colours in front really pop out. Also, don't be afraid to experiment with brighter shades to see what effect they have.'

▶ 'If you're looking for long-lasting colour, pelargoniums are a good choice. The summer flowers come in a variety of pinks, reds, apricots and white, and bloom up to the frosts if deadheaded regularly. Others to try include abutilons, potentillas, penstemons, and sweet peas, which offer scent as well as colour. Let's not forget that green is a colour, too, so plant a few evergreens to introduce cooling shades of emerald and jade.'

Plants for difficult places

Frost pockets

A frost pocket is a low-lying area such as valley, dip or hollow in a cold region where frost travels downhill and collects at the bottom. A garden in a frost pocket is at higher risk of early and late frosts and has a shortened growing season, so whether your whole plot or just areas of it are affected, you will need some tough plants to cope with the icy conditions.

Cold air can also collect behind barriers such as fences or dense hedges that run across the slope. To prevent it becoming trapped in your garden, try making gaps in the barrier to allow the air to drain away down the hillside and reduce the effects of frost on your plants.

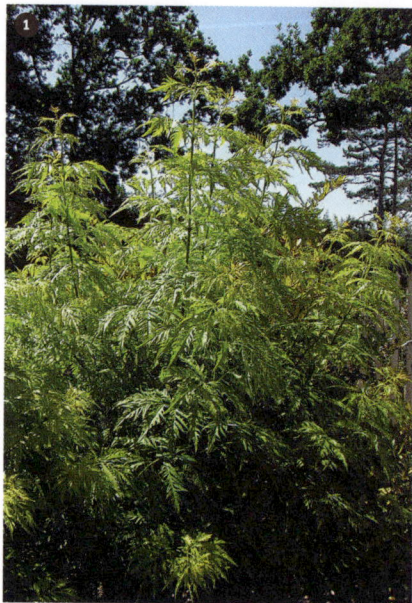

Wet clay soils that then freeze can cause more harm to plants than drier sandy soils, so add mulches (see pp.36–7) to improve drainage and create an insulating blanket over the roots. Planting slightly closer together than usual can also offer some protection.

The plants listed opposite are hardy down to at least –15°C (5°F) and will cope with the coldest winters in the UK. During spring and summer, the *Sambucus* and *Physocarpus* offer attractive foliage and flower interest, while tough little shrubs such as *Potentilla fruticosa* add a sprinkling of blooms later in the summer. The dwarf pine (*Pinus mugo*) and ferns such as *Dryopteris erythrosora* (see p.143) will create permanent evergreen structure and textural interest all year round, while hardy ornamental grasses such as the *Calamagrostis* also offer a sculptural quality for most of the year, their dried stems and seedheads standing proud over winter.

The classic winter flowers of hellebores introduce colour during the colder months, and most will cope in a frost pocket, while dainty little *Iris reticulata* such as 'Harmony' offers much-needed colour as the seasons turn.

CHOOSING FROST-PROOF PLANTS

1 Elder 'Sutherland Gold' (*Sambucus racemosa* 'Sutherland Gold')
Grown primarily for its deeply cut, bright golden-yellow leaves, this hardy deciduous shrub also produces small, conical heads of creamy-white flowers in spring, followed by glossy red berries, loved by birds, in autumn. **H&S:** 4 × 4m (16 × 16ft)

2 Ninebark LADY IN RED (*Physocarpus opulifolius* LADY IN RED)
The young red foliage of this hardy deciduous shrub turns brown-bronze as the season progresses, while domed clusters of pink flowers appear in early summer. **H&S:** 1.5 × 1.5m (5 × 5ft)

Dwarf mountain pine (*Pinus mugo*)
This relatively small conifer produces dark green needles, and small, egg-shaped brown cones in autumn. **H&S:** 3.5 × 5m (11 × 16ft)

Christmas rose (*Helleborus niger*)
Leathery, dark green, divided leaves adorn this evergreen perennial but they are best removed before the white, bowl-shaped flowers appear in winter to prevent the spread of fungal diseases. **H&S:** 30 × 45cm (12 × 18in)

3 Shrubby cinquefoil 'Pink Beauty' (*Potentilla fruticosa* 'Pink Beauty')
A bushy deciduous shrub that produces small, dark green leaves and pink, saucer-shaped flowers in summer and early autumn. **H&S:** 60 × 60cm (24 × 24in)

Iris 'Harmony'
This little reticulata-type dwarf iris produces blue or dark purple flowers with yellow markings from late winter to early spring above grassy foliage. **H&S:** 15 × 8cm (6 × 3in)

RHS gardens to visit

The RHS has five beautiful gardens to visit, which are open all year round and free to enter for RHS members and a family guest or two children (four children for joint memberships). There are also over 220 RHS partner gardens in the UK and abroad that offer free entry to RHS members, the details of which can be found at rhs.org.uk/gardens/ partner-gardens/.

For opening times, visit the garden websites listed.

BRIDGEWATER

The RHS's newest garden, Bridgewater opened in 2021 and has been dazzling visitors with its stunning garden displays ever since. A tour begins in the Worsley Welcome Garden, its ribbons of colourful planting setting the tone for your visit. The jewel in Bridgewater's crown is the Weston Walled Garden, which houses the stunning Paradise Garden, based on the layout of ancient Islamic gardens, and a contemporary Kitchen Garden that showcases a range of innovative productive growing ideas. The wider woodland, meadows and lakes add to the visitor experience, while the sparkling water and Asian-inspired planting in the Chinese Streamside Garden are not to be missed.

To plan your visit and for more details about the garden, head to rhs.org.uk/gardens/bridgewater/

RHS Garden Bridgewater
Occupation Road
Off Leigh Road
Worsley, Salford
Greater Manchester
M28 2LJ

HARLOW CARR

Set deep in the Yorkshire countryside, Harlow Carr offers a variety of beautiful gardens to enjoy, from lush lakeside walks to woodland and wildflower meadows. Highlights include the Main Borders, bursting with colourful, prairie-style planting; the stunning Winter Garden, with its inspiring, cold-season planting; a Kitchen Garden packed with ideas for home growers; and a Subtropical Garden that takes its inspiration from the colourful planting at Great Dixter in Sussex.

To plan your visit and for more details about the garden, head to rhs.org.uk/gardens/harlow-carr/

RHS Garden Harlow Carr
Crag Lane
Beckwithshaw
Harrogate
North Yorkshire
HG3 1QB

HYDE HALL

A jewel in the heart of rural Essex, Hyde Hall offers an eclectic mix of traditional and modern gardens, the most famous of which is the Dry Garden, showcasing colourful, drought-tolerant plants. Other highlights include the Hilltop Garden, with its roses and herbaceous borders; the Global Growth Vegetable Garden; ponds and meadows buzzing with wildlife; and an adventure playground where the children can let off steam.

To plan your visit and for more details about the garden, head to rhs.org.uk/gardens/hyde-hall/

RHS Garden Hyde Hall
Creephedge Lane
Rettendon, Chelmsford
Essex
CM3 8ET

ROSEMOOR

Surrounded by woodland and rolling hills, Rosemoor sits in the heart of the Torridge Valley in north Devon and offers a range of dazzling gardens to enjoy all year round. The Cherry Garden and orchards are decked with blossom in spring, while the romantic Rose Garden and Hot Garden are the stars of summer. The woods and Lady Anne's Arboretum blaze with fiery colours in autumn, and the Winter Garden is a must for cold-season inspiration.

To plan your visit and for more details about the garden, head to rhs.org.uk/gardens/rosemoor/

RHS Garden Rosemoor
Great Torrington
Devon
EX38 8PH

WISLEY

The RHS's flagship garden in Surrey, Wisley houses one of the largest plant collections in the world and offers 24 hectares (60 acres) to explore. From gardens showcasing prairie-style plants, roses and Mediterranean species to those designed for wildlife and wellbeing, Wisley offers something for everyone. The famous Glasshouse sits at the heart of the garden, its huge cathedral-like structure housing a world-class tender plant collection, while RHS Hilltop is the home of Gardening Science, where you can discover fascinating facts about plants and take part in a range of ongoing horticultural research studies.

To plan your visit and for more details about the garden, head to rhs.org.uk/gardens/wisley/

RHS Garden Wisley
Wisley Lane
Surrey
GU23 6QB

Index

Author biographies

ZIA ALLAWAY is the book's co-author (with Guy Barter) and has written many best-selling gardening books. A qualified horticulturist, Zia opens her own garden for the National Garden Scheme in Hertfordshire.

GUY BARTER is co-author and the RHS Chief Horticultural Advisor. Highly knowledgeable in all areas of horticulture and gardening, his specialist subjects are growing edibles and sustainability.

DR NICHOLAS CRYER is RHS Senior Scientist in Horticultural Water Management and an expert in water conservation and usage, national weather and climate change.

JAMES LAWRENCE is an RHS Principle Horticultural Adviser and landscape designer with a special interest in selecting sustainable planting for a range of different garden situations.

JAMES CURTIS, RHS Head Chef, devised the delicious recipes in this book as he does every day in the restaurant at RHS Garden Hyde Hall.

HELEN BOSTOCK is the RHS Senior Wildlife Specialist and promotes wildlife in the garden. She is also a lead on the RHS Plants for Pollinators scheme.

DR HAYLEY JONES, RHS Principal Entomologist and author of *RHS Slugs: Friend or Foe* (published by DK), researches and advises on garden invertebrates, including sustainable, wildlife-friendly management.

DR JASSY DRAKULIC is an RHS Senior Plant Pathologist and Mycologist who provides advice to members on the management of fungi and diseases in UK gardens.

Picture credits

© **RHS / Tim Sandall** 10t, 10b, 11, 12t, 13(4), 20t, 28t, 28b, 30, 32tl, 32m, 32b, 36, 39, 46t, 49(5), 49(6), 50l, 50r, 54, 55, 56t, 56b, 57tr, 66t, 66b, 67, 68t, 70, 77, 79, 82, 83t, 86, 87tl, 87tr, 88t, 88b, 89(1), 89(3), 89(8), 90l, 90r, 95, 97t, 107b, 108t, 108b, 109(2), 117tl, 117tr, 126, 127b, 129(5), 136t, 136b, 137r, 137bl, 148b, 149(4), 156t, 217t, 220b, 222t, 233l; **Jim Young** 12b, 150, 164, 165b, 167(11), 175tr, 175b, 181b, 184t, 186t, 186b, 204t, 204b, 205, 206, 212b; **RHS** 13(1), 13(7), 13(10), 20b, 60, 106t, 122b, 161t, 207(3), 207(8), 232, 233r; **RHS / Neil Hepworth** 13(2), 14, 29t, 37, 47, 57b, 69(5), 76t, 76b, 109(11), 110tl, 110bl, 110r, 114, 117b, 129(3), 130t, 130b, 135, 165m, 166, 167(10), 168t, 168m, 168b, 188l, 188r, 193, 208t, 208m, 208b, 224l, 224m, 224r; **RHS / Joanna Kossak** 13(3), 13(9), 49(9), 63b, 69(2), 69(6), 69(9), 89(10), 103b, 109(8), 149(8), 154, 167(7), 172, 173, 174, 187(1), 187(4), 187(10), 201t, 207(2), 207(4), 221l, 221r, 223(3), 223(8), 223(11); **RHS / Nicola Stocken** 13(5), 13(11), 31(2), 31(7), 43b, 49(8), 74, 102, 109(1), 109(7), 115, 129(10), 142, 149(2), 149(10), 161b, 167(3), 167(5), 167(9), 174l, 181t, 195t, 207(6), 217b, 223(7), 223(10); **RHS / Graham Titchmarsh** 13(6), 38b, 68b, 89(7), 122t, 194l, 228b; **RHS / Carol Sheppard** 13(8), 31(8), 31(10), 49(3), 49(7), 69(4), 69(8), 69(10), 89(2), 89(9), 100, 103t, 109(10), 123, 129(8), 143t, 149(5), 149(9), 149(11), 167(2), 187(3), 187(11), 195b, 223(2), 223(9); **RHS / Georgi Mabee** 18, 21, 57tl, 80, 146t, 158t, 192, 198, 214, 230; **RHS / Jason Ingram** 19, 25, 38t, 58, 69(7), 75, 78, 98, 118, 128t, 138, 149(6), 174r, 175tl, 176, 187(2), 194tr, 194br, 196, 212t; **Michael Ballard** 22; **Rachel Warne** 23; **RHS / Richard Bloom** 24, 31(5), 31(9), 62, 83b, 129(6), 201m, 207(7); **RHS / Barry Phillips** 29b, 69(1), 89(4), 89(11), 109(6), 129(11), 149(7), 187(5); **R A Kearton / Getty** 31(1); **RHS / Leigh Hunt** 31(3), 31(6), 49(1), 143m, 157; **RHS / Sue Drew** 31(4); **RHS / Philippa Gibson** 31(11), 63m, 89(5), 109(4), 129(1), 143b, 149(1), 223(5); **RHS / Andrew Halstead** 40, 99, 119, 120, 139, 229; **RHS / Luke MacGregor** 41, 159, 215; **RHS, Herbarium** 42, 49(4), 156b; **RHS / Mike Sleigh** 43t, 49(10), 69(3), 223(4); **Lokibaho / Getty** 46b; **RHS / Helen Yates** 48, 96t, 187(7), 217m; **RHS / Vicky Turner** 49(2); **Teresa Clements** 49(11); **SA Harrison** 59; **RHS / Mark Waugh** 61; **RHS / Wilf Halliday** 63t, 129(2), 180; **RHS / Oliver Dixon** 69(11), 121, 199; **Wax London** 81; **RHS / Mark Bolton** 89(6), 137tl, 167(8), 181m, 207(1), 223(6); **RHS / Clive Nichols** 94, 223(1); **Dinesh Ahir / Getty** 96b; **RHS / Sarah Cuttle** 97b, 141; **Rebekah Kennington** 101; **RHS / Fiona Secrett** 106b; **RHS / Guy Harrop** 107t; **RHS / Ali Cundy** 109(3), 109(9), 161m, 197; **RHS / Lee Beel** 109(5); **RHS / Jacquie Gray** 116; **RHS / John Scrace** 127t, 213; **William Andrew / Getty** 128b; **RHS / Fiona Lea** 129(4) 149(3), 167(4), 167(6), 187(8); **RHS / Christopher Whitehouse** 129(7); **RHS / Kat Weatherill** 129(9); **RHS / Josh Kemp-Smith** 134, 228t; **Sharon Vos-Arnold / Getty** 140; **RHS / Paul Debois** 146b; **RHS, Hyde Hall** 147; **RHS / Keith Harris** 148t; **RHS / Jon Parker Lee** 155; **Tomasz Klejdysz / Getty** 158b; **RHS / John Trenholm** 165t; **Wendy Wesley / RHS Trials** 167(1); **RHS / Plant Health** 177; **Dr Jassy Drakulic MRSB** 178; **Richard Bloom** 179; **RHS / Trevor Ray Hart** 184b; **Jonas Hanacek / Getty** 185; **RHS / Daniel Bridge** 187(6); **Ashley Cooper / Getty** 187(9); **RHS / David Nunn** 201b; **RHS / James Rudoni** 207(5); **RHS / Simon Garbutt** 207(9); **Jacky Parker Photography / Getty** 207(10); **RHS / Anna Brockman** 207(11); **Ashley Cooper / Getty**; 216; **RHS / Joe Wainwright** 220t; **Julia Sudnitskaya / Getty** 222b; **Paul Madeley** 231